The Discursive Construction of Identity and Space Among Mobile People

Advances in Sociolinguistics Series

Series Editor: Tommaso M. Milani

Since the emergence of sociolinguistics as a new field of enquiry in the late 1960s, research into the relationship between language and society has advanced almost beyond recognition. In particular, the past decade has witnessed the considerable influence of theories drawn from outside of sociolinguistics itself. Thus rather than see language as a mere reflection of society, recent work has been increasingly inspired by ideas drawn from social, cultural, and political theory that have emphasised the constitutive role played by language/discourse in all areas of social life. The *Advances in Sociolinguistics* series seeks to provide a snapshot of the current diversity of the field of sociolinguistics and the blurring of the boundaries between sociolinguistics and other domains of study concerned with the role of language in society.

Titles in the series include:

Becoming a Citizen: Linguistic Trials and Negotiations in the UK, Kamran Khan

Language Ideologies and the Globalization of 'Standard' Spanish, Darren Paffey

Linguistic Landscapes Beyond the Language Classroom, edited by Greg Niedt and Corinne A. Seals

Making Sense of People and Place in Linguistic Landscapes, edited by Amiena Peck, Christopher Stroud and Quentin Williams

Multilingual Encounters in Europe's Institutional Spaces, edited by Johann Unger, Michał Krzyżanowski and Ruth Wodak

Multilingual Memories: Monuments, Museums and the Linguistic Landscape, edited by Robert Blackwood and John Macalister

Negotiating and Contesting Identities in Linguistic Landscapes, edited by Robert Blackwood, Elizabeth Lanza and Hirut Woldemariam

Remix Multilingualism: Hip-Hop, Ethnography and Performing Marginalized Voice, Quentin Williams

Semiotic Landscapes: Language, Image, Space, Adam Jaworski and Crispin Thurlow

The Languages of Global Hip-Hop, edited by Marina Terkourafi

The Language of Newspapers: Socio-Historical Perspectives, Martin Conboy

The Tyranny of Writing: Ideologies of the Written Word, edited by Constanze Weth and Kasper Juffermans

Voices in the Media: Performing Linguistic Otherness, Gaëlle Planchenault

The Discursive Construction of Identity and Space Among Mobile People

Roberta Piazza

BLOOMSBURY ACADEMIC
LONDON • NEW YORK • OXFORD • NEW DELHI • SYDNEY

BLOOMSBURY ACADEMIC
Bloomsbury Publishing Plc
50 Bedford Square, London, WC1B 3DP, UK
1385 Broadway, New York, NY 10018, USA

BLOOMSBURY, BLOOMSBURY ACADEMIC and the Diana logo are trademarks of
Bloomsbury Publishing Plc

First published in Great Britain 2021
Paperback edition published 2022

Copyright © Roberta Piazza, 2021

Roberta Piazza has asserted her right under the Copyright, Designs and Patents Act, 1988,
to be identified as Author of this work.

For legal purposes the Acknowledgements on p. ix constitute an
extension of this copyright page.

All rights reserved. No part of this publication may be reproduced or transmitted
in any form or by any means, electronic or mechanical, including photocopying,
recording, or any information storage or retrieval system, without prior
permission in writing from the publishers.

Bloomsbury Publishing Plc does not have any control over, or responsibility for, any
third-party websites referred to or in this book. All internet addresses given in this book
were correct at the time of going to press. The author and publisher regret any
inconvenience caused if addresses have changed or sites have ceased to exist, but can
accept no responsibility for any such changes.

A catalogue record for this book is available from the British Library.

Library of Congress Cataloging-in-Publication Data
Names: Piazza, Roberta, author.
Title: The discursive construction of identity and space among mobile people / Roberta Piazza.
Description: New York, NY : Bloomsbury Academic, 2020. | Series: Advances in
sociolinguistics | Includes bibliographical references and index.
Identifiers: LCCN 2020034776 (print) | LCCN 2020034777 (ebook) |
ISBN 9781350053502 (hardback) | ISBN 9781350195455 (paperback) |
ISBN 9781350053519 (ebook) | ISBN 9781350053526 (epub)
Subjects: LCSH: Homelessness. | Homeless persons. | Squatters. |
Irish Travellers (Nomadic people)
Classification: LCC HV4493 .P56 2020 (print) | LCC HV4493 (ebook) | DDC 362.5/92—dc23
LC record available at https://lccn.loc.gov/2020034776
LC ebook record available at https://lccn.loc.gov/2020034777

ISBN: HB: 978-1-3500-5350-2
PB: 978-1-3501-9545-5
ePDF: 978-1-3500-5351-9
eBook: 978-1-3500-5352-6

Series: Advances in Sociolinguistics

Typeset by RefineCatch Limited, Bungay, Suffolk

To find out more about our authors and books visit www.bloomsbury.com
and sign up for our newsletters.

This one is for Paul

Contents

List of Illustrations		viii
Acknowledgements		ix
1	Introduction	1
2	Theoretical framework	17
3	Methodology	33
4	Locating the transient self in a transient heterotopia: Squatting as an affective and entrepreneurial proposition	47
5	'We don't need a castle. We need a home.' Desire for place in a Travellers' transit site	81
6	Irish Travellers: Mobility within immobility	115
7	Rough Sleepers: 'Homeless is what I am, not who I am.' Rough sleeping as a liminal condition not the essence of being	135
8	Conclusions	165
Notes		175
References		179
Index		199

Illustrations

1	A squatted boarded up public house (personal photo)	50
2	Concordance list for property/ies	61
3	Inciting hatred towards GRT	87
4	Anti-Roma, Anti-Muslim Sentiments Common in Several Nations	89
5	The transit site (personal photo)	91
6	The site aerial view	91
7	Electrical units at the site (personal photo)	92
8	Caravans in temporary stay in a park	95
9	Caring for the new site (personal photo)	117
10	Shrubs at the entrance to an amenity block (personal photo)	117
11	Artist impression of the permanent site	119
12	Street Homelessness in the town centre (personal photo)	136

Acknowledgements

I am indebted to many people for this project, first and foremost to the people who so generously lent me their voices. I am extremely fortunate to have met them. With some of them I dare say we have developed some friendly relationships. Besides them, the Council Travellers' Liaison staff, the staff at the day centre for the Rough Sleepers and the many charities with which I have been working for many years first and foremost FFT (Friends, Family and Travellers), Anthony McCoubry and Kirsty Pattrick at the Mass Observation Project at the Keep, my inspiring friend Peter Morgan, equally inspiring Emma Higham of RAPT and Richard Dufty of RBDdesign, Sheila Peters, Chris Hall, Daniel Fascione, Rachel Chasseaud, Debbie Simmons, Jackie Whitford, Jim Alexander, Sarah Lee, Deidre O'Halloran, Frank Cotterell-Snow, Terry Green, Ivy Manning, Michelle Buck, Chris Ellis, Mattia Sonnino, Coco Maartens, Pommy Collingwood, Aenum Machin, Charlie Papworth, the Day Centre clients and many others have all made this project possible. I am grateful to the University of Sussex for believing in my project and funding the multiple events and activities through which, in cooperation with FFT and councils, I tried to raise the public's awareness of the reality of these individuals.

1

Introduction

What this book is about

The space each of us occupies is an integral part of our individual selfhood. Who we are is inextricably connected to where we are. The broad concept of 'place-identity' has been widely employed by researchers to investigate this relationship. For Georgalou who explores the relevance of place among Facebook users, 'place identity refers to the ways in which we understand ourselves by attributing meanings to places' (2017: 45). Even in a virtual environment therefore the lack of and exclusion from space is crucial to the construction of selfhood. In line with the significant turn in the 1970s in the approach to space, this is not understood as objective and physical or as 'location', rather as subjective 'meaning' and the context of social action within which human existence is emplaced (Johnstone 2004, 67–8).

This volume investigates the relationship between identity and space in order to find out how people who are in an unstable, temporary and threatened spatial condition discursively construct their self in an interaction with an empathetic outsider, while at the same time taking on board the discourses that exist about them in society.

A multifaceted approach is adopted for the analysis of 'place-identity' that focuses on the identities of three mobile groups or sets of individuals whose lives lack well-defined space in the conventional sense. Being marginalized and generally poverty-stricken, the Squatters, Travellers and the Homeless (capitalized in this study in respect of their condition) are in many ways very different from the rest of mainstream society. Their space is also markedly distinct from Lefebvre's (1991) 'abstract space' that elite groups represent as homogeneous, integrated, ahistorical and functional to the exercise of power in a capitalist world. Their space is borderline and socially non-integrated and, rather than generating profit, proves the failure of corporativism.

These marginal individuals and groups are 'super-diverse' in terms of their social complexity and lack of conformity to mainstream society. Vertovec, who deliberately declines to offer a precise definition of the concept of super-diversity, refers to it as a 'summary term':

> 'Super-diversity' is proposed as a summary term. Whatever we choose to call it, there is much to be gained by a multidimensional perspective on diversity, both in terms of moving beyond 'the ethnic group as either the unit of analysis or sole object of study' and by appreciating the coalescence of factors which condition people's lives.
>
> 2007: 1026

It is significant that the definition of the concept of diversity by Queensborough Community College makes crucial reference to the elements of acceptance and respect as opposed to practices which result in segregation and exclusion.

> The concept of diversity encompasses acceptance and respect. It means understanding that each individual is unique, and recognizing our individual differences. These can be along the dimensions of race, ethnicity, gender, sexual orientation, socio-economic status, age, physical abilities, religious beliefs, political beliefs, or other ideologies. It is the exploration of these differences in a safe, positive, and nurturing environment. It is about understanding each other and moving beyond simple tolerance to embracing and celebrating the rich dimensions of diversity contained within each individual.[1]

While diversity engages with a multitude of differences, diversity studies have often centred on the ethnicity-related pluralism and explored a variety of migratory contexts including multilingual practices in business situations (Cogo 2012) or social work environments (Boccagni 2015) and engaged with issues of integration and 'cultural confluence' (Vertovec 2007: 1026) of various groups (Crul 2016) with very rare exceptions of diversity associated with minority groups (Tremlett 2014).

Contrary to such focus of most (super)diversity research, this study investigates a diversity that is integral to the British urban fabric and as such is domestic and internal to it. These people's existence is blatantly transgressive as much as, if not more than, that of migrants of different ethnicities and provenience and they face enormous challenges in meeting their livelihood needs on a daily and long-term basis. Years of ethnographic work were spent with the protagonists of this volume who are excluded from mainstream society, who do not coalesce with the average citizen and whom many ignore, often deliberately. Exclusion is not simply an economic issue; it is determined by interpersonal behaviour. Naegels and Blomme (2010 in van de Mieroop 2011: 566) argue that people have their personal GPS system, which enables them to avoid problematic individuals such as the poor and needy like the three marginal groups examined in this study. To a degree, therefore, this volume is a tribute to these invisible people and an attempt to give them a voice.

Volume organization

This volume comprises eight chapters. Following this introduction, chapter two presents the study's interdisciplinary theoretical background and the several constructs that are used in the analysis of the discourse of the individuals in each group. Firstly is the notion of *space* as a physical 'geographic location, material form, and a human investment with meaning and value' and *place* as the emotive discursive positioning of a speaker, the 'socially-based spatiality' constructed through the process of discursive interaction and referring to the individuals' affective engagement with a locality (Liebscher and Dailey-O'Cain 2013: 15–16). The three other key concepts that underpin the analytical approach of this study are also presented: the construct of desire or, better, *desires*, plural, referring to continually de/reformulated, non-sexual, momentary, albeit persistent, wants (e.g. for affection, security, material objects and the like) that individuals harbour; *liminality*, as the condition of occupying suspended, unofficial and in-between spaces; and, finally, the Foucaldian (1966/7-1986) concept of *heterotopia* as the place outside all places, the non-place with its value of compensation of an individual's lack of integration but also resistance to and challenge of society's norms. These three constructs are approached from the Gramscian (1971) perspective of 'hegemony' as the ideological control that a majoritarian group exerts on others on economic, and, more importantly, intellectual and cultural levels. For Gramsci, hegemony is reached not through force and subjugation but through consent obtained through the manipulation of language, morality and common sense (in terms of guidance of individuals' private activities) and the circulation of relevant 'narratives' or 'Discourses', with 'big D' (van de Mieroop et al. 2017: 181), in support of specific views of the world that are functional to a group's supremacy. Discourses as 'ways of being in the world, or forms of life which integrate words, acts, values, beliefs, attitudes, social identities, as well as gestures, glances, body positions and clothes', are opposed to 'discourse' with a little 'd', referring to any meaningful and connected stretches of language from a joke, to a conversation or a story (Gee 2005). Therefore (D)discourse is the subject matter of this volume in the belief that individuals align themselves or defy hegemonic ways of being in society (Benwell 2011). As identity is inherently social, the multidimensional consideration of factors external to its construction during the interactional practice of the interview is crucial to a full understanding of what the interviewees produce as a response to a range of narratives that society perpetuates around them.

Chapter three explains the study's interdisciplinary methodology which merges linguistic ethnography and critical discourse analysis. It discusses the benefits of this integrated approach and how the research was based on field notes and conversational interviews (De Fina 2009a) to then examine the practical and ethical issues involved. After these three preparatory chapters, four chapters of data analysis follow. All of them see identity construction as a 'performative achievement' (Butler 1990) against the backdrop of a number of social constraints and expectations by others (Bamberg and Andrews 2004). The chapters touch on, therefore, the existing social Discourses or sets of signs related to Squatters, Travellers and the Homeless that influence people's ways of thinking, and that the interviewees themselves plausibly take into account when constructing their persona.

Chapter four is a case study of a female Squatter in her various temporary locations; the discussion centres on the multiple identities she creates for herself according to two distinct topical configurations in a specific time and space. The focus is on the resistance she opposes to mainstream interpretation of space and the consequent heterotopia she conjures up as she attempts to come to terms with the outside world. The contradiction between contestation and a desire to belong (Benwell 2011) that is the core of her identity construction is emphasized. Chapters five and six centre on a group of female Irish Travellers who were interviewed in a coastal city in the south of England firstly in a transit site (chapter five) and subsequently in a permanent council-provided location (chapter six). Their desires, ambitions, future plans as well as the account of their hardship are highlighted in relation to their space deprivation first and space appropriation later on. Their strong preoccupation with their children and the chiasm between the world they desire for them and their perceptions of mainstream society emerge clearly in the interviews where they construct their personas in dis-alignment with the roles they are aware society has set for them.

Chapter seven examines conversations with male and female clients of a day centre for the Rough Sleepers in a city on the English southern coast; the liminal identities they create in their talk often revolve around their past life or around their projection for a better future, which are investigated against the backdrop of society's discourses around street Homelessness. Chapter eight concludes the volume and brings together the various threads and results' implications through a final discussion of the three groups as well as through a conclusive evaluation of the theoretical framework and the constructs employed in the study.

Rationale behind the choice of study's participants

The three sets of individuals observed in this study are an expression of diversity in so much as they interpret and use space in a very different way to mainstream social groups. In addition, their beliefs and lifestyle defy generally accepted shared norms, which adds to their diversity within the city's urban fabric and contributes to society's response in terms of their exclusion and marginalization. For this reason, they can be characterized as having 'deficit' identities (Reynolds and Taylor 2005 in Van De Mieroop 2011: 566) which are marked by lack, in this case a denied access to space and the deprivation it involves; their identities are also 'poverty-associated' (Van De Mieroop 2011) as the economic factor is undeniably a shared determinant of these groups' collective physiognomy. While more for the Squatters and Rough Sleepers than for the Travellers, economic deprivation is often alluded to, no specific reference to class is deliberately made in this study. This decision will appear clearer when in the methodology the notion of groups is problematized. Here, however, it suffices to point out that class cannot be taken as a uniform variable in defining the destiny of the individuals discussed in this book. While Irish Travellers fall outside traditional economic considerations, the most varied people may end up squatting or sleeping rough. The interviews show how both Martha and some of the Homeless men and women came from middle class, which suggests their condition is not associated necessarily with an economic disadvantage.

As noted earlier, this study is positioned within the mobility and (super)diversity framework (Vertovec 2007, Blommaert 2013). However, instead of exploring the identity of people whose mobile lives are determined by the desire to leave one country in search of better economic, social and cultural opportunities or fear for their safety, the volume offers an analysis of the social difference that exists within the fabric of English society (although very similar realities exist in many other parts of the UK and the world at large). While the lives of Squatters, Irish Travellers and street Homeless (or Rough Sleepers as a sub-category of the latter) have an undeniably dramatic dimension that people generally prefer to disregard, their experiences and choices also represent a challenge to many of the tenets of mainstream society, in particular the notions of permanency, property, profitability and individualism. For this reason, these people are often perceived as a threat and, as much as possible, concealed by dominant society.

The groups analysed in this volume are also often the object of negative media coverage and portrayed as people creating concerns for the hegemonic majoritarian society; the dramatic eviction of Travellers from the largest site in the UK (at Dale Farm in Essex) in October 2011 made the news for months; similarly, the political activities of the anarchist ANAL group occupying a Russian millionaire's mansion in one of the wealthiest areas of London fulfilled all criteria of newsworthiness (Bednarek and Caple 2014 and 2017). In both cases the press strategically tapped into settled people's fear of having their property and land invaded or taken away by unwanted others. Numerous documentaries have been produced on Travellers and Gypsies, most chastising them by representing them as crooks, thus enforcing misconceptions about them,[2] others occasionally attempting to capture their plight and consequent segregation (Piazza 2015a and 2017). On the contrary, the worsening situation of people living on the street in the UK and the continually rising death toll of Homeless people is the persistent concern of local and national press and investigative journalism (cf. the 2019 *Guardian* series in G2 'The homeless death of …'). Such media representation operating through language and visual channels divulges discriminatory concepts, ideas and feelings (Hall 1997) and reinforces negative stereotypes about the three groups discussed in this book. Such Discourses, in a Foucauldian sense, of exclusion, otherness and distrust therefore constitute the macro-context within which this study's participants operate and with which they engage in their identity work, the micro-context being the face-to-face interaction (McNamara 2019: 119).

Beyond such public discourses, very little is known about these groups. Therefore, this volume seeks to inform readers about the diverse and invisible people who occupy the interstices of society, also with the aim of challenging the shared beliefs about them. In this sense, this book responds to the plea of such scholars as Creese (2008) to give due consideration to the area of social action and involvement, whereby academic work can encourage a change in social and cultural attitudes.

The relation between language and place-identity

The post-modernist view of reality as not objective but socially constructed (pioneered by Berger and Luckmann in the mid-1960s) when adapted to identity understands language not as a reflection of a self that is an individual's permanent and fixed property, but as fluid and situated in the speakers' many contexts, interlocutors, aims and intentions, and emerging in the interactional practice in which the individual is involved.

> In the face-to-face situation the other is appresented to me in a vivid present shared by both of us. I know that in the same vivid present I am appresented to him. My and his 'here and now' continuously impinge on each other as long as the face-to-face situation continues. As a result, there is a continuous interchange of my expressivity and his. I see him smile, then react to my frown by stopping the smile, then smiling again as I smile, and so on. Every expression of mine is oriented towards him, and vice versa, and this continuous reciprocity of expressive acts is simultaneously available to both of us. This means that, in the face-to-face situation, the other's subjectivity is available to me through a maximum of symptoms.
> Berger and Luckmann 1966/1991: 43

The self therefore is 'constructed' through language and invoked as speakers choose to (dis)align with the relevant roles that are available in society. Sociolinguists have for many years paid attention to language features associated with particular identities. Labov's (1963) seminal work on the diphthongs /au/ and /ai/ in such words as 'house' and 'right' uttered by the residents of Martha's Vineyard may be seen not only as a study on social variation but the observation of a collective act of identity through which a group of islanders signalled their ideological distance from the mainland residents of Massachusetts and constructed a separate, deliberately distinct social community through the non-standard, local pronunciation of [əu, əi]. Similarly, the /aw/-monothongization of American English in Pittsburgh (Johnstone and Kiesling 2008) may be read as an indication of how a group can index its identity through developing or maintaining distinctive patterns of language use, thus creating borders and delimiting its own social self through language choices. Identity construction, therefore, may be at the basis of the many sociolinguistic processes. In line with this, in a postscript to a special issue on identity in the *Journal of Pragmatics,* Auer explains the move from a traditional sociolinguistic 'variationist' approach to a broader view of identity as a 'useful mediating concept between language and social structure' (2005: 404).

In a similar vein, in a July 2012 interview, the discursive choices of female Traveller, such as the non-standard English register and the voicing of her children through direct reporting, function as Membership Categorization Devices (Sacks 1972 and 1992, Schegloff 2007, Stokoe 2003) encoding the speaker as a woman belonging to a particular segregated and antagonized community as evidenced by her reference to the insults her children receive at school. In the following extract, the relevant linguistic indicators are highlighted in italics:

Excerpt 1: my children doesn't feel like, like most children feel like oh they're getting picked on *'they called me a gypsy, they called me a pikey'*

Similarly, in an April 2017 interview, an Irish Traveller constructs her identity as English and refutes the label of Irishness usually associated with her group. The deictic opposition between 'here' referring to the speaker, and 'Ireland' or 'there', as a space that is associated with her grandparents, leaves no doubt as to the speaker's desire to inscribe herself in the local southern English community. In this extract (as in all others) 'Tr' stands for Traveller and 'Int' for Interviewer.

Excerpt 2: Tr. *I'm not Irish.*
Int. You're not Irish.
Tr. Yeah, *I was born in England.*
Int. Oh you're born in ... but you ....
Tr. But I have an *Irish accent.*
Int. (...) So, where is ... what's Ireland for you?
Tr. *Ireland, my grandparents comes* from Ireland.
Int. All right, okay. So, you don't consider Ireland your place anymore?
Tr. No. *I was born in England.*
Int. So, what do you consider *your place*? Here?
Tr. Yeah, *here* now.

Through the choices that speakers make it is, therefore, possible to identify the individual's persona that is an 'emergent product rather than the pre-existing source of linguistic and other semiotic practices' (Bucholtz and Hall 2005: 19) resulting from the particular moment and the specific situation in which the person finds herself.

At a macro level, the unconscious or not entirely conscious (Kulick 2000 and 2014, and Cameron and Kulick 2003) use of dialect and non-standard forms and the switching between language registers makes the relation between language and identity particularly complex. Bucholtz and Hall (2005) argue that the use of referential identity labels in talks is a very direct index of identity, and work in sociolinguistics has contributed to understanding labelling and categorization as a form of social action. The use of the derogatory label 'hjra', whose real meaning is 'impotent', by one of their interviewees and referring to the way she was ostracized by her family in her childhood was crucial information about the person's identity. Selfhood, however, can be instantiated in more indirect, mediated and elusive ways often in relation to the epistemic certainty or uncertainty speakers express in an interaction (Ochs 1992 and 1993). Alternatively, the roles that interlocutors take up in the interaction provide crucial information about their identity. In a study on the Zanzibar diaspora (Piazza 2019), some of the speakers constructed themselves as defenders of the island Revolution and their identities as non-conforming with the colonialists, while others chose to take a more personal and less political positioning.

Stance as social action linguistically encoded through evaluation, intentionality, and epistemic choices is a further index of identity. More specifically, the speakers' positioning in relation to the interaction, the topic and the interlocutors, and viewed as a subjective and intersubjective process (Du Bois 2007) can shed light on the social alignments speakers make in their talk to invoke a particular identity. Identity indexes are also the result of pragmatic implicature and presupposition and Bucholtz and Hall (2005: 597) point out how a speaker's style is made up of idiosyncratic linguistic choices at a discursive level (grammar, phonology, and lexis) or, for instance, how the preference for quotations can instantiate identity.

Besides the complexity of establishing a relation between linguistic forms and identity construction, an additional issue is that social identities evolve and '[t]he same speakers may shift their acts and stances many times, [and] in so doing, reconfigure the social identities of themselves and others over a brief period of time' (Ochs 1993: 298). A Social Constructivist approach, therefore, attempts to provide a 'non-arbitrary account' of how language determines identity by capturing as much as possible the 'ebbs and webs of identity construction' by identifying linguistic indicators but without, as Ochs says (1993: 298), 'grammaticizing' them or assuming them as permanent and fixed elements. Therefore, the investigation of speakers' style, as the structured combination of resources (Eckert and McConnell-Ginet 2013: 250) and repeated linguistic performance, becomes the way to access identity discursive construction.

Identity, space and narrative

The above examples of language in connection to identity have something in common: they all relate to space, whether indirectly through the appropriation of a linguistic feature that invokes a particular group membership (for example, 'gypsy' and 'pikey' as common derogatory labels used by mainstream society to refer to travelling people), or directly through the clear expression of belonging, as in the last excerpt of the Irish woman who claims an English rather than Irish membership. These examples, therefore, provide a suitable introduction to the notion of *space-identity*, the subject of this book, and the investigation of what Hunziker et al. (2007) term the 'human-landscape relationship'. Physical space shapes and is shaped by the people who live in it. While *space* or the physical landscape has an impact on people in terms of their aesthetic preferences, a geographical locale is changed into a *place* through the person's discursive construction of their emotional relation to it. For example, to draw upon a recent historical event, during the 2011 protest against the European austerity, the physical space of Syntagma Square in Athens was transformed into a political forum by the people's use of it and the surrounding media discourses. 'Since 25 May, when demonstrators first converged here, this has become an open-air concert – only one where bands have been supplanted by speakers and music swapped for an angry politics' (*The Guardian*, 19 June 2011). That area in the heart of Athens then became a public forum for the expression of a rancorous Greek national identity awoken by the imposition of financial hardship; in so doing, its original physicality was overlooked and side-lined. Similarly, in *Desire Lines* (2007), the essays collected by Murray, Shepherd and Hall, the authors explore notions of space and identity, memory and desire, in post-apartheid South African cities and highlight the emergence of 'new-public cultures' (p. 1) that use but also resist the available spatial realities. In a not dissimilar way, the chapters in Martin Rojo's book *Occupy* investigate the various ways in which public spaces are transformed in to radical 'public arenas' (2006: 2) during occupations and protests through which people reject the hegemonic control of the system. This book discusses space as a physical entity that challenges and resists normative spatial ethics through the choices that the three groups of participants, the Squatter, the Irish Travellers, and the Homeless make. It focuses on the power struggle between sedentarist and mainstream spatialities and investigates alternative interpretations and ideologies of space. Space, however, has also an additional dimension that is at the core of this study. De Fina explains the recent interest in space in narrative studies and 'the implications of the reconfigurations of the categories such as space and time' (2009b: 111) for the understanding of story-telling. Central to her discussion is the implication that space is no longer simply structural but is an indexical process invested with social meaning, for which she proposes the term 'spatialization'. Through space references, therefore, narrators 'index different kinds of subjective positions'

(De Fina 2009b: 113) so that spatialization becomes a device for positioning. Modifying spaces into places is a necessary 'existential activity' (Hunziker et al. 2007: 51) through which people discursively emotionalize a physical locale (in the sense of past recall and/or future projection) to satisfy the fundamental needs to belong, have a sense of their self and their role in life. Therefore, this book explores not so much how people simply talk about the space they inhabit or wish to inhabit, but how they discursively give life to that place and how their self emerges as a result. Such a discursive construction pertains to the area of emotions and discourse rather than to the cognitive sphere of geographical mental map studies and space-related behavioural customs through which people appropriate a locale.

Importantly, the space considered in this study is a minority space associated with people with lesser status who are victims of marginalization. Social segregation, for instance in the case of the Travellers' site built miles away from the city centre, has increased because 'the aesthetics of place' has become a priority in contemporary city agendas (Mitchell 1997). Local governments want to make towns and cities more appealing to visitors and inhabitants. The aesthetics of space, therefore, acquires priority and promotes decisions to exclude and relegate to invisible areas aesthetically unappealing human beings. Poverty, Homelessness and other kinds of diversity are interpreted as an economic rather than a social problem and excluded with the pretext that they create anxiety, fear and discomfort among local residents and tourists. This study focuses on the key manifestations of uncertain and threatened space and attempts to understand how people who occupy that space construct who they are. It is concerned with the emotional attachment to place in the case in which, as for the people who are the study's protagonists, the space is only a desire and an aspiration.

The relationship between identity and space emerges in this study through the personal narratives of the interviewed participants, who 'symbolise, transform, and display a stretch of experience from [their] past [...] into linguistically represented episodes, events, processes, and states' (Schiffrin 1996: 168). These narratives offer relative versions of reality and reflect the individual's 'subjective involvement in the world' and their 'struggle to bring experiences to conscious awareness' (Ochs and Capps 1996: 21).

This study's approach to narrative is a long way removed from the most influential structuralist model advanced by Labov and Waletzky (1997), based on a chronological sequence of events and a culminating moment followed by a resolution or conclusion. As Wortham (2000) notes, self-narratives that have an interactional as well as an interpersonal function, are completed only through the positioning of the narrator towards the audience. In a not dissimilar vein, narratives can be seen as the locus of a meeting of the three 'coordinates of space, time and personhood into a unitary frame' (De Fina and Georgakopoulou 2008: 380). Narrative, therefore, is understood here as talk in interaction and the continuous negotiation that is part of a 'social practice', in other words the 'production of social life in the semiotic world' (De Fina and Georgakopoulou 2008: 383). The focus of the analysis is on the dynamic responses to the rhetorical stimulation during the interaction, the strategies speakers use to bridge the gap between what they actually say and what is expected of them to say in respect of society's generic representations, available roles and discourses, and the incompleteness or smallness of some narratives that are subject to revision and reinterpretation. Such a view of narrative is also reinforced by the notion of 'small stories' understood as 'part of a trajectory of interactions rather than as a free standing, finished and self-contained unit' (Georgakopoulou 2007: 40).

Incomplete, fragmented, even told by multiple tellers, projected into the future, only understandable within their contexts, far from Lyotard's (1984) 'grand narratives' as the culturally constructed modes of interpretation for social phenomena, these small stories (Georgakopoulou 2006 and 2007) recount an immediate past or even a present or create links to the speakers' immediate experience. 'By recalling experiences and making choices on narratives, individuals or groups of people could retake their control over life after any major events like displacement or any kind of disaster in life; [...] the term "survivorship" [...] interpret[s] how people could take control over their lives' (Islam 2017: 70).

Although the stories in this volume are usually quite tragic, their narrators often disguise their trauma and suffering by offering a positive vision of the world and express an attempt to retake control over their lives. In a study similar to Islam's (2017) investigation of refugees and his concept of survivorship, Malkki (1992) stresses how, due to their unsettled status, these people reinvent their own space, 'homes and homeland' in an often positive way that echoes what some of this study's interviewees do in their stories. The protagonists of this study can be referred to as 'survivors' both in the moment of their social practice of narrating through which they construct an often future self, and in the preliminary decision of reflecting through the act of narrating on their suspended condition instead of accepting it acritically.

In the narratives of the contributors to this volume, the relationship is not solely between identity and space. Inevitably, space is interconnected with time, therefore the interpenetrations of these two axes is best understood in terms of

Bakhtin's notion of chronotope where the 'spatial and temporal indicators are fused into one concrete whole [...] The chronotope makes the narrative events concrete, makes them take on flesh and blood, causes blood to flow in their veins' (1981: 250). Although complex and elusive, the notion of chronotope (Blommaert 2015) materializes coordinates of space and time and combines them with identity is particularly pertinent to the type of dynamic analysis of mobile and unsettled people, which is the focus of this study, and to the way they combine their narrated stories with the act of narrating (Perrino 2011).

Marked identities

Squatters, Travellers and the Homeless are special people who stand out because of their 'marked identities' (Piazza and Fasulo 2015). This term, first coined by Goffman (1963), refers generally to individuals who suffer from a loss due to the stigma that surrounds them. 'Marked' is also derived from the linguistic concept of 'markedness', originally coined by scholars belonging to the Prague School of Functional Linguistics to express the relation between two extremes: the normal and expected form of the unmarked 'I was given this for my birthday' in contrast to the marked, 'This (especially if accompanied by a rising intonation), I was given for my birthday', where the passive construction with fronting of the direct object indexes the speaker's critical stance towards the present received.

While Goffman (1963) discusses the various strategies used by individuals to compensate for the social mark they carry, it must be remembered that the notion of markedness assumes the presence of an accepted social norm to which the majority aligns. Even though the meaning of social 'markedness' is not necessarily negative (Piazza and Rubino 2015), this does not mean that the stigma surrounding these groups is aproblematically refuted; on the contrary, the echo of the negative discourses that society produces and circulates through a variety of media is ever-present in these individual's narratives. By contrast, this study explicitly adopts a perspective that portrays these individuals in a neutral light. By penetrating the reality of the lives of Squatters, Travellers and Homeless people, this book attempts to understand the experiences behind their words and appreciate any potential positive aspects of their life style.

Two choices made here are in line with this intent. The first is the use of capitals as the first letter for the names of the three groups of individuals interviewed in this book. While Travellers, as a legally recognized minority group in its own right, already bears a capital, in the other two cases of the

Squatters and Homeless people this is the chosen practice in this study in order to highlight the respect these people deserve. The second choice has an impact on the level of the theoretical framework of the analysis. It concerns the adoption of the theoretical construct of 'liminality' that guides the investigation of the identities that these individuals evoke through their language. According to Turner, liminal personae or liminals are 'neither here nor there; they are betwixt and between positions assigned and arrayed by law, custom, convention and ceremonial' (1997: 95).

A key argument of this study is that liminality is a more useful construct to understand place-identity than the more traditional concept of marginalization because the 'talk' of the individuals who are profiled in this study eludes the classifications and roles that society normally confers upon them. Furthermore, this study's participants are in a process of transition, not solely in terms of the uncertainty of their residence, but in terms of their general suspended and transient condition. All three groups want to create alternative existences for themselves. In particular, Travellers (and Gypsies) want new forms of settled residence that would still allow them to pursue their traditional peripatetic way of life when they, and not the evicting bailiffs, decide. Therefore, the concept of liminality bestows on these participants the opportunity of change and transformation rather than ensnare them in a subaltern condition from which they cannot escape.

The choice of the three groups of participants was dictated by a number of factors, some fortuitous, others deliberate. Having been interested in mobility and in alternative forms of existence and being curious about the phenomenon of nomadic people in the south of England, I first made contact with a group of Travellers who were residing at the only Council-run site in the area where I live. I received a warm welcome that encouraged me to return numerous times since then. Similarly, with regard to the Squatter group, I was fortunate to know some Squatters, ended up befriending a woman in a squat through a close friend and set to meet with her. The picture at that point started shaping up and an investigation of people in different forms of temporary and insecure accommodation began to appear possible. Finally, in 2017, while I was doing archival work at the Mass Observation Project at The Keep in Brighton & Hove on a 'directory' or collection of people's responses to the topic of Homelessness, I was introduced to a man, who had been volunteering for years at a day centre for the Rough Sleepers and who inspired me to continue my field work with this last group of people.

In conjunction with research activity, a series of community-engagements and events were held over a period of four years with the aim of sensitizing the general public to the reality of these communities and engage in a productive dialogue with the responsible authorities about how the services and other support for these groups could be improved. These events funded by the HEIF (Higher Education Innovation Fund) and RIF (Research Impact Fund) at the University of Sussex are an attempt to reach a degree of that social praxis arising from academic research to which this entire project aims.

2

Theoretical framework

Introduction

This chapter presents the theoretical framework that underpins the investigation of the identities of individuals who can be termed Squatters, Irish Travellers and Homeless. As discussed in the opening chapter, they pertain to the area of diversity that Appadurai (2013) positively associates with infinity of possibilities and wealth of variation. However, in contrast to how diversity is usually understood in contemporary research, these people's social diversity is not associated with migration but is within English society and contesting some of its most basic values and beliefs.

After a brief review of the literature on *identity*, the discussion focuses on the *place-identity* as indicating the relationship between personhood and space. The chapter continues with the conceptualization *of space as essentially ideologized* and as a point of contestation of hegemonic forces, to then present the notion of *liminality* as a way of understanding the suspended state of the individuals investigated in this study, caught as they are between the authoritative spaces that shape the expectations of mainstream society and the uncanonical spaces they manage to appropriate. The condition of liminality that the interviewees experience determines their response in terms of a *desire* or volition for space and, more specifically, the construction of a *heterotopia* as the space outside all spaces that acts as a form of either contestation of the space deprivation which these people suffer or, vice versa, as the creation of a comforting zone into which they can retreat.

Postmodern theories of identity

Reflecting on the connection between identity and language, Llamas and Watt remind us that '[l]anguage not only reflects who we are but, in some sense, it *is* who we are' (2012, p. xv, emphasis in the original). Language is the means by which people describe themselves and assign identities to self and others. Hall (1996, pp. 5–6 in Edwards 2009: 16) observes that identity does not exist in isolation or in a vacuum. As we construct our identities through language, we take into account many capital –d Discourses (Gee 2005) or master narratives (Bamberg and Andrews 2004) that are both 'socially constituted and socially constitutive' (Reisigl and Wodak 2009: 89). We exist discursively in alignment with or, vice versa, in opposition to the specific subject positions available within the context-dependent semiotic practices in which we engage.

'In critical discourse research, subject positions refer to the possibilities for social identity that are available at particular times and places. The notion of subject positions is thought to capture the idea of social identity as multiple, complex, dynamic, locally situated, and open to negotiation' (Pomerantz 2000: 27). By way of illustration, the identities constructed by a Saudi student during her interview greatly differ from those of a similar woman in the same situation and location. Through the account of her decision to leave behind at home her four-month-old child and a five-year-old daughter with her husband and mother while she would be studying for her PhD, she presented herself as an emancipated woman prepared to sacrifice temporarily her family in order to advance her career goals; at the same time, however, she was keen to clarify her role as a traditional and obliging Saudi woman married to what she defined a conservative man. By balancing these two opposing identities, this woman shows that 'interviews are sites of struggle where individuals strive to construct representations of themselves [. . . and] utilize a variety of linguistic and social resources over the course of an interview encounter to create a publically recognizable self' (Pomerantz 2000: 27–8). According to Bakhtin's (1981) concept of *heteroglossia*, words always historically 'entangled' with the voices of others and echo the social, political and historical voices of others. In this case, several women's roles, discourses of womanhood, therefore other voices of and about women were interpelled by this student during our interaction, partly in contestation of home old traditions and association with the new definition of femininity in Saudi, partly in alignment with more established discourses of womanhood.

Postmodernist identity studies (Beck 1992, Giddens 1991) understand identity as fragmented, reflexive, constantly changing and even contradictory. Importantly, identities are performative (Butler 1990) and subject to the local contingencies of time and space. In this sense, identities are 'socio-culturally constructed ongoing narratives, which develop and evolve across different spatio-temporal scales, ranging from the micro, local and immediate to the macro, global and long term' (Block 2015: 527 echoing Lemke 2008). Such fluid identities are not pre discursive and it is only through the social practice of interaction that people construct their selfhood and (Simon 2004: 45) particular aspects of their identities emerge.

Given that identity components have no constant value, identities can change even during a single interaction if the subject changes focus and goal.[1] Nevertheless, to counter the notion of identity fragmentation, a degree of continuity and stability (Edwards 2009: 19, Seul 1999: 554) is assumed to exist between the various identities that individuals construct in different contexts. Zimmerman's (1998) old concept of transportable identities that 'travel with individuals across situations and are potentially relevant in and for any situation and in and for any spate of interaction' (1998: 90) acts to safeguard the essence of a person's identity. Similarly, Giddens (1991), who argues that the self is not something individuals were born with but something that is consciously constructed, perceives modern or 'post-traditional' identity as complex and multi-faceted but still as a non-fragmented continuum. 'Self-identity, then, is not a set of traits. Self-identity has continuity – that is, it cannot easily be completely changed at will – but that continuity is only a product of the person's reflexive beliefs about their own biography or observable characteristics. It is a person's own reflexive understanding of their biography' (Giddens 1991: 53).

Identity is personal as much as social. Individuals' identities are forged by their membership in a positive and comfortable 'in-group' preferred to the 'out-group' (Tajfel 1974: 68). Also, participants self-categorize themselves and ascribe to each other membership in social categories (cf. Turner and Reynolds 2011, Hester and Eglin 1997). Identity scholars therefore assume a 'close association between categorization and identity construction' (De Fina 2019: 3). The notions of selfhood vis-à-vis otherhood and categorization will appear very salient in all discussions with the three types of individuals whose self is determined by their perception of others and their awareness of how others see them. The interviews will also show how otherhood causes these people to construct a border between their selves and the rest of society (Watt et al. 2014).

Hall and Bucholtz (2012) list a number of principles defining identity. The 'relationality' principle emphasizes that identity is not isolated or independent but the product of intersubjectivity (p. 23) resulting from a variety of identity relations, the most obvious of which is similarity or 'adequacy' between speakers sharing the same views and, vice versa, difference or 'distinction' by which people highlight their distance from others. The 'positionality' principle refers to the local and 'ethnographically specific' positions as well as to the 'temporary and interactionally specific' stances that, at a micro level, can be taken up by participants within an interaction, in addition to the 'macrolevel demographic categories' (Bucholtz and Hall 2010: 21). Therefore the 'local identity categories' (p. 20) capture the subtle nuances of the moment-to-moment construction of identity in an individual in stark opposition to large-scale sociolinguistic studies.

Finally, 'indexicality' refers to the way particular linguistic features become linked with social meaning and relates 'the micro-social to the macro-social frames of analysis of any sociolinguistic phenomenon' (Silverstein 2003: 193). Linguistic indexes derive their meaning from the social context and ideological structures and, like the linguistic choices in a person's talk, indicate their association with a particular view of the world and contribute to their identity construction. Such indexical relation is problematic as there is no one-to-one mapping of forms and social meaning. Ochs (1993) problematizes the language and meaning relation as 'non-exclusive' in the sense that the same linguistic indicator can be associated with both men and women rather than exclusively with one gender, and as 'constitutive' in the sense that more than one individual feature can indicate social meaning. 'The relation between language and social identity is predominantly a socio-linguistically distant one', Ochs (1993: 288) concludes. Identity is, therefore, 'mediated' by the interlocutor's understanding of the social conventions regarding certain acts (Ochs 1993: 289) and can only be inferred by the linguistic choices that a person makes.

Constructing a safe identity is a human necessity (Bloom 1990, Breakwell 1986). As will be discussed in the following chapters, this study's protagonists struggle to satisfy such basic necessity as they lack the material conditions conducive to security. The temporariness and suspension of their lives impact their personhood in addition to the awareness of their relegation to the margins of society and the racialization of their condition as a consequence of the public discourses around them.

Place-identity

The geographical environment is both shaped by and shapes the people who live in it. The identities of this study's speakers are linked to space because of the 'located nature of subjectivity' and the inevitable association of questions of self with questions of space (Dixon and Durrheim 2000). Proshansky et al.'s (1983) definition of place-identity incorporating both space and time is along lines that are explored in this volume:

> a sub-structure of the self-identity of the person consisting of, broadly conceived, cognitions about the physical world in which the individual lives. These cognitions represent memories, ideas, feelings, attitudes, values, preferences, meanings, and conceptions of behavior and experience which relate to the variety and complexity of physical settings that define the day-to-day existence of every human being. At the core of such physical environment-related cognitions is the 'environmental past' of the person; a past consisting of places, spaces and their properties which have served instrumentally in the satisfaction of the person's biological, psychological, social, and cultural needs.
>
> p. 59

Korpela observes the way place is humanized, recalled, and controlled and reflects on the 'mechanisms connecting the physical environment to psychic self-regulation' (1989: 241) and ensuring self-esteem. Similarly, De Fina explores the recent interest in space in narrative studies and 'the implications of the reconfigurations of the categories such as space and time' (2009: 111) for the understanding of narrative. In her view, space is no longer simply structural but it is an indexical process invested with social meaning, for which she uses the term 'spatialization'. Through space references, therefore, narrators 'index', in the sense of 'constructing' and 'evoking' (Johnstone et al., 2006: 81) different kinds of subjective positions so that spatialization becomes a device for positioning.

Opposing Proshansky et al.'s (1983) cognitive perspective on space, Sarbin advocates a 'humanistic stance' and refers to the concept of 'emplotment' through which subjects construct their place-identity by creating a plausible narrative 'complete with plots and subplots, dramatis personae, settings, goals, beginnings and endings, climaxes and anti-climaxes, etc. In construing a self from the referents for "I" and "me" in spoken or silent monologues, the person does not simply chronicle experience, he/she renders experience.' (Sarbin 1983: 340)

Most of the studies on place-identity in the areas of social and environmental psychology and human geography agree on the relevance of belonging to a space for the definition of self.[2] Dixon and Durrheim (2000: 29) point out the limitations of an individualistic interpretation of place-identity that obscures the collective dimension of the relationship between identity and physical setting.

The approach to place-identity adopted in this study is very much in line with the way in which identity as a general concept is understood. It is informed, in particular, by the work of Dixon and Durrheim (2000) in the field of environmental psychology and, more recently, of McNamara (2019) in applied socio-linguistics. Both identity and place-identity are understood as personal and collective constructions of individuals and groups and resulting from their relationship with the physical reality surrounding them and in consideration of the discourses that circulate in society about it. Through the available discourse affordances such as narrative emplotment and through interaction, individuals make sense of their self and their relation to space and 'locatedness', to use Dixon and Durrheim's terminology.

Many theorists link the initial impulse to construct a secure sense of self to the survival instinct of the infant (Bloom 1990, Breakwell 1986). As one develops, and assuming one gains in the confidence that physical needs will be met, increasing energy is devoted to the satisfaction of the 'higher-order' needs, firstly systematically identified by Abraham Maslow (1954/1970) and including the need for psychological security, and for love (or belonging), self-esteem, and self-actualization.

Individuals seek 'continuity across time and situation' (Breakwell 1986: 24) to reduce uncertainty in social affairs which contributes to psychological stability and a positive sense of self (Goffman 1963). Efforts to achieve a sense of connection or belonging, self-esteem and even self-actualization help people establish and maintain positive, secure identities (Bloom 1990, Breakwell 1986, Stein 1996). Failure to establish or maintain a relatively positive identity produces severe psychological discomfort, or even a total personality breakdown, which may be experienced by the individual as a threat to survival (Bloom 1990).

Space

Space is becoming increasingly scarce and, as such, more and more valued and sought after (Shields 2005: 165, in Palladino 2016). It is not neutral, innocent, harmless or 'empty' rather it 'always embodies a meaning' (Lefebvre 1991: 154). Sibley's (2006: 401) comment that '[t]he geographies of inclusion and exclusion are rooted in particular histories and space-economies' is pertinent to this study's individuals who have a long history of exclusion and occupy marginal spaces. The spaces allotted or denied to the three groups in this study reflect the exercise of power in the society to which these people do not belong and by which they are strongly ideologized.

For Lefebvre, spatiality can be understood in a number of ways: as 'material space' that we experience physically, as 'represented space' in terms of how a space is portrayed and interpreted culturally including for instance maps and graphs,[3] and as 'space of representation' or lived space (Harvey 2005: 15). Two of these three conceptualizations of space are particularly relevant to our understanding of the concept. While the material space is based on our perceptions and we experience it with all our senses, spaces of representations 'refer to the way we humans live – physically, affectively, and emotionally – in and through the spaces we encounter' (Harvey 2005: 15). We may derive great joy from a view of the sea; vice versa the waves can conjure up our memory of the uncertainty and fear we experienced in trying to reach the Sicilian coastline if we are African migrants. Such a distinction between material space and spaces of representation is to a degree close to the already mentioned discrimination in the social sciences between space as 'geographic location, material form, and a human investment with meaning and value' and place as 'socially-based spatiality' constructed through the process of discursive interaction (Gieryn 2000: 464–5 in Liebscher and Dailey-O'Cain 2013: 15-16; also see Blommaert et al. 2005 and Hult 2014). In this study, therefore, the two constructions of space and place are discussed in terms of the hegemonic and counter space that the interviewees deal with as well as the individuals' recreation and expression of locale constructed through their words, memories and aspirations. In light of this distinction, therefore, while this study's focus is on place-identity mainly, it follows Setha Low (2014) in an attempt to operate within the area of 'engaged anthropology to space and place' to address inequality and the 'systems of exclusion that are hidden or naturalized and thus rendered invisible' (p. 34).

Some recent studies consider spaces as modern 'heterotopias' (Foucault 1967) or counter spaces suspended between utopia and dystopia. For example, Hocking et al. (2019) investigate the post-conflict reality of Northern Ireland by looking at seemingly innocent spaces such as parks, which instead of being open to all, have 'effectively been 'privatised' for the exclusive use of certain sectarian groups' (p.166). By adopting a novel methodology of walking interviews in three of Belfast's main parks, Hocking et al.'s study shows that place-identities strongly impact the way people feel about these green spaces and, consequently, the way they use or avoid them. In a similar investigation of peripheral spaces, Scully (2019) focuses on Cornish place-identity and finds that the participation in spaces where local music and dance festivals are held considerably reinforces an authentic Cornish and Celtic identity.

In her investigation of the spatial heterotopia of Gypsies and Travellers, Palladino (2016) focuses on the Foucaldian idea that especially within a sedentarist ideology, space is the means to exercise power and impose hegemonic norms. In response to dominant society, Travellers' place is

> 'a place without a place', [and their caravans] a mobile home [that] visits different spaces and all the same encompasses all these sites within itself. [...] a mobile home for Travellers is a 'reserve of the imagination', it involves the anticipation of movement, imaginary travel, it triggers memories of spatial travel and, by definition, it embodies the possibility of dislocation.
>
> p. 26

Liminal identities

The last studies by Hocking et. al., Scully and Palladino, in particular, introduce the type of space-identities considered in this volume; such identities are 'marked' in a sociological sense (Piazza and Fasulo 2015) because of their mobile and unstable relation with space. One term to define the people discussed in this study is 'nomads' whose lives are an 'intermezzo' (Deleuze and Guattari 1999: 443). Postmodern theories of identity do not capture completely the relationship between identity and elusive space. An important exception is the work of Deleuze and Guattari (1999) which, by analysing nomadism as a social and spatial practice, highlights the difference between a migrant and a nomad in the following terms:

> The nomad is not at all the same as the migrant: for the migrant goes principally from one point to another, even if the second point is uncertain, unforeseen, or not well localized. But the nomad goes from point to point only as a consequence and as a factual necessity; in principle, points for him are relays along a trajectory.
>
> 1999: 443

This particular formulation of space and nomadology is very much in line with the approach to understanding mobile space adopted in this study. The trajectories and trails nomads follow may be customary but are definitely very different from sedentary roads, which are designed to '*parcel out a closed space to people*, assigning each person a share and regulating the communication between shares' (1999: 443 emphasis in the original). The nomadic lifestyle contradicts the sedentary one as it provides an open space for people, that is not 'striated' (1999: 444), that is enclosed and regimented by borders and walls, and is not programmed to convey a specific meaning. In opposition to such a space, a counter-hegemonic mobile space is 'smooth' in its being unregulated and natural. In addition to Deleuze and Guattari's very pertinent notion of nomadic space, this study relies on the specific concept of 'liminality' centred on the idea of temporariness and suspension that enables a good understanding of the place-identities of the three communities.

The concept of liminality was originally proposed by the French ethnographer, Arnold Van Gennep. His 1909 study, *Rites de Passage*, analyses the process of passing from one stage of life to another. Liminality is the second of three stages of a ritual rite of passage which initiates must go through. During this intermediate stage of suspension between the 'separation' from their previous state and the 're-assimilation' in a transformed condition, liminals experience an anomalous condition and are separated from society on the grounds of their sacred or infectious status. Van Gennep's work never had the impact it deserved, but in the late 1960s the concept of liminality was revisited by Victor Turner who focused on the central stage of identity transition.

Scholars have interpreted liminality in a number of ways. Some researchers focus on the spaces and processes intended either to facilitate transitions into educational institutions and normative states within those (Bettis 1996, Irving and Young 2004, Manning 2000, Rushton 2003) or to promote resistance to those normative states (Cook-Sather 2006). Others concentrate on the transitional state of the passenger, for example, the ambiguous positions within organizations of temporary employees (Garsten 1999) or consultants (Czarniawska and Mazza 2003), the re-integration in society of ex-prisoners (Maruna 2011) and the networks and temporary teams that cross organizational divides (Tempest and Starkey 2004).

Of particular relevance to this study is Anfara's work (1997) which focuses on the dis-affective and disengaged behaviour of school children in response to teachers treating them 'as not yet formed' subjects. Similar to Anfara's school children, this study's three groups of liminals engage in forms of resistance to a dominant, mainstream society that in view of their very different ways of living, treats them as incomplete individuals. As they are separate from society, in this stage of transformation, the people who are 'betwixt and between' (Turner 1967), are 'structurally invisible'. Importantly, there is a power dimension to liminality. In the case of the three groups, liminality is a form of contestation of society's beliefs and rules; at the same time, however, society responds by relegating them to segregated liminal spaces to curtail their interference with the politics of productivity and sedentarism.

Turner differentiates liminality from marginality and inferiority. While marginality relegates individuals and groups to the edges of society, inferiority attributes to them a lower and less dignified state than other people. Conceptualizing this study's three social groups as liminals is, therefore, a political decision. Moreover, liminality is temporary and limited in time in contrast to the marginal and inferior conditions that imply permanency and 'no cultural assurance of a final stable resolution of their ambiguity' (Turner 1974: 97). While I leave to one side the problem of who Turner defines as inferior and marginal or indeed outsider, (hippies, for example, are outsiders while hobos are inferior) as this raises complex issues that are not directly relevant to this study, I argue that liminality is a useful construct for this study of people whose identities are suspended between states and constructed on the grounds of the possibility to resolve their present problematic state of being. What characterizes Squatters, Travellers and Homeless people's existence as liminal, however, is the presence of two further constructs that make it possible to understand their construction of personhood in relation to space. The two constructs are that of *heterotopia* and *desire* that will now be discussed in what follows.

Heterotopia

Foucault's famous and 'confusing' (Cenzatti 2008: 75) discussion of *heterotopia* was part of a lecture he delivered in 1967 and published in full in 1984. He uses the concept of heterotopia to frame the history of space in western societies during the nineteenth century (although his analysis extends as far back as Galileo). For Foucault, heterotopias are situated between the unreal spaces of utopia and the negative spaces of dystopia. As such, they are counter-spaces or 'other spaces' and sites 'outside of all places, even though it may be possible to indicate their location in reality' (Foucault 1967: 24).

As mentioned, Palladino (2016) refers to the concept of heterotopia in reference to the sites occupied by Gypsies and Travellers. She argues that these heterotopias are especially deviant spaces that 'do not fit into established social (and spatial) order' (p. 8). Being also spaces of possibility where things that are extraordinary and different can happen, heterotopias thus define new spatial opportunities.

The boarding school, the army and even the honeymoon trip where the bride is taken to an unknown location for her symbolic deflowering exemplify heterotopias. As some heterotopias disappear, others emerge, some of which are spaces for individuals whose conduct is deviant and not in sync with mainstream society. The psychiatric hospital is the most frequently discussed heterotopia of contestation but so is the Travellers' unauthorized camp which is a space outside the law and where the law is suspended. Modern heterotopias or 'other spaces' have, therefore, lost their original connotation as 'transient concepts' (Cenzatti 2008: 77) and spaces of passage and have become instead 'other spaces' for deviants who do not meet society's requirements and whose conduct is a challenge of majoritarian beliefs and values.

Heterotopias are ephemeral and 'fluctuate between contradiction and acceptance' (Cenzatti 2008:79) as will become apparent in the interviews with the three sets of participants as 'subaltern counter-publics' (2008: 83) who both desire and refute the normalcy of mainstream society.

In addition, heterotopias 'always presuppose a system of opening and closing that both isolates them and makes them penetrable' (Dehaene and De Cauter 2008: 21). The contradictory features of closeness and penetrability are crucial aspects of the lives of this case study's communities. As will be discussed, Squatters, Travellers and especially Homeless people are in front of our eyes, visible to all, and as such seemingly penetrable. Yet, this penetrability is illusory since, in reality they are closed communities, both because the people in them choose self-segregation as a defence strategy and because mainstream society blocks them out by excluding them.

About heterotopias, Foucault further argues that,

> [e]ither their role is to create a space of illusion that exposes every real space, all the sites inside of which human life is partitioned, as still more illusory (perhaps that is the role that was played by those famous brothels of which we are now deprived). Or else, on the contrary, their role is to create a space that is other, *another real space, as perfect, as meticulous, as well arranged as ours is messy, ill constructed, and jumbled.*
>
> 1967: 8 emphasis added

Such interpretations of heterotopic space will be found in the words through which some of the study participants construct their place-identity. In particular, their need of a place and the exclusion they all suffer from contributes to the construction of an idealized spatial reality. The function of this counter-space is that it is flawless and perfectly harmonious in opposition to the imperfection of real spaces. The individuals who belong to this study's liminal groups occupy, therefore, a very complex space that merges contradictions of openness and impenetrability as well as perfection and fantasy accomplishment.

Desire

Foucault's sixth principle of heterotopia, namely the aspiration to a space and the discursive creation of a perfect locale, is closely associated with the concept of *desire*. Understanding the liminal individual's direct and indirect desires for space and the language used to express these adds important insights into the way people construct their place-identity.

Non-sexual desire may be a longing for a number of realities, both material and immaterial, determined by the conditions of incompleteness and powerlessness in which the three liminal groups live. It is often an indirect desire but the speakers' attempt to encode it even in a circuitous manner is a way of capturing and understanding it. These individuals' desires are realized through their linguistic choices that transform their experience into meaning.

The construct of desire has long been a core topic in a variety of disciplines from feminist research (Butler 1987, Kristeva 1980), philosophy and psychoanalysis (Deleuze and Guattari 2004, Kristeva 1980, Lacan 1977) and postcolonial studies (Young 1995, Stoler 1995). More recently, it has been adopted as a core construct in studies of identity (Canakis 2015) to understand motivation in language learning and L2 identities (Motha and Lin 2014) and partly as a tool for research into emotions (Prior 2016). As for space, it is argued that desire is not spontaneous or natural, rather, it is society and culture-driven. Thus, in its relation to a sedentary space and its hegemonic role in society, desire acquires a particular meaning and becomes the aspiration to confirm or contest a hegemonic conceptualization of space. In the introduction to their special issue on the topic, Cameron and Kulik (2003) distinguish between, on the one hand, plural *desires* as the momentary drive to obtain specific wants (e.g. food) and, on the other hand, a singular *desire* which refers to a more continuous and generalized drive. As is well known, in psychoanalysis both Freud and Lacan associated desire with sexual impulse and libido; on the contrary, for Deleuze and Guattari (2016), sexual desire is only one expression of such an internal drive among the many non-sexual manifestations and forms of longing such as the desire to walk, to listen to music, to swim, and have a drink. For these authors '[d]esire is lack', a lack that can be 'assuaged by pleasure' (2016: 179), but interpreting it only in relation to sexuality overlooks how desire works and is expressed. Cameron and Kulik (2003) point out how Deleuze and Guattari chose not to develop a whole theory of desire in exactly the same way that Foucault did not develop a theory of power. They follow how desire works and develops but without a theory that, like psychoanalysis, would have forced them to reconnect every human move to this drive (Cameron and Kulik 2003: 98).

Crucially, desire does not exist in isolation; it is inextricably linked to the context that triggers a given sense of something missing and/or the aspiration to resolve this lack. In Sara Ahmed's words, 'desire is both what promises something, what gives us energy, and also what is lacking, even in the very moment of its apparent realization' (2010:31 in Motha and Lin 2014: 334). To understand desire, therefore, one needs to understand what caused the sense of lack and what triggered the willingness to pursue what is not available.

Rather than an inner phenomenon or process, desire is a consequence of social conditions and 'constituted through social, discursive activity' (Billig 1997: 140 in Cameron and Kulik, 2016: 99). For example, Italian children more than their American counterparts are socialized into a desire for and appreciation of food that is healthy or tasty (Ochs, Pontecorvo and Fasulo 1996).

As noted earlier, few studies explore non-sexual desire although scholars are now attempting to capture the discursive construction of longing for a place. Building on their study of an agoraphobic American woman (1995), Ochs and Capps (2009), for instance, identify her conflicting accounts of fear of open spaces which are directly linked to strong desire to free herself from her deep-seated agoraphobia. Koven suggests 'making desire more central to the discourse-based study of place' (2019: 57). Her analysis contrasts the expressions of longing for the homeland by a second-generation Portuguese migrant in France during two different moments of her life. In both these examples, the desire to avoid fear and the desire for a lost place is realized through the woman's accounts before and after her move to Portugal.

In the above studies, as in the interviews in this book, desire is not produced in isolation but is relational and co-constructed by the speaker and the interlocutor, because 'our desires are not solely our own but are inter-subjectively constituted and shaped by our social, historical, political, and economic histories and contexts' (Motha and Lin 2014: 333).

Desire is inextricably linked to identity (Norton 1997) and expressed through the want for a particular membership, for security and place, and for being surrounded by particular things or people. For Norton, the identity question of 'who am I?' must be responded to with another question, namely 'what can I do?'; in other words, who we are depends on the access we have to services, structures, and, ultimately, power. Norton claims, therefore, to be in line with Bourdieu (1977) and his concept of symbolic power as the non-material form of cultural and social domination which is available to some individuals more than others.

As will be shown, the participants in this study display powerful wants for a place but also a clear ability to elaborate on their desires. Thus, the concept of first and second order desires lends itself particularly well to an understanding of their identities. According to Harry Frankfurt (2010, also cf. Norris 2010), personhood is the capacity to discriminate between ordinary, first-order basic wants and reflective, second-order volitions. 'Nothing but common sense (...) prevents an individual from obsessively refusing to identify himself with any of his desires until he forms a desire of the next higher order' (Frankfurt 2010: 91). It is, therefore, exactly the ability to move away from and rationalize impulsive drives what characterizes a person. The distinction between first and second order desires is relevant to this study's interviewees who show an ability to understand and demonstrate a degree of reflection with regard to their aspirations and wants.

The identities invoked by this study's individuals are a direct consequence of their non-sexual desire for respect, safety, security, dignity, recognition even integration, to a degree, that can all be encompassed in their longing for space. At the same time, the spatial choices made by them amount to an unambiguous contestation of sedentarist dominant society. They are, therefore, perceived by settled people as failing to support the profit-making values that underpin the neo-liberal economy and, as a result, they are relegated spatially to invisible spaces or spaces that can be ignored. Given their condition, it is not surprising that these people's identities are strongly moulded by their desire to fill this void although in ways that are still not consonant with the majoritarian hegemonic spatial ethics. It is also not surprising that their desire is inextricably linked to the discursive construction of a heterotopia as the space that counters and defies mainstream society's spatial ethics.

To summarize, the two key constructs of desire and heterotopia express a longing to resolve a lack and fill a void, which is inextricably linked to the condition of suspension and temporariness that characterizes liminality. The in-depth analysis of the speakers' interviews will show how such a concept of liminality is most useful in furthering our understanding of the nature of the individual identities belonging to these three sets of people.

Conclusion

This chapter has presented the theoretical framework of the study by exploring the concepts of place-identity, as situated and discursively constructed by the individuals in an interactional context. The linguistic analysis of the interviews adopts a number of specific constructs that, it is argued, are suitable to an understanding of the individuals' relation to space. Turner's notion of 'liminality' as the condition of suspended temporariness allows us to view the study's participants as people with potentials and not reified in a permanently marginal condition.

Foucault's concept of 'heterotopia' as a 'counter-site' on the margins of society is very much in line with the sense of space and in-betweenness experienced by liminal individuals. For Foucault, heterotopias are 'real places, effective places, places that are written into the institution of society itself, and that are a sort of counter-emplacements [...] the kind of places that are outside all places, even though they are actually localizable' (Foucault 1967: 17). The Squatters, the Irish Travellers and the Homeless people interviewed in this study physically occupy a liminal heterotopia, but also discursively construct that heterotopia with different functions.

The construct of desire or 'desires', which refers to continually reformulated, non-sexual, momentary, albeit persistent, individual wants (e.g. for affection/ material objects) is expressed directly and indirectly in the individuals' talk. As will be discussed, these desires are diverse, from the desires expressed by the Squatter for security and an alternative yet productive life, the Travellers' need to have their own space and be independent from any institutional control in the authorized site or the Homeless' attempt to justify and/or change their condition. The conceptual construct of desire, therefore, usefully supplements the linguistic creation of heterotopia. It is here that the link between space as another emplacement positioned between a reality of contestation and one of compensation relates closely to and shapes the identity of these individuals.

The next chapter discusses the methodology of the study and the issues involved in working with vulnerable people. Following that, the analysis chapters will show how the theoretical framework and constructs presented here are applied to the investigation of the participants' language.

3

Methodology

Introduction

This chapter explains how the study's theoretical framework is operationalized; it also discusses the methodological and ethical concerns inherent to the investigation and the general issues concerning data collection, while more specific information is contained in the individual analytical chapters. The core assumption of this book is that place-identity is realized discursively therefore the lexico-grammatical/syntactic, discursive and pragmatic choices as well as the rules of language use (turn taking patterns, conversational conventions etc.) that speakers make and the stance they express are the devices through which they construct their experience, transforming their feelings, volitions, pain, memories into social and personal meaning.

This book analyses the language affordances that the three types of liminal individuals resort to in order to encode their desire for place that informs their identity work. This is in line with the view of identity as arising from social interaction, being locally situated, fluid and co-constructed that was discussed in the previous chapter. The study's discursive constructionist focus is on how the specific information is presented and negotiated between speakers and how 'stance' (Du Bois 2007, Kiesling 2018) and evaluation are realized in terms of the way speakers position themselves to each other, to the interviewer, to the topic of the interaction and to society's shared knowledge and Discourses.

In terms of framework, this study is informed by Critical Discourse Studies (Fairclough 2010, van Leeuwen 2008, van Dijk 1993, Blommaert 2005), Conversation Analysis (Sacks et al. 1974, Hutchby and Wooffitt 2008), discursive psychology (Edwards and Stokoe 2004), ethnography (Copland and Creese 2015, Blommaert and Jie 2010), the ethno-methodological work of Garkinkel (1967) and Goffman (1981), anthropological approaches (Bauman 1986), and the research on interactional narratives (De Fina 2003 and 2015, De Fina and Georgakopoulou 2011).

Linguistic ethnographic, interactional and discourse analytic perspectives are therefore combined in this study. Linguistic ethnography studies local action as produced by actors embedded in a wider social context. Thus, it 'investigate[s] how language resources are deployed and what this can tell us about wider social constraints, structures and ideologies' (Creese and Blackledge 2016: 277). In addition, following Blommaert and Rampton (2011), ethnography is combined with a discourse perspective in order to unravel the ideologies that lie behind the identities constructed by the study's participants. In this way, this study's methodology responds to the call for 'an ethnography enriched with highly developed heuristic frameworks and procedures for discovering otherwise under-analysed intricacies in social relations' (Creese and Blackledge 2016: 278). On the other hand, the Critical Discourse Analysis focused on the interviewees' strategies of reference, predication and legitimation (van Leeuwen 2008) realized semantically, lexically and grammatically. To this effect, the qualitative analysis focuses on the speakers' recurring choices through which they construct their situated persona, which are identified both manually and with a concordance programme.

The post-structuralist social perspective of this study informs the way the interviewed individuals are conceptualized as social actors or 'subjects' (McNamara 2019). This follows on from the Foucauldian notion that identity is always constructed against the set of the discourses circulating in society which 'provide a language for talking about – a way of representing the knowledge about – a particular topic at a particular historical moment' (Hall 1997: 44 in McNamara 2019: 3).

The consideration of the role of discourses in the construction of subjectivity does not solely concern the study's participants. In qualitative investigations, in particular, the researcher is the 'primary research instrument' (Heigham and Croker 2009: 11) who is inevitably influenced by society's discourses or 'cultural scripts' as 'the tacit norms, values and practices widely shared, and widely known (on an intuitive level) in a given society' (Wierbizca 2010: 43). In some cases, a process of triangulation, through which different and even contrasting information is obtained from various sources, can limit the effects of the researcher's own subjectivity. However, a post-structuralist social interaction-based approach goes beyond such limitations since it openly admits the consideration of the researchers' role and thus rejects the notion of their neutrality (see Prior 2016: 3). As will be discussed, this is both a methodological and ethical issue.

The data: Theoretical issues

The study is based on one-to-one interviews as a popular research method in qualitative research that seeks to elicit rather than constrain speakers' accounts (Dörnyei 2007, Potter and Mulkay 1985). The interviews were semi-structured based on a set of standard questions, but still giving the interviewees plenty of leeway to steer the conversation in their preferred direction. The questions aimed at finding out about the interviewees' relation to place, attempted to elicit their emotions towards it and offer them an opportunity to reflect on their life history but also their plans and volitions for their future.

The Squatters, Travellers and Homeless are prime examples of the social marginality and exclusion in contemporary society due to their refutation of a dominant space logos. Following on from McNamara (2019), therefore, this study views the individual as adapting to and engaging in resistance towards the various forms of violence through which minority groups are kept in a condition of subalternity and disempowerment. However, as explained earlier, while fully recognizing the extreme social marginalization of these three groups, the theoretical construct of liminality involving the view of these individuals as occupying the 'interstices of society' (Turner 1967) is preferred in this study.

The topics discussed in this study are politically sensitive and the data collection was very challenging. The individuals interviewed stand in a controversial relation with society and do not easily open up to an outside researcher, however well-intentioned they may be. Not only do these people suffer from the negative media stereotyping but even well-meaning individuals and institutions who try to support these groups can constrain, often unintentionally, their agency and autonomy. It is not surprising, therefore, that, in these situations, gaining the interviewees' trust is a lengthy process which necessitates considerable personal involvement.

For studies that are situated within such an interactional framework, 'it is axiomatic that researchers' own biographies cannot help but shape their research' (Prior 2016: 7). More generally, the growing complexity of qualitative research has led to major concerns about the shortcomings of the positivist approach (see Heigham and Croker 2006). As many scholars have pointed out (Prior 2016, Denzin and Lincoln 2011, among many others), the aspiration to perfect objectivity is illusionary. The centrality of researcher's positionality and reflexivity has been stressed by a number of authors within the tradition of social constructionism, feminism and post-structuralism (e.g. Talmy 2011). The explicit recognition of the impact of the researcher's self on the research process is also fully consistent with the social constructivist framework informing this study that views meaning as continuously constructed by individuals. Similarly, from the Foucauldian theoretical perspective that underpins this investigation, no social reality can exist outside discourse and all interpretations are, therefore, conceived only within the subjectivity and relativity of discourses. Finally, without embarking on epistemological discussions, the relativist perspective taken in this study is based on the belief that all knowledge is socially situated and hence partial (Rolin 2006: 126).

The direct implication of these concepts is visible, among other things, in the socially grounded perspective according to which space is understood and interpreted in this study, in the recognition of the hegemonic management of diverse and less powerful communities by mainstream society and in the attempt to take sides with the people investigated.

On the methodological level the 'cultural and epistemological relativism' (Rolin 2006: 126) and the belief in a discourse-created identity imply that, as an interviewer, I positioned myself not just in relation to the participants but to the overall goal of the study, which admittedly has an influence on the investigation. The questions I posed to the interviewees, but also the pauses I allowed, the comments I made, the empathy I expressed and the ensuing narratives that emerged were all strongly and inevitably dependent on my stance towards these individuals. Since all data produced in such interactions as interviews are context-bound, no neat separation exists between the observer and the observed. Identity construction is an intersubjective process in which the portable identity an individual evokes depends crucially on who they understand the interlocutor to be. An interview is not simply the revelation of a personal truth but a collaborative achievement (Talmy 2011) between two or more parties situated in particular social, linguistic, cultural contexts. Interviews are not neutral and objective ways of gathering data; '[w]hat speakers say in interviews cannot be taken as texts produced in a "transparent context"; rather they are recipient oriented and designed to try to answer specific questions' (De Fina and Perrino 2011: 27). Therefore, interviewees' responses reflect the speakers' interpretation of the situation and their natural desire to present themselves as positively as possible (van De Mieroop 2011). The veracity of the accounts may be less relevant than the telling: 'Being interviewed is not about telling some inner truth about ourselves [. . .] This does not mean that respondents are not being truthful; it just means that they are producing appropriate answers in keeping with their understandings of the interview situation' (Duran Eppler and Codó 2016: 307).

Interviews and the personal stories within them can be understood as both 'accounts' and 'performances'. While accounts are understood 'in terms of their rhetorical, persuasive properties, and their functions in constructing particular versions of events, justifications of actions, evaluations of others, and so on', through a performative act 'identities are enacted, actions are justified and recounted events are retrospectively constructed' (Atkinson and Delamont 2006: 166–7).

Viewing interviews as opportunities for self-representation undeniably has important methodological implications for research on place-identity. Context plays an integral role with respect to the data produced and the researcher's illusionary neutrality. Blommaert (2001) for instance opines that, differently from Critical Discourse Analysis and Conversational Analysis, in ethnography, the situatedness of the data and their origin are crucial to the research together with the reasons that led a researcher to investigate them at that particular moment. Blommaert's analysis of the narratives of asylum seekers when they abandoned their usual underground status to protest openly against the killing of a Nigerian woman by the police in Belgium shows just how much context can impact data. The narrative collection was only possible because that event had changed the identity of the asylum seekers to that of protesters, which shows how the context was so integral to the data.

Beyond such methodological considerations, however, this study affords other more complex responsibilities as is discussed later. The interviews in this study are the main source of data, although they are accompanied by a wealth of field notes.

Transcriptions

Interview transcriptions are not neutral representations of spoken discourse; some scholars even go so far as to define them as a political process (Jenks 2011). In this study, for instance no phonetic transcriptions have been provided and only occasionally have comments been included about the speakers' prosody. Such a methodological choice is justified by the focus on the discourse level, in terms of the lexis/syntax and the pragmatics in the interviewees' talk, while other features of the delivery are considered less salient. All the interviews extracts were transcribed according to conventions loosely following Gail Jefferson's.[1]

> If the process of transcription involves choices so does the decision about what elements of the interviewees' language are worth analysing. One feature that

stands out especially in the talk of the Travellers is the use of non-standard English and such set phrases as 'You know what I mean?' These two elements, however, are not given much attention in this study. In the latter case, the interrogative phrase is not exclusive to the Travellers but is in frequent use among myriads of speakers in an interactional situation. The use of non-standard English among the Irish Travellers on the contrary is more complex. Of all the women interviewed, only one used standard English and did not show an Irish accent. When I commented on it, she told me she could change her speech according to the situation and interlocutors to avoid difficulty in being understood. For the other Travellers non-standard English is instead the norm. To use Johnstone's words, '[a] sign (a word, a gesture, a glance, a hairstyle, or anything else that can be meaningful) is indexical if it is related to its meaning by virtue of co-occurring with what it is taken to mean' (2016: 633). The example Johnstone gives is thunder and its association with lightening, dark skies and rain. Like thunder, the Irish women's dialect, therefore, is an indication of the Travellers' identity. However, it is not a form of 'enregisterment', the process 'whereby performable signs become recognized (and regrouped) as belonging to distinct, differentially valorized semiotic registers by a population' (Agha 2007: 81 in Johnstone 2016: 633). Not being systematically exposed to other forms of English due to their only occasional contacts with settled citizens, the Travellers are generally only familiar with non-standard dialect and unable to produce any other register. The non-standard English so apparent in the interviews, cannot therefore be taken as a meaningful act that is semiotically linked with the 'culturally-relevant ways' (Johnstone 2016: 634) of being a Traveller. This restricted code (Bernstein 1964) therefore is not discussed as the speakers' deliberate choice.

Representativeness

This study is not an investigation of gender and language, and femininity versus masculinity is not a main concern. It is undeniable, however, that the majority of the speakers are female for reasons that range from the participants' availability for the interviews to the greater ease I, as a female researcher, had in addressing women. This raises two main concerns. Firstly, how representative the data are, given that the women in the Travellers' community are the primary object of investigation with men being very much behind the scenes. Secondly, in spite of the fact that the majority of participants are female, the present analysis is not centred on gender specifically, although inevitably there is clear recognition of the role of female speakers as mothers and guardians of their community. Therefore, this study does not claim to have complete representativeness in terms of the degree to which a data sample reflects the general situation of a community (Biber 1993: 243). The study's results cannot be generalized to all the individuals associated with space deprivation, but they are strongly indicative of how people in that particular context construct themselves in an interaction with a sympathetic interlocutor. What this study offers is an opportunity for, in Bakhtin's (1981) words, a 'heteroglossic' engagement with diversity as a window open on to the alternative voices, especially those that are rarely heard or are 'muted' (Atkinson and Delamont 2006: 166). Echoing Baxter (2008: 247), this means 'giving space to marginalised or silenced voices (such as certain girls who say little in the classroom settings, or those women whose voices are overlooked or silenced in management settings).' While female voices are investigated as such and women's role within the communities under study duly recognized, what emerges from the field notes is that often the few men's testimonials are not very different from the women and very much complete the picture that their partners, friends or spouses have depicted.

Issues of terminology in data collection

As mentioned earlier, the data for the four analysis chapters come mainly from semi-structured or conversational interviews accompanied by field notes. During the interviews, researchers generally make sure to show understanding and appreciation, especially through eye-contact, while limiting back-channelling to avoid interfering with the speaker's narrative. However, 'the interview is an exchange in which the interviewer has to contribute to get quality conversation back' (Feagin, 2006: 31). At times, therefore, showing my enthusiasm for something the interviewees said or occasionally sharing a similar experience with them produced the positive result of encouraging the speakers to talk more about the topic.

The term 'narrative' appears throughout the book to refer to the often-minimal stories provided by the speakers. It is used interchangeably with the term 'accounts', in agreement with De Fina (2009a) who highlights how narratives in interviews are different from unsolicited stories:

> ...the mode of emergence of narratives has consequences for the types of narratives that get told and it shapes and reflects a certain kind of relationship between the interactants. When accounts are produced, the relationship

established between the participants tacitly implies that one of the partners is in a position not only to elicit a certain kind of narrative, but also to evaluate it. The nature of this relationship and the weight of this asymmetry needs to be defined based on the type of activity in which accounts are embedded and the specific social roles and power relations between interactants, but in general terms one can safely argue that in situations where accounts are produced it is assumed that the interlocutor, more than the narrator, has the primary responsibility in evaluating the validity and/or adequacy of the narrative in its context'.

2009: 240

Accounts or narratives in interviews, therefore, are highly negotiated between the two parties involved and, since the narrative structure changes according to the context of production, any attentive analysis must consider them as the situated product of an interaction.

As noted earlier, referring to the individuals interviewed in this volume as members of a 'group' or a community is problematic for the very reason that group in itself is not an easy word. Conversation analysts, especially Benwell and Stokoe (2006: 158), have criticized the tendency of researchers to ascribe external categorizations to individuals. The relevance of the categorical meaning of 'group' is similarly doubted in this study. Some definitions of the term emphasize that sharing a purpose or goal 'turns a mere aggregate of individuals into a bona fide group' (Forsyth 2014: 2), while for some others it is when people form relationships that they can be considered as part of a group or community. The variety of interpretations of the term 'group' justifies a researcher's perplexity in adopting the notion for the three sets of contributors to the volume. Moreover, especially in the context of marginalization, the term 'group' does not seem to take into account the agency and free determination of the individuals to associate effectively with each other. It seems that most definitions of the term are to a degree juxtaposed onto an aggregation of people without interpelling the individuals inside it. This point in particular raises concerns that border with ethics. It can be argued that, for the community of Irish Travellers, the notion of group does to a degree fit that association of people in the name of their declared shared interests, beliefs and ideology as well as the frequent self-naming. However, do the Travellers observed in this study effectively share such common features without reservations and exceptions? Are they representative of Travellers in the UK or worldwide? More to the point, is it appropriate to use the term 'group' with, for instance, the Squatters or, even more problematically, the Homeless clients of day centres? As identity construction is not neutral, one must not ignore issues of power and ideology. Therefore, it is legitimate to ask whether the choice of the collective term 'group' is not in reality a way of easily distancing or 'negative othering' (Riggins 1997) a most varied and diverse set of individuals with idiosyncratic experiences and very discrete and private history.

Two risks are therefore associated with a study like the present. One is the risk of reproducing a hegemonic classification for a set of individuals who are already victims of social exclusion; the other is the risk of accepting a label that ends up essentializing these people on exactly the same grounds as those used by society to marginalize them.

A possible answer to these concerns comes from Spivak's work (Spivak and Grosz 1990). In one of the interviews in *Criticism feminism and the institution*, Spivak uses the example of the category 'intellectuals'. She argues that 'there isn't, in fact, a group that can be called "a group of Intellectuals", that exercises the same sort of role or indeed power within social production. I mean a figure like Noam Chomsky, for example, seems very much an oddity' (1990: 177). Similarly, phenomena like the French May '68 or Berkeley riots in the US a year earlier are for Spivak too context-specific to be interpreted in a general way. Following on from her suggestions, therefore, people who form associations can reasonably reject common labels like the members of various subcultures in Widdicombe's (1998) study, in spite of their still undeniably sharing some common elements. Vice versa, as in the case of this study, the concern is with using the label 'group' solely because some people tend to live in the same conditions and spaces. This methodological concern would, of course, determine the choice of a continuous context-specific relativism and the rejection of both categorizations and generalizing reflections. However, although starting from a clear stress on the role of context, Spivak proposes a way out of this conundrum when she admits that a degree of 'strategic essentialism' is necessary and indeed inevitable as in studies on sexuality and anti-sexist work. 'Even as we talk about feminist practice, or privileging practice over theory, we are universalising – not only generalising but universalising' (1990: 184). The present study faces these methodological and ethical issues and, while it accepts that the strategic choice of essentialism is inescapable from any research, it problematizes issues of classifications especially concerning people in a condition of lower power and status.

Practical matters of data collection

The study's interviewees are undeniably in an inferior position to the rest of society. Approaching them and obtaining their consent to be interviewed was as expected, difficult. It involved getting their trust not just in me as a person but in my project and declared goal to learn about their community and then raise people's awareness about it. In spite of the fact that consent was obtained orally and recorded at the beginning of the interviews, the ethical issue remained. The case of the Irish Travellers is paramount. As will be explained in more detail in the relevant chapters, I spent a long time in the transient encampment starting in 2012 prior to the completion of the permanent site in June 2016. In both contexts, my aim was to understand who the Irish Travellers are, their needs and aspirations. My broad questions were, 'Who are they? How do they live? What are they after? How could their conditions be improved? Do they relate to the outside society?' As the community lived on an authorized site, liaising with the relevant Council staff was an important and necessary step. My work was always appreciated by them as a way of finding out more about the Travelling community due to the fact that the Travellers would open up to me more than they did to them. However, I still felt the responsibility of sharing with the Travellers' Liaison staff the information the interviewees gave me; this was in spite of the fact that the Travellers' comments contributed to a better understanding of their desires and needs and could be used by the local authorities to make that community more satisfied with their living arrangement. For a number of years since 2012, I organized a series of events for the Irish Travellers and Gypsies as well as for the Homeless in coordination with local authorities in the south of England. This was a deliberate ethical decision, the intention being to continue community engagement work for these people beyond the academic work. The interviewees were strongly encouraged to participate in the public events and occasionally contributed. The goal was, on the one hand, to talk about these individuals who are invisible and muted, unknown to most people, and raise the general public's awareness that there are alternative ways of living beyond the general logos of sedentarism. On the other hand, the intention was to open a dialogue with the institutions and offer them an opportunity to discuss publicly their strategies with regard to these communities. To a degree, therefore, my research with these liminal individuals turned into serious community-engagement aiming at realizing the social praxis that Creese (2008) advocates as the outcome of linguistic ethnography. In spite of this, the awareness of my condition as outsider never completely siding with or being able to appreciate the full complexity of these people's lives was always very present in my mind.

In a linguistic ethnographic study of this kind, it is not always clear whether the overall goal is to make the different and largely unknown lives of the

Squatters, Travellers and Homeless more familiar or, conversely, make their known social practices stranger (Creese 2008). Ethically, both these goals could mispresent these research participants who may end up being portrayed as odd, unusual, and 'marked' (Piazza and Fasulo 2015) as they stand out against the conventional and hence 'unmarked' people who follow society's norms. The difficulty of approaching the three groups can be viewed as an integral part of the context that had an expected effect on the interview. As an outside researcher, I showed an interest in and empathy for the interviewees and this inevitably influenced the identities they constructed. Following on from this, the relationship established between us also had an impact on the discourse produced. Martha, the squatter, for instance, was given access to the transcripts of her interviews; while this was an important choice in terms of responsiblizing the interviewee by making her into a participating actor (according to the tenets of 'reciprocal anthropology', Lawless 1993: 60-61) rather than an object of observation, it is not unlikely it contributed to a crystallization of her identity throughout our encounters.

Similarly, it is not easy to enter the Traveller community. This issue has been extensively discussed in a number of studies (Matthews and Velleman 1997, Hester 2000) and recognized in Home Office research on police engagement with 'hard to reach' groups. Jones and Newburn (2001) and James (2007) report on the difficulties of interviewing Travellers and their preference for note-taking as a less invasive technique. For this study gaining the Travellers' trust and obtaining their agreement to being recorded was not an easy task. It involved explaining who I was, why I was on the site and why I was keen to talk to them. The explanation I provided that I wanted to know that community and their needs was generally accepted. Occasionally, however, I encountered some resistance and was told that they did not have time to talk to me, that they were not well, that they did not like the sound of their recorded voice or that their mother, sister, daughter or friend was more articulate than they were and I should talk to them instead. However, when interviewing was successful, the respondents often recommended other potential interviewees, which proved that the use of snowball sampling is particularly successful to accessing hard to reach people associations (Waters 2014)

I arrived at the Council-run Traveller transit site with a student in spring 2012. I explained our intentions to the site guardian and obtained the Council's permission to enter the site by explaining my project to a member of staff on the phone. Initially, the Traveller women were taken by surprise but were won over by our casual and friendly attitude. However, as with the asylum seekers in

Blommaert's study (2001), I suspect they agreed to be interviewed in the hope that we would provide support for them in their discussions with the Council about the proposed permanent site.

Working with Travellers is not easy. However, the reason for this is not, as I have repeatedly heard even by Council support staff, that Travellers are 'private people'. Rather, being interviewed for no apparent reason can make the interviewees feel like they are being treated as circus curiosities. Thus, when feelings of this kind are engendered, their lack of interest or openness to engage with a researcher is quite understandable. In a book for the general public based on these interviews (Piazza and Morgan 2018), I reported an episode that occurred at the permanent site that is symptomatic not solely of the Travellers' attitude but also of the ethical responsibility involved in the present study. Surprised at finding a huge mobile home in the open space outside her bungalow, one day I asked a woman Traveller whom I know relatively well how many rooms it had. While she launched in the account of the ordeal her family went through to set up the four-bedroom home, her partner started asking me a number of increasingly odd questions. 'Where do you live? How many rooms have you got in your house? Have you got pets? Have you got rats?' to the final 'Do you want rats?' The woman Traveller told him to stop, while under his breath the man said something along the lines of 'what right do some people have asking questions?' The woman apologized and urged me to ignore her partner although I decided to leave, with a clear sense I was intruding on the privacy of that family. The researcher's ethical responsibilities are beyond doubt in studies like the present one. Within a linguistic ethnographic and a Critical Discourse Analysis approach, however serious the belief in interventionism and political praxis can be, the investigation of such liminal communities as Irish Travellers or the Homeless can undoubtedly be perceived as exploitative by the participants. This is true in spite of the aspiration of this study to encourage advocacy for the groups and, by working alongside the local authorities, improve their life standards.

Over time, a relationship developed with the Traveller women. I was often invited into their caravans, offered a cup of tea, showed around and frequently thanked for my interest in their cause. My field notes were filled with comments about the objects found in the caravans, from richly decorated plates to religious paraphernalia. I was particularly struck by the plastic sheeting under which precious items like tables and sofas are kept in the caravans. Protecting valuable items without ever enjoying them to their fullest was something I had seen before in migrant Italian communities in Australia and my enthusiasm for such a custom clearly ingratiated me to the women and increased my familiarity with them. The women's devotion to Padre Pio or Saint Pio of Pietralcina, who was a mystic friar and alleged stigmatist now venerated as a saint in the Roman Catholic Church, was another discovery. Statuettes of the saint were very frequently present in the caravans; my expression of positive surprise and the fact that I told the women I came from the saint's original country was another trigger for a rapport with them. Finally, the fact that I am not a native speaker put me in a positive light with them; like them, I was, to a degree, a cultural outsider, a further reason for bonding.

Developing a relation with the clients of a local day centre for the Homeless was equally problematic. Thanks to a volunteer in the day centre,[2] I gained access to a transient community of Rough Sleepers. The term 'transient' is most appropriate in this case as these people wander about dividing their time between the various resources available in the city where the study was conducted. Their presence is, therefore, erratic as they may be 'regulars' for several weeks and then disappear completely because their situation has changed for the better or the worse. Homeless people go through serious difficulties not solely triggered by the lack of a home; they have histories of abuse, violence, loss of possessions, ill health and much more. As a result, they are often not emotionally stable and have low and less low days. Day centres are only a momentary station in their turbulent days. In this situation of precariousness, establishing a good rapport with these people and gaining their trust was challenging. The data were collected during two periods; one, when I first approached the centre and the second, when I participated to some artistic activities with two groups of clients that a colleague ran at the centre. This study only considers the first set of interviews while the others will be part of a further study (Piazza in preparation).

Finally, accessing the Squatter in this study through a friend who shared the same experience of squatting was an achievement and through Martha I learned not solely about the hardship of people who lead her life but also the resources that are available to them. Issues of representativeness have been discussed already; however, such rare interviews with a woman in this transient condition can provide some insight into her and others' life. Given the one-to-one relationship with Martha, the type of talk ensued was more intimate and the stories she shared with me were longer and more revelatory than the other interviews. The analysis however takes into account these differences between the various study's participants.

In conclusion, the collection of the data from the three types of mobile and transient individuals presented in this book was a complex process that involved serious ethical issues and a commitment to their cause. The chapters that follow will give the reader the sense of how individuals without a home construct their personhood and create their own heterotopic reality. Although the three investigations are based on interviews and field notes, the first one is a case study where the same individual was re-interviewed several times in different places. Further details about the methodology are given in the individual chapters.

4

Locating the transient self in a transient heterotopia: Squatting as an affective and entrepreneurial proposition

Introduction

Place-belongingness is not only one aspect of place identity, but a necessary basis for it. 'Around this core the social, cultural and biological definitions and cognitions of place which become part of the person's place-identity are built' (Korpela 1989: 246). In line with such concerns, this chapter investigates situated place-identity defined as the relation between an individual's self and the location they occupy, which is integral to personal identity (Dixon and Durrheim 2000, Kabachnik 2009 and 2012, Massey 2013, Moss and Dyck 2003 among many others). The physical space of one's environment is what allows 'the psychic balance of pain and pleasure, and the coherence of one's self and self-esteem' (Korpela 1989: 241). In light of this, the chapter's main focus is on 'affect' (Martin and White 2005) and the aspirational and imaginative dimension of the individual's relation to place by which the speaker compensates the precarious situation in which she is. The attention therefore is on the impact longing and desire have on the self seen in terms of 'who we *think* we are' or better 'who we want to construct ourselves as' rather than 'who we are'.

This is a case study of a female squatter in a major city in the south of England whom I followed in some of her temporary accommodations. As with the subsequent chapters, this investigation of her real and imagined relation with space and the role it occupies in her identity construction is based on one-to-one interviews.

Underpinning the study is the view of places as 'dynamic arenas' in continuous evolution rather than fixed 'containers of social action' (Dixon and Durrheim 2000: 27). As will be discussed later in relation to Foucault's (1966/7) concept of 'heterotopia', places are the result of top-down interests of majoritarian groups but also the consequence of the bottom-up efforts of less powerful communities. A political dimension therefore also characterizes this study, which responds to Dixon and Durrheim's (2000) plea against the marginalization of the political dimension in individual space representation in place-identity studies (p. 28). Such a political dimension is integral to the choices made by the particular individual in this study, who resists mainstream society's sedentarist spatial logic; it is also reflected in the way she articulates such relation by constructing her space as suspended between a critique of capitalist ideology and an appreciation of its potentialities for alternative goals.

This first analysis chapter reflects on a squatter as a liminal individual representative of groups and communities perceived as threatening in that they challenge many of the majoritarian society's norms. The considerations that can be drawn from the analysis of the interviews with Martha, the pseudonym for the squatter in this chapter, cannot be generalized to all squatters and certainly not to those 'hard core' squatters (as the participant calls other more radical squatters) who are less approachable than the individual belonging to the group with which I established a long time relationship. In spite of this note of caution, however, Martha's story contributes to understanding both the reality of precarious residences and the identity that individuals who choose them construct discursively.

Squatting as an alternative life-style

The quote below from a no longer available URL provides an introduction to squatting and some of the reasons why people may choose it:

> Squatting – an alternative lifestyle, a political statement, or a solution to a housing problem? If you're thinking about squatting, make sure you know where you stand legally.
> Why should I squat?
> A lack of decent housing is still a major reason for squatting.
> All kinds of people squat – those with regular jobs who don't earn enough to pay the rent, ex-armed forces people who are unable to find work. And then there are people who choose to live alternatively due to political beliefs such as artists, musicians, travellers, and those who disagree with private housing ownership.[1]

Squatting can be a choice of necessity (to ensure accommodation) or political activity (to send a message to the authorities).

Piotrowski and Polanska (2016), who trace the origin of the term *squatting* to 19th-century US, describe it as 'the taking-over of unused property by the Settlers (it also meant taking the land from Native American people), regulated in 1862 by the Homestead Act' (p. 55). Vasudevan (2017) reminds us how in the 19th century squatting was often connected to rent strikes and public unrest, which is probably one of the reasons why governments have always been opposed to squatters in spite of some occasional support from citizens. While in one of the chapters, Vasudevan analyses the situation in Vancouver, Piotrowski and Polanska (2016) examine the squatting situation in two cities in Poland and find out that the media have changed their attitude to squatters from scepticism to interest in their campaigns for accessible space thanks to the activists' accurately planned moves. Born as a practice to provide cheap or free accommodation to the needy, in the 1970s squatting became a political manifestation of counterculture and DIY[2] culture in an attempt to redistribute economic resources in a more egalitarian way (Piotrowski and Polanska 2016: 55). In spite of the distinction between need-based and politics-based squatting, often the two types of building occupation seem to merge. Piotrowski and Polanska also distinguish between 'house projects (living projects, social shelters etc.)' and other squats that 'after the Italian anti-hierarchical left Autonomia movement activists from the late 1960s and early 1970s, are usually called social centers' (2016: 55).

Dee and Debelle (2015) compare squatting in England, Wales and Catalonia. As squatters in Barcelona are granted a much longer time in their occupied space, the Catalan nationalist movement has facilitated negotiations between squatters and local authorities and has also led to the formation of a separate political group for squatters. Contrariwise, the squatters' movement in England and Wales[3] is 'diffuse and fairly disorganised, with the average lifespan for a squat being three months' (Dee and Debelle 2015: 130). The authors also confirm that squatters are not interested in talking to the mainstream media given their coverage is generally negative.

The passing of the Legal Aid, Sentencing and Punishment of Offenders Act (2012) has made squatting of empty residential properties in England and Wales a criminal rather than a civil offence. Occupying commercial buildings on the contrary is still accepted for short periods of time until, through legal measures, eviction is sanctioned. 'In the English context it is interesting to note that the Land Registration Act of 2002 made it harder for squatters to gain ownership of buildings or land through adverse possession, by notifying the owner of a claim and thus giving them the chance to begin eviction proceedings. (...) [T]his adjusted approach takes a moral stance which sees property owners as blameless' (Dee and Debelle 2015: 131).

In the conversations with Martha, the consequence of the criminalization of squatting in England, caused by a mostly media-inspired moral panic, is evident, 'legitimised by a narrative concerning the vulnerability of private property (whilst the counter narrative emphasised the vulnerability of people squatting)' (Dee and Debelle 2015: 131). Martha indicates that once a suitable commercial property for squatting has been identified (schools, churches or boarded-up pubs as in Figure 1), a group of people moves in and adjusts the site to their residential needs. In some well-organized and well-run squats, people of all ages, ethnicity and gender can lead a harmonious commune-style life very different from the private, individualistic existence of mainstream people. Squatters' life, however, is generally stressful and uneasy as they are always on the brink of eviction and continuously faced by bailiffs. Prosecutions are frequently avoided, however, because 'when challenged (...) most guardian companies back down and come to a deal, rather than allow the issue to go to court'.[4]

Against this backdrop and in the *hic et nunc* of the interview contexts, this study shows how Martha constructs her squat as a real but also an aspirational

Figure 1 A squatted boarded up public house (personal photo).

place, and as a heterotopia of both deviation and transgression as well as illusion. As discussed in chapter two, the notion of heterotopia is in sync with the understanding of the study's participants as liminal individuals. Martha always occupies in-between spaces, she has slipped into the interstices of English society and, while there, she is longing for a different life. The place she constructs during the interview and the way she portrays herself are therefore inextricably linked to her condition of liminal suspension.

The discourses around squatters

To understand liminals like squatters and their identity construction, it is useful to consider the prejudices and narratives that circulate around them and which the interviewees will resist or assuage in their desire to distance from or align to society's roles. In contrast with the other groups and individuals profiled in this volume, squatters are not considered a minority or a group suffering from marginalization; rather, they are perceived as usurpers of public resources, and 'othered' as deviant. Only very rarely, therefore, are their motivations behind the occupation of private property objectively or even sympathetically considered by mainstream society.

Dee and Debelle note how the stereotypes of squatters as 'possessing such supposedly deviant values as being foreign, young, criminal, anti-capitalist, drug-using and so on' encourage a 'moral panic' and heats up the debate about squatting criminalization that facilitates repression (2015: 120). In an earlier study, Dee commented that 'there is a certain shorthand at work which enables "good" squatters who are protesters, occupiers or an art group to be distinguished from "bad" squatters who are aggressive, lifestylists, serial, unlawful and unwanted' (1993: 257).

As expected, negative press coverage clusters around particular newsworthy events that further inflame the discourse about squatters. However, this moral panic has emerged only relatively recently. In particular, after World War II, due to the chronic shortage of accommodation, the mass appropriation of living spaces by the Homeless was strongly supported by the public at large. In a BBC article on 22 November 2011, ninety-year-old Eileen Milton remembers squatting in a 'former Italian prisoner-of-war camp in the Bristol area' without ever suspecting squatting could be illegal.

Some squatters are part of the 'social movement scene', in that they 'share a common identity and a common set of sub-cultural or countercultural beliefs, values, norms' (Creasap 2012: 182). Being part of this 'scene', squats provide spaces of resistance and urban contestation. Against such a background, squatting is the expression of a claim to space and squatters represent 'attempts to intervene in the urban landscape in response to increasing neo-liberalization and gentrification' (Creasap 2012: 184). For some, squatting is an intelligent response to the housing crisis and a contribution to grassroots movements. In this case, their presence is synonymous of a 'gentrifying imaginary' (Cattaneo and Martinez 2014) when they save buildings from dereliction and transform seedy and down-at-heel areas of cities into upmarket places. The choice of occupied spaces often indexes a clear political choice as in the case of a preference to squat in buildings located in working-class neighbourhoods away from wealthy and corporate areas (Creasap 2012: 186).

Dee (2013) scrutinizes the coverage of squatting in three national newspapers and one local newspaper in Brighton: *The Guardian* (a left-leaning quality broadsheet), *The Daily Mail* (a right-leaning tabloid), *The Daily Telegraph* (a right-leaning quality broadsheet) and the *Brighton Argus* (a right-leaning local paper). By contrast with the positive view of squatters in other European countries such as the Netherlands where they are regarded as 'actors participating in city planning' (2013: 3), in the UK, national and local newspapers portray squatters as drug addicts and modern hippies. An article in the *Brighton Argus* on 10 May 2009 highlights the very poor condition of a recently squatted building, while another (24 September 2004) describes a squat as 'typical of those occupied by many students, littered with books, videos and clothes' (p. 3). Such negative discourse is supported by the polarization referred to earlier between, on the one hand, bad, anti-social and destructive squatters, and good, socially progressive and constructive squatters, on the other.

In summary, the dominant narrative around squatting is strongly shaped in a way that facilitates their criminalization and exclusion. Even when a squat is an explicit act (as, for example, when the ANAL group, in 2017 occupied the empty, London mansion of Russian billionaire Andrey Goncharenko), the general attitude to squatters is that they take what is not theirs and live at the expense of tax-payers. Little attempt is ever made to understand the rationale behind their choices, the political motives that underpin their actions or the needs that they try to fulfill when occupying properties.

The theoretical approach

An interpretation of space as discursively constructed and situated in the *hic et nunc* of its specific interactional context fits in well with a social constructionist vision of identity as locally situated and negotiated. Within this view, 'human actors are cast as imaginative users of their environments, agents who are able to appropriate physical contexts in order to create, here, a space of attachment and rootedness, a space of being' (Dixon and Durrheim 2000: 29). During the interviews, Martha shows different strategies to discursively express her affect to the squat, from the use of particular lexis and pronouns to 'emplotment' strategies (to use Ricoeur's term) by which she constructs 'personal narratives complete with plots and subplots, dramatic personae, settings, goals, beginning and endings, climaxes and anti-climaxes etc.' (Sarbin 1983: 340).

Like many other squatters, Martha leads a precarious life in residences that deviate from the majoritarian conceptualization of permanent space. Thus, her choice bears a crucial dimension of resistance to a dominant interpretation of living space and the traditional modalities of individualistic social life. In light of this, the present study considers Martha's identity as resulting from the relation she has with her squat. The place Martha constructs and in relation to which she negotiates her identities is interpreted as a form of Foucault's (1967) heterotopia.

Heterotopias are 'real places, effective places, places that are written into the institution of society itself, and that are a sort of counter-emplacements (...) a kind of places that are outside all places, even though they are actually localizable' (Foucault 1967: 17). The discussion in this chapter draws on Foucault's complex concept by analysing the way in which as a liminal subject, Martha constructs her place as a site that although real, is 'situated outside all other spaces and [is] destined to efface, to neutralize, to compensate or purify the spaces [it] oppose[s]' (Boyer 2008: 53). Close to the concept of utopia and dystopia, heterotopias appear ambiguous, indecipherable and suspended between suitably normal or 'eutopic' and undesirable or 'dystopic' realities (Dehaene and De Cauter 2008: 25). As is discussed in the course of the analysis of Martha's interviews, heterotopias are spaces of both contestation and illusionary compensation. Martha challenges the dominant settled spatial discourse, while at the same time she aspires to assuage her lack of fit in society with a series of propositions that while illusionary, still well reconcile squatting with a corporate vision of reality, and position her as a potentially productive individual.

In the contemporary world, heterotopias defy the 'hegemonic' logic of sedentarism according to which space is stable and fixed and individuals can exert control on it. It is from this perspective that the heterotopia constructed by such liminals as squatters and other non-sedentary people – as will be discussed in the subsequent chapters of this book – is deviant in that it proposes an often functioning non-hegemonic counter space that does not align with a logic of control and ownership, whether permanent or temporary. Today's heterotopias, therefore, are made 'other' by the very same deviant groups that inhabit them (Cenzatti 2008: 77). In this way, the notion of heterotopia helps us to understand the choices that some individuals make in particular contexts. Such choices reflect a 'diversity' or 'super-diversity' (Vertovec 2007) in our society, which although beyond the context of migration, still pertains to the reality of mobility. In this study, the life style of the group to which Martha belongs is a choice that needs to be fully understood if we want to move away from an assimilationist vision (Crul 2016) and build a more open perspective that is respectful of alternative ways of social living.

Importantly, as Cenzatti notes, heterotopias of deviance are not permanent because deviance in itself is a 'transient concept': '[a]fter all, power flows in all directions, and regulatory controls are not just produced by top-down interests. They also respond to movements from below' (2008: 77). Such a concept of deviant heterotopia as transitory is not only crucial to the understanding of the space that squatters occupy and the way they relate to it in terms of desire and aspiration. It is also crucial to the concept of identity that is conceptualized and explored in this study. It will be shown how Martha resorts to linguistic practices to construct the identities she has forged from the instability and ephemerality of her life in several residences. The analysis shows how, across the conversational interviews (carried out in different squats) and even within the same conversation, Martha claims multiple identities and offers differently connoted representations of her heterotopia.

A word on the methodology of the study

The conversational interviews analysed in this chapter were collected over a period of two years during which I followed Martha in different squats in a major city in the south of England till the moment when she started sofa surfing while preparing for a trip to an ecological farm in a European country where she had planned to establish herself with some friends. She was always happy to let me record our exchanges that were later transcribed; Martha is her pseudonym to protect her privacy and references to places in her talk have been deleted to make her unidentifiable. While I spent some time with Martha in her squats and took notes about her and her friends with whom I also talked, this study is based on four one-hour long interviews. A crucial aspect of this study's methodology is the democratic and responsibility-encouraging cooperation between the participant and researcher. Following the principles of 'reciprocal ethnography' (Lawless 1993: 60–61), I shared the transcriptions of our exchanges with Martha together with the conference presentations I gave on the data; I encouraged her to comment on and reflect on what she generously shared with me. Martha was always treated with respect and humility rather than condescending patronage and over the years a friendly relationship ensued between us. This does not, however, rule out or resolve in any way the ethical concerns arising from an ethnographic study of this nature in which the researcher in a situation of stable comfort cannot avoid feeling like an intruder when observing how people in much less fortunate situations lead complicated and challenging existences.

Apart from such ethical preoccupations, a limitation of the present case study is that the repeated exchanges with Martha and, at a later stage, the open access I offered her to the transcripts may have contributed to some degree of crystallization of her identity in the sense that is discussed below. Martha became a particular kind of squatter in my eyes and once she had constructed that identity (something I suspect she was aware of) she continued to strengthen and support it discursively.

Arguing that this study's methodology is replicable is not easy. I was lucky to find an entry in a squatters' collective; however, other times I managed to speak to other squatters in other locations and found they were willing to open up to me. In brief, engaging with marginal people requires a personal commitment to and a tangible interest in their cause. After all, in spite of some initial resistance, people are not insensitive to a show of care for their condition, therefore gaining an entry into closed groups simply requires persistence and kindness. As an example, sometime later during the Corona pandemic crisis, I tried to interview an English Traveller I befriended and his wife on issue of debris and dirt that Travellers are accused to leave behind. I made very clear I wanted to hear their voice to counter-balance the widespread discriminatory discourse around mobile people and they were very keen to share their views. In respect of social distancing, however, they did not allow me to visit their site. After some insistence, we agreed to have a video call that I recorded with his permission; this, I hope, proves that perseverance and show of honest interest in their condition are the strategies to approach vulnerable individuals.

The counter dimension of Martha's heterotopia of deviation and transgression alternates with a heterotopia of illusion and compensation, both clearly visible through the language she uses to refer to her site. Martha's heterotopia is realized through the discursive construction of two different yet mutually sustaining 'frames' (Tannen 1993) in terms of ways of organizing the experience linked to the 'structure of expectations' of a particular scenario, e.g. the supermarket till or the medical consultancy frame, which an individual's discourse construction can raise in the hearer. These frames have been termed the *corporate frame* and the *self-defence frame* respectively; through them Martha's heterotopia appears both as a site of contestation of mainstream places and a compensatory site. Through the referential identity labels Martha uses (Bucholtz and Hall 2005: 594), indicators at grammatical and lexical level, stance and pragmatically expressed meanings, this speaker instantiates very clear identities and chooses specific alignment roles suggesting her complex relation with the space she inhabits.

As is discussed below, Martha is and constructs herself as a liminal person. She is liminal as she inhabits those interstitial contested spaces that society allows to exist. She also constructs herself discursively as a liminal by centring her talk not on her present but rather on the expression of a longing and desire by which she attempts to provide an imaginary structure to her life. The following analysis discusses how these two realities of heterotopia and liminality shape up in Martha's talk.

The first frame: The corporate frame

The most immediate way in which Martha discursively constructs her place is through a vision of corporate productivity at the service of an alternative community.

Insight from lexical analysis

'[T]he analysis of particular words used in a [text] is always the first stage of any discourse analysis' (Richardson 2007: 12). The entry into Martha's interviews begins, therefore, from a basic search for the most frequent words she uses, accompanied by the analysis of the textual context in which they occur.

The word *people* is a suitable starting point. With 198 instances in a small corpus of four interviews amounting to about 35,000 words, it is the 21st most frequent word. The various uses and contexts of this word are immediately revealing of Martha's relation to the squat. Her choice of processes, for instance, indexes the way she feels about the space she is occupying. Although she chooses 'relational' processes that 'construe being' through attribution and identification (Martin, Matthiessen and Painter, 1997: 106) as in 'we have a real balance', these elements indicate Martha's agency; they suggest how she feels in charge of her community or 'crew' who, in squatter lexicon, is the group of people who live together in a squat, and how she refers to it as if it were her own business organization. In the following excerpts Martha's talk is not preceded by my questions, as they follow from the general opening stimulus 'tell me what it is like to live in a squat'. Martha loves talking and carries on telling her story with little or no prompt.

> *Excerpt 1:* Martha. *We've got people* in their 20s, 30s, 40s, and I'm 50, so you know *we have a whole range*, [proper name] is the youngest and I'm the oldest. So *we have a real balance,* age and number wise, *we have quite a balance* (Int 1).

Similarly, Martha portrays herself as an agentive person who, through the choice of slogan-sounding phrases, e.g. 'community living works', identifies strongly with her community to which she refers as if it were a well-established business institution.

> *Excerpt 2:* Martha. *We call ourselves the Creative Collective and we have a couple* of artists, a DJ, a filmmaker, a film editor, writer, comedian, a photographer, and one, two, three, four, five, six musicians, *so we all have* some form of creative [inaudible] in our work that we do and we just want to be able to live together in a community because it works, *community living works*, you all help out, *everybody contributes something to the greater of the whole*, and it works. You know it is a great way to get back to basics (Int 1).

The collective pronoun *we* 'primes social representations of the self that are more inclusive than that of the personal self-concept'; *us* and *we* therefore 'carry positive emotional significance that is activated automatically and unconsciously' (Brewer and Gardener 1996: 87). By labelling herself (Bucholtz and Hall 2005) a planner and theorist for her crew, Martha constructs a salient collective identity that allows her to emphasize the positive values of her group against, as will be shown, other less valiant squatters. Martha calls herself a 'solutions theorist' (Int. 1) and appreciates how her squat offers her an opportunity to show her entrepreneurial creativity. In the following excerpts from Interviews 1 and 2 respectively, the word 'incentive' that has a corporate ring to it (financial incentive, additional payment made to employees as a means of increasing production, Cobuild dictionary[5]), introduces Martha's interpretation of the council plans, while the unmitigated expression of her desire in 'I want people to', 'I want a forum' together with the use of the future tense expressing strong volition, 'I'll set it up', betrays her vision of the perfect commune.

> *Excerpt 3:* Martha. (...) there's *incentives for people* to be honest, there *incentives for people* to buy their own homes. Council does not want to own properties

anymore, they want to get rid of them, they want to be in the property management. They just want to collect their council tax (Int 1).

Excerpt 4: Martha. I'll set it up so that *people* can actually um post their CVs and skills
Int. mhm
Martha. and have a forum where and have a forum where *people* are talking about it because what I want is (.) and the reason I want a forum is *I want people* to try to create and find their own projects and the council to see wow . . . (Int 2).

Martha's identity claim as the person able to run a well-functioning democratic squat is supported by general statements as the one below in which she neatly opposes happy and satisfied people versus unhappy individuals who revolt.

Excerpt 5: Martha. If everybody's needs are met then they are happy. Somebody once said, '*People* don't want to be . . . the government doesn't want *people* to be autonomous.' But I disagree; they are the easiest *people* to control. *Happy people are easy to control, unhappy people revolt* (Int 1).

As the physical and emotional space of the squat allows people to be happy, it becomes the harmonious location where each crew member has a role and is in charge of specific duties: 'some *people* do the cooking, and, everybody (.) does the chores together, and, you know, (0.2) I kind of like the idea that in about five years from now some of these *people* will start settling down, start having children . . .' (Int 3).

Martha constructs herself as a city planner who can propose intelligent and novel solutions to the housing crisis, while her squat becomes more and more a heterotopic counter space. Such heterotopia compensates for what society is missing out on especially in terms of rationalizing space, presented as a scarcity; similarly, the squat is constructed as a place that brings to the surface the good in people and guides them away from abusing the system.

Excerpt 6: Martha. And then *for every five single parent-child combination you put in communal living you free up five council flats.* And also you need to have *incentives for people* who were taken advantage of the government and there are *people* that are doing all kind of benefit fraud and housing benefit fraud. You've got *people* that claim to be single because they get more benefits in housing, but their partner lives with them, the partner is renting out their council flat, so they're preventing someone from getting on the list. But if you've got nice community living spaces like some of these big, old commercial buildings where you can have these amazing luxury apartments and you can get six families that all know each other, it would be like a housing cohort. *Since they are living with the community and helping each other and you are happy and your needs are met, there is no benefit in screwing the government.* There's no benefit for you. Why would you want to have these two tiny council flats when you could have a big beautiful modern new home *living with people* that you like? And so there's *incentives for people* to be honest and they get more from it and eventually everybody can become homeowners (Int 1).

Disempowered individuals do not have the opportunity to create their own meaning but are only the recipient users of signs that have been defined for them by dominant groups. In these interviews, however, Martha changes her disempowerment to a situation of agency in which she takes her own responsibility for the acts she describes. She offers a clear rationale for the dutiful behaviour of her crew members who do not have any incentive to abuse the system and prefer living in cooperative accommodation where everyone has a role and a duty rather than in small individual flats. Once again, Martha flaunts an identity as economic planner who can offer figures and quotes for a solution to the accommodation shortage, as in 'and then for every five single parent-child combination you put in communal living you free up five council flats'. The very same is true in the excerpt below where Martha refers to percentages that are meant to add credibility to her calculations and portray herself as authoritative and legitimate (van Leeuwen 2008).

> *Excerpt 7:* Martha. So you take ... *I'm proposing* that of the 720,000, we can only get our hands on half, that's 360,000 properties, so 60% is for social housing, 30% is for the *people* who had worked on the scheme, the *people* that have done the physical labour and have earned points, so they can buy them and then 10% social enterprise (Int 2).

Besides *people*, Martha's vision is realized by many other lexemes that have a high frequency in her talk. As expected, the modal *can*, reflects Martha's ability to plan and offer futuristic solution to social problems: 'you *can* have film houses and theatres, you *can have* so-' (Int 1); 'well *I can get on* teaching English and presentation skills and it pays well, it's 30 euros an hour' (Int 3). Similarly, personal pronouns and adjectives underline Martha's attachment to the squat as her own space, the heterotopia she protects and about which she has a clear vision. At the very same time as Martha portrays herself as the squat theorist and guardian angel of her crew, and the squat as the counter-site where human fulfilment is a reality, these linguistic indicators mark the spatial segregation of which Martha and the squatters become victims, which 'reflect[s] the processes of fragmentation of our society' (Allweil and Kallus 2008: 192). Martha's squat is an isolated and marginalized counter site that is too often besieged by the antagonizing authorities but also a space that is appreciated by the same actors who eventually have to follow the legal procedures of eviction.

> *Excerpt 8:* Martha. There was a commercial property that's been emptied there's been a *commercial property that has been empty* for a year
> Int. mmm
> M. they have guardians in there and uh *the property managers said 'I'd rather have you guys in'*
> Int. what do you mean? What do you mean? Guardians? They're just paid to to make sure that the properties not occupied by
> M. yeah they basically are *property guardians* they live in an empty property to prevent it from being squatted or vandalized (Int 2).

Although she is marginal to the productive sections of society, through her portrayal of the squat as a profit-making site, Martha appears as a contributor useful to the estate market. Noteworthy is Martha's use of her performative reported direct discourse.

One other lemma stands out as particularly indicative of Martha's discursively ideological appropriation of a dominant mainstream logic within the frame of the squat as counter-space: p*roperty/ies* with seventy-eight occurrences in the interviews. It is through the articulation of the concept of property that Martha constructs the squat as a heterotopia of resistance to and deviation from capitalist society's spatial logic; the squat is therefore a 'steam-releasing' space of vibrant 'social critique' (Allweil and Kallus, 2008: 191). At the same time, however, the squat functions as a heterotopia of compensation in that Martha describes it as the space that can provide the salvation of humankind and that can guide people out of dishonest and individualistic habits. Such a compensatory heterotopia helps Martha soothe the trauma of the provisionality and ephemerality of the space she is occupying as well as the marginality of her existence unfit as is for the productive sector.

The collocates of *property/ies* are most revealing of Martha's sophisticated control of professional corporate lexis, far beyond the expected association with *empty*, *derelict* or *listed* properties and the discrimination between *commercial* and *residential* spaces, with the consequent criminalization of the occupation of the latter ('squatting residential *property* is not a criminal act', Int 1). Through the association of *property/ies* with such words as *portfolio, sell, commercial, guardian, developers, proposal, firm, fix up, list, owners, negotiate, finance, manager/ management company, scout, research* as shown in excerpts 9 and 10 and the concordance list in Figure 2, Martha portrays the crew of squatters as security guardians of abandoned commercial places who live in those occupied properties as rent-paying licensees. In so doing, she claims for herself an identity as a 'corporate squatter' as she defines herself, who proposes alternative solutions to the housing crisis:

> *Excerpt 9:* Martha. . . . we constantly scout and find *properties* and there are a couple of solicitors who have (.) there's a solicitor's office that has a *portfolio* of *properties.* (. . .) *We do not charge for our service* and what is in it for us is we want to build up a *portfolio* of *properties* that we have taken care of there are so many empty *properties* while [inaudible] I will get into the *alternative housing proposal* after I tell them (Int 1).
> *Excerpt 10:* Martha. we will continue to put *love and light and energy* into the *property*, we will continue to cover and paint it, because we can get free paint (Int 2).

In conclusion, the collocates of the lemma property/ies suggest a semantic prosody pertaining to the domain of alternative corporatism and a capitalistic view of housing. Therefore, Martha discursively creates a new space where 'macrocosms of society' are reinterpreted and revolutionarily inverted, in 'a blurring of public-private distinctions [the abolition of] a conceptual or physical border or boundary separating heterotopia from everyday file' (Low 2008: 153).

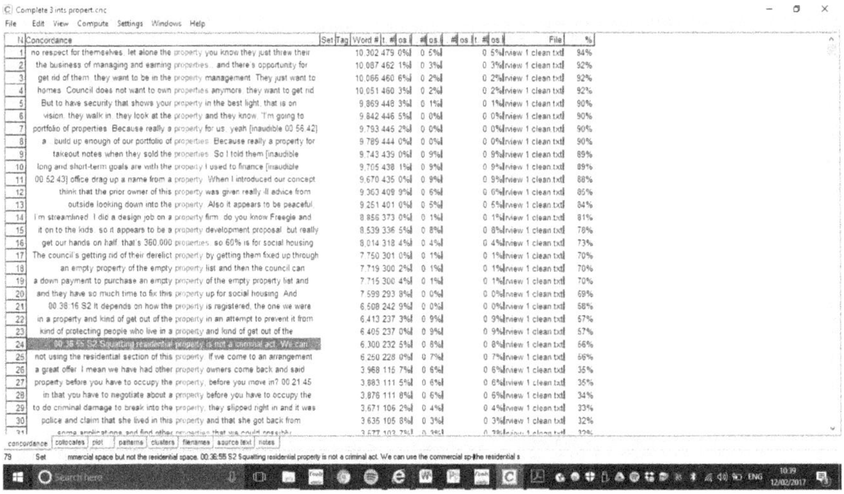

Figure 2 Concordance list for property/ies.

The role of self-naming/labelling

As squats are counter-sites, they are also heterotopias of 'absolute otherness' 'distinctively disconnected from the dominant spatial order [which] severely limits their ability to affect hegemonic society' (Allweil and Kallus, 2008: 192). As was discussed in the previous section, Martha claims an identity of ethical and alternative yet corporate entrepreneur. Her use of such self-defining phrases as 'corporate hippie', 'fantasy developer' or 'solutions theorist', on the one hand, underlines her identity as organizer of a marginal, yet compensatory and conciliatory heterotopia, by which she recreates reality in an alternative and healthier way. On the other hand, however, these catchy phrases index how she is scrupulously creating her identity by searching for cogent labels that summarize her position to the crew.

i. Corporate hippie

> *Excerpt 11:* Martha. Well, I kind of think of myself as a *corporate hippie* (…) but my background's very corporate (.) you know (.) I used to be employed by (bank's name) in the nineties (Int 2).

ii. Fantasy developer

> *Excerpt 12:* Martha. The joke amongst me and my crew is I play *fantasy developer*. Welcome to fantasy developer, on this episode. We have created a beautiful communal living space (…) for 20 people on the derelict warehouse and *I play the fantasy developer thing*. But I digress, I was talking about something else and *I went back to the fantasy* (Int 1).

iii. Solutions theorist

> *Excerpt 13:* Martha. The community's never going to allow six buildings to be built there, but I have a *proposal* for it [inaudible] build the houses on stilts, you can do three subterranean and five trees [inaudible when you build the old club house (…), turn that into a cafe and sell chutneys and jams and everybody in the community would like that because they [inaudible] just right solutions to the- … *I'm a solutions theorist* (Int 1).

Through self-categorizations and self-naming that highlight her central role within the squat and vis-à-vis the crew and through the explicit account of her futuristic plans for an egalitarian alternative space, Martha constructs herself as a good person (van de Mieroop 2011), who, while forced into a situation of building occupation, has made the best of it for herself and others. Although seemingly self-ironic, the labels she uses for herself are linguistic devices of 'self–aggrandizement', which are 'designed to place the narrator in the most favorable possible light' (Oliveira 1999).

In her fourth interview, although Martha had abandoned her squat, she continued to propose sound political and environmental solutions to the housing situation. She immediately starts the exchange with the question about Earthship, the model for solar earth shelter designed by architect Michael Reynolds, and launches into one of her enthusiastic lectures on the topic. At this stage of our relationship, Martha has consolidated her identity as ecological planner, while I have developed mine as learner of environmental issues. Later on, reference is made to Tristan Stuart and his plan to stop the haemorrhage of wasted food in the world. This is another example of Martha's pedagogical attitude. She told me to google Stuart and watch his informative Ted talk. The mention of Earthship at the very beginning of the conversation without any preface is an indication of such a role negotiation. As usual, Martha provides figures and exact information about her project in her desire to construct herself as a competent and legitimate (Van Leeuwen 2008) advocate of changes.

> *Excerpt 14:* Martha. *Ever heard of an Earthship?*
> Int. No
> Martha. *An earthship is a home that's built out of recycling materials*, it was created it was *invented by the architect Michael Reynolds*, he's an American architect.
> Int. Ok
> Martha. It's built from recycle materials that harvest all of its own rain water.
> Int. yeah
> Martha. And uses four times so the rain water goes through into the tanks goes through the filtration system that's your drinking water, your shower and your kitchen, then that grey water goes through the gravel pit where it's cleaned up and then it goes under your green house and your plants can drink from their roots up then it goes into the flashing toilet (. . .) So you're harvesting rain water and using it four times and even using your waste.
> Int. And why are you telling me this?
> Martha. Because you can build an earthship for abo:ut (0.2) o:ne twenty fifth of the cost of a house in London.
> Int. Alright
> Martha. I've got some photos on my phone I have some and some fantastic documentaries about it but what I've decided was I would like to take the positive aspect from the squatting role.
> Int. yeah

Martha. And and first people were talking about Spain there's over 2000 villages for sale in Spain.
Int. You were telling me about this, I remember.
Martha. You can buy an entire village for less than a house in Spain but after we did our research we discovered that Portugal embraces ah sustainable living
Int. uh uh
Martha. (...) so I wanna just do a basic survival earthship and this is what it looks like (shows drawing) (...) *so the idea is to take to buy land* in (name of a European country)
Int. uh uh
Martha. *And build a communal land* so that we'd have a big commercial kitchen, a guest area and a lounge a library that'll be our communal one (...) so everybody has their own space but there's also a community (...) some people would take care of the bees, some people would take care of the animals, some people would take care of the vegetables, some people would take care of the fruit trees, some people would cook prepare meals for those who are out in the fields working and I figured that a community of 20 to 36 is a good number because we'd have 24 people to run it to have everything that you need to run it like a finely oiled machine but what's the point of living free if it's your prison? That means 12 people can be travelling at any time and you have rotas (...) so *I see this as a solution to capitalism* (Int 4).

iv.   Not a conspiracy theorist

> *Excerpt 15:* Martha. So I see this *as a solution to capitalism* because it *doesn't work*, it isn't working people are sleeping rough you know on the streets I find the super elites=
> Int =It's only the super elites isn't it?
> Martha. it's a mental illness (...) So there's the plan. I'm not a *conspiracy theorist* I see it happening (Int 4).

Giving herself labels and providing definitions that encapsulate her visionary and prophetic role within the crew, Martha claims an identity as a principled leader. She refuses to partake in the consumerist capitalist world and wants nothing to do with the dirty games the elites play on people that are always at the expense of the poor and disadvantaged. While she positively aggrandizes herself as an ethical planner, she also defines the boundaries of her identity by detaching herself from other forms of contestation of the capitalist system as represented by conspiracy theorists. As she does that, Martha attributes to herself the capacity to see in the future with clarity together with the desire, expressed very directly through the verb 'want', to take herself out of a system of inequality and oppression.

Excerpt 16: Martha. And there are the super elites obsessed with controlling the little people, it's like a game, *I want out of the game I want out of the system I want out of the game I want to live off the grid* I *wanna* live in a community where we empower one another (Int 4).

The idealized squatters

The discursive construction of the squat as a heterotopic counter-site also relies on the depiction of its members as a special group. The analysis of the personal pronouns (*us/our/we*) defining the squatter community as the in-group (Tajfel and Turner 1986) confirms Martha's attempt to depict her space as a 'sanctuary or safe heaven such that a special kind of community develops expressed in inclusion/exclusion or insider/outsider distinctions' (Low 2008: 153). In Martha's words, the squatters inhabiting the commercial spaces where I met her, are a well-meaning crew endorsing a number of positive social values. In her description, they are hard-working, inventive, supportive, international, multilingual ('We've got, two English, Dutch, Danish, Turkish, Lithuanian, Latvian, Hungarian, Estonian, German, Italian, [inaudible] So yeah 12 countries, 15 from 12 countries and sorry Poland. Did I not say Poland?' (Int 1).

Such a representation that Martha offers can be seen as an attempt to counter the dominant discourse around squatters as deviant subjects, who are homeless, foreign, slovenly and unclean. This othering process draws a very clear line between hard-working tax-paying citizens and squatters, and is clearly in sync with a hegemonic discourse along the lines of the vulnerability of private property which squatters threaten (Dee 2013). In contrast, Martha's crew is ethical and law-abiding, as it respects the separation between commercial sites in which squatting borders with legality, and private ones, whose squatting is a penal infringement. This glorified representation of the crew mirrors Martha's self-aggrandizement or the attempt of a narrator to highlight their 'meritous' qualities which Oliveira (1999) postulates is often present in self narratives.

Martha and her crew behaved in a very law-abiding manner. For example, they never used the top floor of the boarded-up pub where I interviewed her for the first time; this was a precautionary measure because this part of the pub was registered as residential space. The interviews, however, took place upstairs to avoid the noise of the band practising down below. We sat on the bare floor as that residential space was totally inhabited by the squatters.

Excerpt 17: Martha. *We* can use the kitchen, if *we* wanted to have *our* own catering business, *we* can use it for commercial- but to avoid that any misunderstanding or ambiguity in the law we [use?] the kitchen downstairs, the pub kitchen. *We're in the commercial kitchen not the residential* (Int 1).

While Martha refers to entrepreneurial possibilities for herself and her group (if *we* wanted to have *our* own catering business, *we* can use it for commercial), her positive portrayal of her crew resists all sorts of mainstream society's malaise, proposing new solutions to capitalist excesses. For instance, following people like Tristan Stuart fighting the 'global food scandal',[6] Martha and her crew don't buy meals; rather they 'skip' for food that is still edible and nutritious but is disposed of by shops and supermarkets once the expiry date has been reached. As a group they contribute, therefore, to on-going efforts to stop the 'haemorrhaging out' (Stuart 2012) of food waste.

In the several small accounts interspersed in the interviews, it is striking how Martha identifies completely with the squatting community and how, through her crew, she presents an idealized self to her interviewer. The heterotopic place she is constructing is flexible, open and collective, challenging the rigidity of the capitalist individualism at its root. In the squat, there are no specific roles for people, rather everything is an organic shared practice like the fry-up described in the excerpt below. The non-structure or anti-structure that Turner describes as associated with the liminal individuals in *Liminality and Communitas* (1974) therefore is transformed in an associative spontaneous yet well-orchestrated activity that indexes the multiple potentialities which the squat as a liminal and heterotopic space unleashes.

> *Excerpt 18:* Martha. *We* had a recycling section, a general waste and it was nice and the guys were just about ... *they were making a fry up*, it was Wednesday morning about noon, they just decided, 'hey *let's* have brunch, *let's* have a fry up and then the band would practice'. You know different people would go and *skip for food we* had and the neighbourhood *we* were in we met several other restaurants in the area and a couple of the sushi places *we* would be waiting and they will just walk out and hand it to *us* (Int 3).

Worthy of notice is Martha's use of direct discourse ('hey, let's have brunch') that adds to the immediacy of her narrative and the vivacity of the scenario she conjures up. Overall, however, she aims to construct her crew as a dynamic, forward-looking group in an environment that engenders positive responses in the surrounding context.

In Martha's talk, squatters are constructed as also enforcing democratic rules to ensure safety and harmony within the community.

Excerpt 19: Martha. I remember one (@) day I was sitting in the lounge with two other people. They were fairly new and they had been actually *voted in*. They had come and asked us if they could join us, we said 'we'd give you *two week trial* and then if it's a fit you can stay and *after that it's one month probation probatory period*']
Int.   [uh uh
Martha. because what we discovered everybody is on their best behaviour for those two weeks if they want to join your crew and once they get in then you can see their real colours so it was like two week trial then *one month probation* (Int 4).

As Branigan (1992: 315) notes, '[n]arrative is a recursive organization of data; that is, its components may be embedded successively at various micro- and macro levels.' In this small story, the recursive organization of details is meant to construct the squat as a perfectly functioning place where only truthful behaviour is allowed and truthful people reside. As usual, the choice of the inclusive 'we' suggests the crew's democratic and collective decision to give the squat applicants a probation period. Davies and Harré (1990: 47) believe in the centrality of 'positioning' to identity construction 'because by positioning, people commit themselves practically, emotionally and epistemically to identity-categories and discursive practices associated with them' (Deppermann 2013: 4). Bamberg and Georgakopoulou identify three different levels of positioning in narrative as: i. positioning at the story level is concerned with how the characters are positioned vis-à-vis one another within the story, ii. positioning on the interaction level refers to how narrators position themselves to the audience, iii by self-positioning vis-à-vis the existing dominant discourses, the narrators establish their self-identity (2008: 385–391).[7]

In terms of level two positioning, that is in terms of how the speakers/narrators position themselves and are positioned by others in the interaction, Martha does not appear to be the individual speaker, on the contrary, she seems to be animating (Goffman 1981) the crew's deliberation. While the first part of the story conjures up the scene of the meeting and develops from a personal memory ('I remember one (@) day I was sitting in the lounge') to a collective recall ('we said'), the last section of the story reinforces the sound rationale of the choice to put the new comers on probation. To this purpose, Martha insists on the trial period and explains why it is necessary ('once they get in then you can see their real colours'); from the story proper, she switches to a less narrative genre that, through the use of 'you', generalizes people's behaviour. From animator of the crew's deliberation, therefore, Martha changes her positioning to 'principal' (Goffman

1981) in that she endorses convincingly the words of the crew to the point of justifying them to the interviewer.

In the second interview Martha's identity is different. Her liminality comes to the fore again in political terms. Playing the principal by strongly endorsing Stuart's concerns about food waste, Martha here campaigns in favour of people who skip for food. The interspersed negative evaluations ('that's just sick') position her vis-à-vis the general market discourse of supply and demand (positioning level 3) to which she juxtaposes a scenario of food foragers who seek for alternative to shopping.

> *Excerpt 20:* Martha. Because the the public outcry was like this is ridiculous you *you carelessly throw away food then you fiercely protect it from no one else having it* (0.3) some places like Marks & Spencer I was told Marks & Spencer and [unintelligible] put blue dye in their food, some people put bleach in it so you can't eat it and that's just sick
> Int. yeah to prevent the market from going down and from=
> Martha. =the thing is the kind of *people that skip for food are not the kind of people that show up in your store* (.) typically
> Int. no 'course not (.) course not
> Martha. and that's what he said (0.3)
> Int. yeah but
> Martha. that's what Stuart said in his article (0.5) he said the people that I (.) when I bump into people out and about skipping *they're not doing it like me as a form of protest they're doing it because that's how they put food on their table because they can't afford shopping in stores* uh (Int 2).

In the closing of this excerpt, Martha constructs herself as a political actor who wishes to distinguish between her motivation for skipping and the needy condition of people who do not have the money for shopping. She aligns herself with other politically-minded squats that in England have organized into groups, such as the Squatters Network of Brighton, Birmingham Tenants & Homeless Action Group, Manchester Housing Action and Squatters Action for Secure Housing (SQUASH) (Dee and Debelle 2015). These groups attempt to encourage positive discourses around squatters while, at the same time, provide housing for the needy and create opportunities for artistic and cultural expression and alternative enterprises.

As the following four excerpts show, Martha's crew is always categorized positively against other less well deserving and respectful squatters; it is ethical, loving, able to provide a useful service to property owners, and respectful of the country's welfare system which it refuses to exploit in contrast to a huge out-group of others that comprises unethical security companies, obtuse councils, ruthless bailiffs, and the suspicious settled community who only pursue profit and show no sensitivity to human concerns. In these excerpts, Martha combines her imagined animator's voice addressing potential property owners ('we'll be your free on-site security') with small stories of theft by bailiffs ('somebody's hard drive was missing') as well as appreciation of the crew's work ('the solicitor company that I contacted regarding the property ... they really liked our proposal'). In all cases in the hands of the crew the squat is constructed as a positive healthy and ethical space within which people give their best and are at their best. The crew's liminality in a continuous situation of threat and uncertainty therefore constructs in the squat a restorative heterotopia that both compensates for their shortage of opportunities and contests the profit-orientated logic of mainstream society.

> *Excerpt 21:* Martha. *we*'ll be your free on-site security to prevent *other squatters* getting in and *we* will continue to put love and light and energy into the property, *we* will continue to cover and paint (Int 2).
>
> *Excerpt 22:* Martha. Well, now *most squatters* (...) *don't believe in taking benefits. It goes against their basic ethos.* (...) I don't even think *we* have anybody in *our* crew on benefits (Int 2).
>
> *Excerpt 23:* Martha ... and *they* were giving them time to go through all *our* possessions. I guess that was part of *their* pay ...
> Int. Mm
> Martha ... to take what they wanted. So, *somebody's hard drive was missing* ... (Int 3).
>
> *Excerpt 24:* Martha. But the *solicitor company* that I contacted regarding the property in (place name), they *really liked our* proposal you know there are a lot of *security companies* that are quite *unethical* and since there are so many, I should say, the change in the laws regarding squatting, people squatting commercial buildings, and then all these *security companies are trying to get rich quick* off the change of the laws and they come in and they *steal* from the squatters (Int 1).

Self-narratives

'Place identity is an integral part of the self' (Sarbin 1983: 337) and the construal of personhood is mainly but not solely realized, as has been shown, by the contextualized use of particular words and personal pronouns that 'take on their meaning from the predicates in uttered or implied sentences' (ibid.).

Therefore through utterances containing material processes in the active voice (or relational processes that are positively associated with them), Martha portrays herself as agentive and resourceful, determined to make the squat a site of positive opportunities: 'I *did* a design job on a property firm, (...) And, I *did* a complete design job, I *had* a king size bed, beautiful furniture. I *had* even like kitchen all the contents of my kitchen came from either France, streets of London (...). I even *had* a bread maker' (Int 1). In such active processes, Martha is the main actor, who combines 'self-conscious thinking' with the competent use of 'self-referential language' (Bermudez 2016: 7); in other words, by insisting on 'I', Martha is 'intentionally self-reflexive' as she is the subject of her own reflection, and 'intentionally self-ascriptive' in that she is communicating information about herself (2016: 8). In both cases when talking about the squat and her life within it, Martha shows the strong awareness that, according to Turner (1974), is typical of the state of occupying the liminal space between society cracks. Through such a condition of awareness, Marta systematically contrasts herself and her squatter community with others so that where she and her crew are the actors of positive processes, they are at the same time the goal of other people's negative actions ('The taxi drivers are watching *us, they're watching our* every move and then reporting back and that's why *we get so upset*...Int 3).

Sarbin's (1983) still thought-provoking paper presents what he calls the 'vigilance formula' according to which individuals in problematic situations in order to survive engage in various 'epistemic actions' that locate their self within the relevant reality (1983: 338). Beyond the use of pronouns and specific words, it is through 'emplotment' in terms of the construction of personal narratives, that individuals respond to the question *What is this place/situation? And Who am I in relation to it?* Sarbin explains that through emplotment and poiesis, that is through a narrative transformation of the order of things more than through simple reporting, individuals construct the self. And this is even more the case if they find themselves in precarious situations (1983: 340). A focus on Martha's narratives of survival can, therefore, shed light on her performative identity (Butler 1990) and the way she positions herself and responds to what she feels is others' positioning of her (Bamberg and Georgakopoulou 2008).

Using her accounts as a resource for self-construction, Martha negotiates her affiliations with the squat and the people within and outside it. By so doing, she merges space with time in evocation of the experience that brought her to the squat and equally compresses the past of the narrated event with the present of the act of narrating (Perrino 2015: 146).

Excerpt 25: Martha. This *was* my third trip, so I *lived* in (city name) since 2002 and I *do* stand-up comedies, so I *used* to pop over to see comedy shows and (...) network with other comedians when I *was living* in (city name). It *was* on my third visit to London that I *met up* with some squatters, and it *wasn't* at all what *I expected*, I *was shocked* (...) *it was beautiful, it was pristine, it was clean, and it was a home*, they *had* a cleaning rota, they *had gone in* and *fixed up* a property, they *had been* there for three and a half years. They *re-plastered* the walls, they *tore out* all the old carpeting and *redid* the floors, it *was* beautiful, it *was* lovely and when they *went* to court, they *offered* to pay the council £1000 month rent plus council tax (Int 1).

Such an account of successful squatting is constructed through an emplotment in which Martha, as Ricoeur (1981: 176) suggests, 'inverts the so-called natural order of time' and juggles between three different tenses: the present ('I do stand-up comedies') that defines her identity then and there but also here and now as an artist and entertainer; the past of her visit to the clean and pristine squat; the pluperfect of what had determined the immaculate conditions of the squat, in terms of the work the people living in it 'had carried out' for three years to the walls, the floors and carpets. The '*retrospective* dimension' (Freeman 2019: 27, original emphasis) of her narratives that entails looking backward to the events she witnessed is at the basis of Martha's construction of herself as the main interpreter of the squatting reality. Her account is, therefore, another example of how squatting could be the business solution for unused properties and the people involved should be viewed not as scroungers but as purveyors of a new positive social order.

The various temporal indicators in Martha's text above are associated with different locales, in terms of a previously decadent premise transformed in a restorative space by the squatters. This combination of time and space can be explained with the notion of the chronotope that captures the inseparability of time and space in human action. 'Specific chronotopes produce specific kinds of person, actions, meaning, and value' (Blommaert 2015: 109); therefore, through the chronotope of the squat as a positive place, Martha expresses her 'historical and momentary agency' (ibid.) and her self-portrayal as a creative and ethical crew leader and competent economic planner.

A similar example is the excerpt below narrating a less fortunate episode in which, again, Martha switches from the past to the present while constructing herself as the bridging link between the crew and the authorities. While the above segment displayed considerable use of positive 'valuation' as a token of 'appreciation' (Martin and White 2005), here Martha's negative 'judgment' expresses her 'social sanction' against the opponents of her in-group. As she narrates the misfortunes of her community whose personal possessions were taken surreptitiously by the bailiffs, Martha returns to the present to chastise the authorities and blame the new law about squatting responsible for encouraging unhealthy capitalist greed.

> *Excerpt 26*: Martha. On one of our evictions, the security company actually *stole* some of our valuables, a flat screen TV, a DVD player, a Nintendo DS, a stone carving of an elephant, someone's aftershave and *went* through everybody's personal possessions with a fine tooth comb. So we *filed* a police report because that *is* wrong. A security company *should* (.) that's what they do, if they *are going to steal* from the people that you just evicted. They *are going to steal* from you and yeah they *can rip up* the electrics, the plumbing, *do* all kind of criminal damage to the property and then *blame* the squatters. *So we are seeing ourselves as the ethical free alternative and what we are looking for is to build a portfolio.* We *want* to show before and after pictures 'this is what we did with the property while we were residents' and 'this is how we took care of it' and 'this is how you know' (...) So, yeah, anyway how I *ended up* with this crew *was* a matter of theft and deprivation crime report, the report that *we filed* because it *is* quite unusual (Int 3).

This small narrative, as many others in the interviews, alternates between condemnation of the others and an emphasis on the squatters' resourcefulness who filed a police report to react to a morally wrong episode. Once again, the incident gives Martha the opportunity to highlight the ethical conduct of her group and its commercial potentials when they plan to take before and after pictures of the spaces they transform.

Similarly, in the second interview, Martha reports on how her crew won the IPO (Interim Possession Order).[8]

> *Excerpt 27:* Martha.... we *won* the initial court hearing for IPO, that's an interim possession order (.) now with an IPO (.) they *have* 48 hours to serve you papers and once *you're served* you *must be* out within 24 hours or *you're committing* a criminal offence (.) um we *won* the IPO out of technicality, they *didn't serve* the papers correctly there *were mistakes* in the paper work and so we *won* (.) when *we went* through the full possession hearing last week.
> Int. This is what the previous place right?
> Martha. No, here no, here *we won* the IPO hearing (.) *we lost* the possession hearing
> Int. Oh okay

Martha. (1.5) it's a shame it really *depends* on the judge, on the judge's mood (1.0) this judge *was* in a foul mood and he *wanted* to make everybody's day miserable (0.3) he *came in* and the first judge *we had really wanted* to know the facts and *he had* to make it and *he said* 'I'm sorry you haven't (.) you did not provide the court or the defendants with proof of ownership and you can't just blatantly claim we want possession of this 'cos we own it (.) you have to provide it by proof so that's why we won the IPO (1.0)' the second judge *was* really awful he *was very rude* to the claimant (0.3) um *wanted* to know how can you prove it and *she's* like 'well sorry if you go to (inaudible)' and just the way *he was talking* to her (.) he *was talking* quite rudely to her (.) *there's no need* to be rude to the claimant or to the defendant' (Int 2).

As in other instances, Martha's lexical competence in this case in the legal domain is striking. She alternates between the time of the event retold and a generalizing present within which she sanctions what in her view is unfair, unethical or illegal. In the above excerpt, for instance, she contrasts the two judges, one rude and moody, the other determined to ascertain facts, and by voicing them, she makes them come alive in the narrative worlds or 'story world' (Bamberg 1997, Wortham 2001).

In conclusion, Martha's accounts construct her as a squatting theorist and a proponent of an economic profitable way of living that she offers as an alternative to mainstream society's way of life: 'When *they need* the property *we just need ample notice*, we need 30 days. (...) *We do not charge for our service* and what is in it for us is we want to build up a portfolio of properties that we have taken care of' (Int 1).

One more excerpt from the second interview shows how Martha's use of the present tense functions as projection into a well-planned future that redresses the present obtuse inequalities of the UK housing system.

Excerpt 28: Int. Would the people (.) would squatters like what you propose? Or would you think that—
Martha. Oh I think they would! I think the squat community would be the ones that could make it happen (1.0) because I really think *it's* kind of funny and *we were sitting* round talking one day and *I said* (1.0) with *we're all* on the brink of the failure of capitalism (.) we're on the ve:ry beginning of it (.) it *was* just the very beginning (.) I *might not be around* to see it (.) the changes in the future (.) but from the very beginning of that falling apart it always *gets* much worse before it *gets* better and *it's the poor illiterate that are going to have to teach the rich how to live* (.) *we're going* to show them how to be self-sufficient (.) because *they're used* to using currency to get whatever they want and people

to bring it to them, but when currency no longer *has* value and it's about sharing skills and barbering again (.) and if you don't have any skill (.) and you don't have any barbering ability (.) then *you're gonna have* to learn how to be self-sufficient (.) but I think *it will be* the people from the squat community (.) the people that *dropped out* of the system and *became* self-sufficient and *will teach* the others how to live.

In this case more than in others, Martha's tone is prophetic in depicting a world in which people are devoid of skills and currency is no longer a valid means of trading. At this point Martha's prophesy is that liminality will come to an end and from within the heterotopic place that she and her crew have built a new army of people dropped out of the capitalist system will come forward who will rescue the world by sharing their skills with the formerly powerful survivors.

The second frame: The self-defence frame

So far, the discussion on Martha's liminality has focused on the corporate frame that emerged from her talk; such frame, as was argued, contributes to discursively constructing the squat as a heterotopic site of positive deviance and transgression. The discourse that Martha encourages is that of a squat as both a solution to the housing problem and a political statement that challenges the logic of greedy capitalism. This main frame is realized through a number of linguistic strategies ranging from the use of particular lemmas usually associated with the business and financial worlds, pronouns that construct the squatters' community as a positive in-group, the choice of self-labelling ratifying Martha's role vis-à-vis her crew, an insistence on an intentional self-ascription and self-reflection and small stories (Georgakopoulou 2007) showing a retrospective and projective as well as a visibly evaluative dimension. However, as Ochs and Capps (1996) argue, 'selves evolve in the time frame of a single telling as well as in the course of the many tellings that eventually compose a life' (p. 23). Besides, and in accompaniment to the corporate frame, Martha's self evolves and changes and she constructs her heterotopia through a second frame that allows her to claim a completely different identity.

In it, Martha's talk seems to have several functions. In the first place, it points to the emotional role that the squat and her crew fulfil for her. Her interpretation of the squat, therefore, summarizes her resistance to a homogenizing spatial logic (heterotopia of deviation); however, this second frame also expresses her desire to reinvent traditional society's structures devoid of patriarchal connotations and compensate for or justify her social marginalization (heterotopia of compensation). Compared with the previous corporate frame, this second one seems to occupy a smaller space in Martha's talk; however, it is already visible in the first interview, where the general tone is optimistic and energetic, and also later on when Martha shows how emotionally taxing squatting has become for her. Although less discursively evident, this frame is crucial to the understanding of Martha and the toil and difficulty that squatters generally experience.

> *Excerpt 29:* Martha. Yeah for me, [the squat] *has filled a huge void in my life, I am an only child*. My mother, my parents are deceased, so I do not have the brother, sister, nieces, nephews, immediate network going and that is one of the things about our crew which truly are our family. You know, after the interview we just go sit down and hang out with everyone and you know it is, *we are a family*. (…) *A squamily, a squat family, a squamily,* you know, we say that *we're squamily* (Int 1).

In Martha's words a *squamily* is the heterotopia where individuals free of social constraints express their creativity in togetherness and in the name of a return to natural non-capitalist simplicity. The neologism, *squamily,* refers to the entity that ensures emotional stability to the liminals' suspended existence. The semantic resources Martha uses to express 'affect' (Martin and White 2005: 46) in terms of her feelings about the squat can be seen here in the choice of a 'material process' when she admits that what she has at the moment 'has filled a huge void in my life'. By such a confessional statement, Martha claims the identity of a person who has specific needs (for friends' company and support) and is able to make specific choices to satisfy them (the squamily). Once again worthy of note is Martha's intentional deictical self-ascription and her ability to analyse rationally her situation, very much in line with the clarity that Turner identifies in liminality: 'I see liminality as a phase in social life in which this confrontation between "activity which has no structure" and its "structured results" produces in men their highest pitch of self-consciousness' (1974: 255).

At a later stage in interview four, Martha states clearly the supporting function she attributes to the crew when she explains that a squamily is a positive construction empowering the individuals who belong in it and her in particular.

> *Excerpt 30:* Martha (after talking about some people she stayed with in 'place name') we just became GREAT friends.
> Int. But I mean you've got so many- you're positive all the time aren't you? You're very- I remember even when you were having lots of problems with your cat and the eviction you were always – you weren't–

>   Martha. that's because=
>   Int. =you were trying
>   Martha. *I had a crew*
>   Int. That's right with the crew
>   Martha. *when you've got your squamily you're strong* (Int 4).

Other times, even within the same interview, Martha unveils her fear of loss which she fends off by adopting a self-protective strategy to screen her displaced self from being hurt by the surrounding antagonistic reality. The following excerpt again from interview one brings together the memory of a positive much coveted place and the dread of losing it.

> *Excerpt 31:* Martha. It *was quite stable* and we had an agreement, *we were told we'd get notice* and all of that, so it is a *quite unstable place. You always know it is temporary* (...) switched rooms with somebody that was moving out. (...) So I had this vision of a secret garden (...) it *was beautiful*, I had a big south facing window and then three west facing windows overlooking this *old overgrown garden*, so *there were blackberry bushes and ivy* and I *didn't even curtain it* was so beautiful (Int 1).

The space Martha is constructing here is 'unstable', temporary, not permanent, under threat, and she knows she is bound to lose it. There is in her account and the description of the place surrounded by a secret garden that screens her from the intrusive outside world, an echo of a fear of the city as 'a jungle of brick, stone and smoke, with its greedy predators and apathetic victims, its brutal indifference to either communal value or individual feeling' (Nochlin 1971: 151 in Slater 2002: 136). The threatening monstrosity of the city disappears in the recollection of her peaceful place for which not even curtains are needed because the ivy on the windows naturally ensures privacy.

The excerpt continues with Martha giving more voice to her fear of losing control of her space.

> *Excerpt 32:* Martha. and I remember thinking, okay, this is *my dream room*, (...) *don't get too attached* and that is what *you have to do* when are living in this lifestyle. It helps *you practice a form of detachment not to get too emotionally attached* to where you are at (Int 1).

In his discussion of American country music, Fox (1992) contrasts two metanarratives. Although Fox's paper refers to a different scholarly domain, what he proposes seems to resonate with the present study. One metanarrative Fox describes is of Desire associated with reification and objectification of things, while the other metanarrative of Loss resists the former and transforms '"things" in to speaking, feeingful presences' (p. 54). The distinction seems appropriate to the representation of the squat that Martha offers. In the earlier section where the 'corporate frame' was discussed, Martha constructed a metanarrative of desire by objectifying the squat through which the offer of a potentially profitable alternative to greedy capitalist society is realized. While ensuring a comfortable shelter away from the consumerist and insensitive world, the squat can be described as an object that can still produce healthy profit and that fits in with a cleansed, not greedy, corporatist logic. At the same time, to protect herself from the always impending loss of her space, Martha attempts to establish a separation between her feelings and her place. Once more therefore she constructs her identity as a woman imaginative enough to bounce off negative affect. In this metanarrative of loss, Martha attaches to the squat, or to the secret overgrown garden as a metonymic part of it, the anthropomorphic ability to screen her from the menacing reality.

At other times, an attitude of despondency can be perceived in Martha's talk as in the third interview in an abandoned church where the crew was in contestation with the minister who called up the *Evening Standard* and said in Martha's words that 'there were squatters in the church and that they [the congregation] were gonna be forced to have their Christmas service on the street'. The number of people who wanted to re-appropriate the church was actually five and Martha is hurt by the repeated lies of the 'man of cloth' who feistily fights the crew in spite of the unusable conditions of the premises (broken windows, pigeon defecation all over, damp and more) and negatively influences the surrounding neighbourhood by blaming them for being like any other squatters ('as far as they're concerned we are like the other people').

> *Excerpt 33:* Martha. There's a paint recycling place down the street but (.) they (0.5) are deeply offended by our presence being here, they didn't wanna meet with us, they didn't wanna talk with us, *as far as they're concerned we're just like the other people, and the other people were (.) I mean (.) they were offensive.*
> Int. These are the people that did all the graffiti on the walls?
> Martha. Yeah I'll show it to you, I'll take you on a tour (Int 3).

The emotional self-defence frame through which Martha recounts her squatting experience, albeit less optimistic than the corporate frame, like that one shows her resistance to mainstream society. It is also a frame resulting in a systematic evaluation of squatting as a solution to modern society's wrongdoing as suggested in the following excerpt where Martha recollects a period of fear and threat before she was invited by some friends to join a new squat.

Excerpt 34: Martha. We got the drills out, us girls fixed the broken stair. (Squatter's name) and I got the drill out (drill noise), fixed the stairs. And he became really aggressive and threatening and saying, 'Get outta here.' And then I finally realized *it was not safe* for me and my cat. When is it a bad decision that I stayed too long, when I come home and *I find my cat was dead* because one of my friends tires got slashed on the bike, the other one got stolen, *anybody who came over to help me, help her, for something was vandalized*. And we can never prove it was him, it was clear and obvious to all of us who it was. So I was in a pickle, so I sent some texts out to the crews that I knew and *this crew immediately were like, 'Martha, don't even think about it. Get over here right now.'* (Int 2).

This excerpt contains blunt othering (Riggins 1997) of bad squatters, who are very different from Martha's crew; instead of caring for their occupied space, they are aggressive and insensitive, rip their space apart and ruin it so the squat 'was thrashed, it was a shit hole'. This opposition functions to delineate the boundaries between moral and conscientious behaviour of which Martha is proud and the lack of respect of other squatters and reflects the general media discourse that breaks up squatters into the 'good' and the 'bad'. Good squatters are those who save properties from decay and dereliction for use as social centres as the London-based Oubliette, an arts collective London (Pidd 2009) whose occupants constantly attempted contacts with the owner and offered to vacate the premises when needed; on the contrary, by abusing spaces for personal or political purposes, bad squatters challenge the logic of capitalism without a plan. Story titles are an easy indication of this tendency of extolling or chastising squatters, as in the two examples from Dee and Dos Santos (2015: 121): '"Squatters refurbish £3 million mansion" in the *Sun* versus "Rave hordes in 18 hour spree of destruction at former Royal Mail depot in central London" in the *Daily Mail*'.

The words in the semantic area of violence, 'aggressive', 'threatening', 'not safe', 'dead', 'slashed', 'stolen', 'vandalized', conjure up an atmosphere of ominous uncertainty. Not only are Martha and her friends subject to bailiffs' evictions, they are also at the whims of authoritarian and threatening neighbours and other squatters. Through this small story and the focus on the self-reflexive and self-ascribing 'I', Martha communicates her intention to talk about herself and share with the interviewer her feelings, 'I was in a pickle'. The choice to animate the friends' reaction ('Martha, don't even think about it. Get over here right now') is in line with the performativity of her story and the expression of her vivid emotions.

Conclusion

Space fulfils a crucial role in identity construction and it is not possible to talk about personhood or subjectivity outside a real or imagined space. This chapter has shown how a liminal individual who challenges the constrictions of mainstream society in a creative way discursively constructs a heterotopia by proposing different yet not incompatible frames. Martha's complex place-identity construction hinges on the desire to renegotiate property rights and offer a solution to the housing problem while making a clear political statement. In so doing Martha evokes a persona that in most cases is a capable and resourceful planner who can contribute effectively to a better society. Her discursive heterotopia of transgression and deviance but also of compensation is a perfect site where she constructs her positive self that emerges in the numerous small stories she shares with the interviewer. In Martha's talk, the squat becomes a place like Cinecittà, Beaubourg or Disneyland (Shane 2008: 263) where other realities take shape that counter, contest and compensate for the surrounding non-gratifying society.

The abandoned commercial sites that squatters occupy can be defined as *terrains vagues* (Doron 2008) as their destination is left uncertain and suspended; however, as Foucault comments, '[t]hese marvellous empty zones at the edge of cities' (1997: 355) have never been empty. They are often populated by marginalized communities and have certain physical and non-physical qualities that are unique to them (Doron 2008). Squatters, like planners, 'rearrange them' (Lang 2008: 223) or more precisely, reclaim life from such provisionally dead and void zones and transform them into living residences. Through a complex discourse in which two different frames alternate and in which she prophesizes about the revitalization of specific sites, Martha constructs herself as the positive and creative 'colonizer of the void' (Doron 2008: 205).

As was argued, the heterotopic reality Martha evokes that is counter to the 'dominant, metropolitan understanding of space' (Palladino 2016: 2) is in tune with the construct of liminality as suspension between uncertain states. Both the temporal and the spatial dimension in Martha's liminality are crucial to her identity construction. While she engages in a complex emotional relation with her space that results in her portrayal of the squat as a very special counter place, the temporal dimension, present in her personal narratives, equally provides the frame that allows Martha to construct her heterotopia. Both space and time are therefore the means through which Martha expresses her longing for stability, albeit within an alternative spatial logic, and emotional certainty outside traditional social parameters. Although such verbs as 'wish' 'want' or 'plan to' are not too often present in her talk, her clear insistence on projecting the future of her crew and on ascribing to herself the ability to guide her squamily towards an ethical and still profitable solution is still very much in the realm of her desire for a resolution to her present liminal condition.

In the chapters that follow the exploration of liminality and place-identity continues with two more groups of individuals who live in the interstices of society. Through their own words and voices, we will get a sense of the aspiration and volition in relation to their heterotopic space that is an integral part of their identity construction.

5

'We don't need a castle. We need a home.' Desire for place in a Travellers' transit site

Introduction

This chapter continues the investigation of desire and heterotopia as discursively constructed through the observation of a different group of itinerant and unsettled people. These are individuals whom, like Martha, society does not understand and perceives as a threat. The element of desire once again strongly pervades these new liminals' discourse. Like Martha, these interviewees are all women and, because of this, their gender liminality is of a special kind.

The aim of this chapter is to examine how the women belonging to an Irish Travellers' community in the south of England construct their self through discourse, understood as 'talk, text, speech' (Blommaert 2001: 14) in relation to a space that is systematically denied to them or granted only for a short time. In the first part, background information is provided on the Travellers' community, including details about the site history that are necessary to understand the interviewees' relation to that space. Attention is devoted to the discussion of the dominant discourse about Travellers and Gypsies in the media. Following that, the main findings of the study are presented in two parts; firstly, a geographical analysis of the Travellers' particular space is presented, followed by the in-depth analysis of the interviews.

Travellers are traditionally nomadic people similar to Gypsies, a generic term with a still negative connotation within settled society, which tends to describe more often Romany or Romani (English) Gypsies, who in turn are different from Roma communities in Eastern Europe.[1] Traditionally, these groups embraced fully nomadic lives travelling around the UK; increasingly, however, Travellers' preferred accommodation is their caravan or mobile home on an authorized and serviced site as Elaine below confirms.

Excerpt 1: Elaine.[2] *Not a house*, but I'd rather have a settled place on the site.

Int. Is that what you kind of like, why wouldn't you live in a house?
Elaine. I don't know about a *house it's too hard* for a travelling person=
Int. yeah
=Elaine. to be put in a house, because there's walls, there's wall and *you're trapped in*
Int. @ yeah
Elaine. but when *you're in a caravan you can open the windows and you can open the doors, you can do whatever you want.*

Gypsies, Romany and Travellers (GRT) feel constrained living in conventional houses, especially in urban areas. They cannot usually be accommodated as extended families but only as nuclear entities, which they are generally averse to; also, they tend to be housed in deprived urban areas whose marginalized and disempowered inhabitants resent their presence and thus discriminate against them.

Some Travellers continue to aspire to a fully nomadic life away from urban centres. Given the growing shortage of available spaces, they usually have no other option but to illegally occupy sites (in both rural and peri-urban locations) where they are evicted by the police after a few days. Not surprisingly, this type of Traveller tends to be very private and inaccessible to outsiders. I would have liked to have included them in this study, but even with the Council staff working with GRT as gate-keepers, they refused to engage.

The chapter centres on a group of Irish Travellers who live in an authorized transit site on the outskirts of a coastal town in South-East England, that is serviced by the council, requires a rent and, at the time of the investigation, allowed only a three-month stay. In this case, the contestation dimension of the Travellers' space is dramatically reduced as an established institution provides a living space to suit the mobile community's needs.

This study focuses on a single group of Travellers over a seven-year period (from 2012 to 2019) who, after living intermittently at the transit site over many years, were able in 2016 to transfer to the newly established permanent site. The attention is on the discursive construction of place-identity of these people when they lived at the transit site, while the following chapter explores how these changed once they moved to the permanent site.

The context: Travellers' mobility

In the 20th century Gypsies and Travellers have increasingly been subject to laws and government policies that aim to curb their nomadic lifestyle and largely enforce their settlement. Despite a period of time in the post-war era when Gypsies and Travellers lived relatively harmoniously alongside sedentarists [...], when the countryside started being privatised Travellers and Gypsies (around 300,000 Gypsy Roma and Irish Travellers) lost their freedom to roam; then tensions around where and how they should live have been particularly enhanced since the closure of the commons in the 1968 Caravan Sites and Control of Development Act.

James 2007: 368

Government legislation has played a large part in this process. In particular, the 1968 Caravan Sites and Control of Development Act closed previously common land where Travellers could encamp. The Criminal Justice and Public Order Act 1994 (CJPOA) then further transformed the lives of these mobile groups. This Act and the subsequent Anti-Social Behaviour Act 2003 give local authorities full legal powers to police and evict mobile people with the severity that accompanies public order measures against for instance protests and has transformed institutional intervention to what can be described as 'the dominant discourse of punishment' (James 2007: 369).

Although marginalized and discriminated against, GRT (together with Circus people, Showpeople, Bargies, and New Wave Travellers) have legal protection as minority groups which obliges Local Authorities to provide serviced sites and ensure they have decent accommodation. According to the 2011 Census, 198 GRT resided in the area where this study was conducted of which 88 were housed. Nationally, still according to the 2011 census, about 42,500 GRT families were in permanent houses and around 13,500 in temporary accommodation (Salford University survey, 2014: 35). Throughout the country, therefore, GRT alternate between accepting permanent housing and sticking to mobile accommodation in accordance with their traditions.

According to Costas (2013), attitudes towards GRT nomadism can be broadly divided into two schools of thought or approaches. Sedentarists (Crang 2002, Hoskins and Maddern 2011) tend to criticize their mobility as disruptive and destructive and advocate for greater stability and permanence. By contrast, there are those who celebrate mobility as a way of life, particularly for its resistance to hegemonic reactionary norms of permanency (see Cresswell 2006, Urry 2007 among others). However, this simple dichotomy fails to capture adequately the 'empirical' complexity central to the development of 'a critical stance on the current mobility ideal' (Costas 2013: 1473). In order to redress this oversimplification, Costas proposes the metaphor of stickiness that was first presented by Sartre in *Being and Nothingness* (2003: 627–8). As a source domain, the metaphor uses the image of snails continually moving yet strongly adhering to a surface or that of an ambiguous fluid that has thick texture and solidity but rolls away leaving little or no trace behind; the metaphor, therefore, conflates the two meanings of mobility and stability.

Sartre's metaphor perfectly captures the essence of modern Travellers' life in mobile self-contained accommodation. The trailer's door that opens up to the outdoors grants Travellers a flexible dwelling of variable sizes according to the weather and the times of the day. Travellers 'roll' and move, yet they would preferably 'stick' to the area of their choice possibly for long periods.

The reasons for GRT mobility are often beyond their control. In particular, the law prevents them from setting up even short-term encampments in open spaces. The 2014 Public Space Protection Order (PSPO) closely controls a wide range of behaviours in public spaces and permits local authorities to restrict activities that are deemed to have detrimental effects on local communities such as sleeping in cars or tents or lighting fires. Where local authorities strictly follow the legal provisions of the PSPO, this invariably leads to the swift eviction of GRT from illegal sites.

Up until the mid-20th century, GRT participated fully in the local economy working in a variety of occupations and trades especially harvesting, tin/blacksmithing, carpentry, and horse trading and slaughtering. These have been supplanted since then by tarmacking, scrap metal collection, gardening and dog-breeding. Illegal activities and unemployment are high among GRT.

A recent change is towards sedentarization as GRT want their children to be educated and for this reason they aim to have some stability. In the first interview a Traveller's words unequivocally express this desire: 'Like, if I had a permanent pitch . . . well then my children would be in school . . . all year round (. . .) children need to know what they are going to be doing.' In July 2016, the community observed in this study was transferred to a permanent site built next to where the old transit camp used to be. The twelve Traveller families selected to live in the new site, therefore, became a hybrid between itinerant and stationary and best exemplify Sartre's metaphor of stickiness. This newly constituted group will be discussed in the next chapter.

GRT are a distinct ethnic group with a strong collective identity and Travellers rarely leave their community. In a 2012 interview, one of the Travellers explains how her mother became a settled person ('country person' or 'Gorja/Gorger' in Travellers/Gypsies' language) through marriage.

> *Excerpt 2:* Lisa. Oh, you mean with the country people . . . yeah, my kids are very used to mixing with country people . . . *my mother's a country woman*
> Int. Oh, really?

Lisa. Yeah, my *granny's a country woman* ... so when we go to visit my granny and my like other family, my first cousins are there and my children mixes with them, so they're used to mixing with ...

Similarly the following excerpt from an interview with an English Traveller highlights the strength of her ethnic self-concept and community membership.

Excerpt 3: Int. So, tell me, how does one become a traveller or a gypsy?
English Gypsy. *You can't become it*, love.
Int. No? Tell me why.
EG. You can't (unintelligible overlapping conversation).
Int. Tell me why, tell me how.
EG. Because, it's what we're brought into.
Int. Yeah. But, originally, you probably had a place or.... No?
EG. Oh, yeah. We originally have places, but *just because you're in a caravan don't make you a Gypsy.*
Int. Right. So, what is it that makes you a gypsy?
EG. *Your blood.*
Int. Your blood?
EG. Yeah.

While this woman talks about 'Gypsy blood', later in the same interview she prefers to define her social identity in terms of traditions and rules that effectively characterize Gypsies as a special group. This confirms recent views of ethnicity as 'not a genetic given but a historical, cultural, textual and linguistic construct' (Joseph 2004); ethnic self-consciousness, therefore, cannot be understood in terms of biological difference but in terms of the complexity of cultural capital they have accumulated over time, in which they firmly believe.

Excerpt 4: English Gypsy. We've got ... *we've got our own rules and ways of life* and you've got your own rules and ways, but ....
Int. So, tell me, what are the rul-=
EG.= What are the rules? [...] *Our rules are* we have to ... *we're not allowed to go with anyone before we're married.* Even if we're courting them, we're not allowed to go with them. *We are not allowed like drinking* and things like that.
Int. So, you never drink?
EG. No.
Int. Okay.
EG. When we ... *when we take ourselves a husband, then we got to stick by him. We go where he wants to go; we do what he wants to do.* It's all about taking care of family, really.

GRT believe in communal life with extended families and children gaining their independence earlier than in settled society but still remaining in close contact with their parents. There is no hierarchy in GRT communities, which may be regarded with suspicion by mainstream society since such strong family bonds are perceived as replacing a commitment to public institutions and laws.

Women especially find support in communal life.

> *Excerpt 5:* Ivonne. Everyone on the site is *friends ... everyone mixes* with each other (...) *your things is kept right,* your *kids is properly looked after.* And everyone, everyone does that . . . . the kids are properly looked after [...] and you just kinda keeps to yourself, like everyone in here now knows each other and like you mix around, like there's always people coming on and off so we mix like, you can just, like *if you needed something you could run over,* or if I ran out of milk I'd run over and be like 'have you got any milk until I get back from the shop' like I did yesterday, like a community.

Tight knit communal life, therefore, ensures children's protection, shared childcare and support in an emergency while at the same time does not deprive families of their private space ('you just kinda keeps to yourself') and respect for private ownership ('your things is kept right'). As in many other cases, the vividness of this speaker's report is realized by her voicing herself asking another Traveller for milk. For the sake of the interviewer, through 'a pattern of verbal and non-verbal acts [...] express[ing her] view of the situation and [... her] evaluation of the participants, especially [her]self' (Goffman 1967: 5), this woman conjures up a scenario of female camaraderie and a supportive network.

Travellers in the UK are subject to ghettoization and objectification (Okley 2014). Mainstream society's dominant narrative is that Travellers are anti-social outsiders with strange values, attitudes and behaviours who lead an archaic lifestyle. Generally, people feel threatened by Travellers and do not want them near their properties because, as Brenmer (2010: 5) points out somewhat ironically, 'in the contemporary world, the idea of dwelling alongside strangers is increasingly unwelcome. Diversity is seen as dangerous.'

This, then, is the social context of the GRT communities under investigation. In line with the analysis of Martha's talk, the two chapters devoted to the Travellers focus on an analysis of liminal place-identity capturing, in the language of these women who are responsible for their families' wellbeing, the aspiration to a different and more stable life.

Discourses around GRT

Due to their mobility, GRT belong to a culture of resistance in the same way that New or Hippy Travellers are (James 2007: 380). In a society that has been organized around stability and sedentary boundaries since the Enclosure Acts of the 18th century, the fluidity of nomadic living is threatening as it escapes the control of institutional agencies and contests the sedentary and private space culture of western societies (Sibley 1995: 72).

Gypsies and Travellers are subject to continuous policing, control and surveillance by governmental agencies that often have the task of removing them from their temporary accommodation in ways that 'require[s] scrutiny in order to provide any sort of social justice' (James 2007: 385). In spite of this, GRT are strongly committed to continuing with their nomadic lifestyle, making themselves as little visible as possible, hiding in marginal areas and camouflaging their homes to escape institutional policing (James 2007: 385).

The press contributes significantly in exacerbating the negative stance towards GRT. Although the media may be echoing negative public opinion towards nomadic groups, 'in reflecting it they condone, encourage and confirm racist assumptions whereas, some might argue, it is part of their role to counter such bigoted simplifications' (Morris 2000: 213). Inflaming racist sentiment is common in tabloids (Figure 3).

Figure 3 Inciting hatred towards GRT.

The following excerpt from the front cover of The Birmingham Evening Mail, Tuesday 29 June 1993, quoted in Morris (2000: 214) is a typical example:

> KEEP THIS SCUM OUT (And it IS time to hound 'em, Chief Constable). They call themselves tinkers. Itinerants, new age travellers. We call them parasites. The scum of the earth who live off the backs of others. They contribute nothing but trouble ... They set up filthy, disease-ridden camps on roadsides and in parks and offend every decent citizen.

GRT are among the most maligned minorities in the UK and Europe and Romaphobia, the demonization of Romany Gypsies especially by the media, is the last accepted form of racism, especially in Eastern Europe (McGarry 2017).

Documentaries similarly contribute to spreading a negative image of GRT. Piazza (2015 and 2017) highlighted the various techniques which result in the serious misrepresentation of these nomadic groups in the UK. Through topic choice, a seemingly neutral narrator's voice-over and interviewer's questions, most documentary films encourage a very negative characterization of GRT either as criminals or exotically rare examples of deviance.

'A Briefing: Gypsies, Roma and Irish Travellers in the media' produced in 2012[3] underlines that the UN Human Rights Committee has fully recognized the extent and seriousness of the negative media coverage of GRT based on grossly inaccurate stereotypes. Other prominent human rights organizations including the UN Committee on the Elimination of all forms of Racial Discrimination and the European Commission against Racism and Intolerance (ECRI) have also made similar observations. A recent ECRI briefing paper highlights the link between the pervasively negative portrayal of GRT and the level of violence inflicted on these minority groups. The briefing also confirms the misrepresentation 'in particular in the tabloid press, where [GRT] are frequently portrayed, for example, as being by definition associated with ... sponging off British society, making bogus claims for protection and being troublemakers.' This has a devastating effect on Travellers' self-esteem and identity. Thomas McCarthy, a traditional Irish Traveller singer and rights campaigner, states in the briefing: 'When I see the headlines, it feels like a physical blow. It feels like we have been knocked backwards when we are trying to step forward' (ECRI, 2012: 3).

On BBC news on 5 April 2019 Romany Gypsy activist, Ivy Manning, complains bitterly about the discrimination faced by her children when they started primary school. She cites such derogatory phrases as 'pikey', 'trailer trash' 'living in the Jippo site' which are similar to the label 'stinky pikey' she was herself given when she was at school twenty years earlier. She pleaded with the government to address inequality. A new report by a group of MPs says Gypsy, Roma and Traveller communities are being 'comprehensively failed' by councils and the government.[4]

Although Gypsies, Romany and Travellers are considered ethnic groups by the Race Relations (Amendment) Act 2000, the press generally avoids using capitals for their names.

A 2016 report by the Human Rights Commission[5] confirms the persistence of inequality following previous research by the same Commission in 2009, while the Global Attitudes Survey (2014) found 50 percent of UK respondents held negative views of Roma (although Roma in Europe are very different from British Romany groups):

> Views of minorities vary widely, both between countries and about specific minority populations. Roma are viewed unfavorably by a median of 50% of those surveyed, with Italians (85%) holding particularly negative sentiments. A median of 46% hold anti-Muslim views. Again it is Italians (63%) who see Muslims in the most negative light. And Jews are seen negatively by a median of 18%, with Greeks (47%) harboring the strongest anti-Jewish sentiment. Negative sentiments about all three groups are consistently more common among people on the ideological right.

Anti-Roma, Anti-Muslim Sentiments Common in Several Nations

% unfavorable

	Roma* %	Muslims %	Jews %
Italy	85	63	24
France	66	27	10
Greece	53	53	47
UK	50	26	7
Poland	49	50	26
Germany	42	33	5
Spain	41	46	18
MEDIAN	**50**	**46**	**18**

*In United Kingdom, asked as "Gypsies or Roma."

Source: Spring 2014 Global Attitudes survey. Q37a-c.

PEW RESEARCH CENTER

Figure 4 Anti-Roma, Anti-Muslim Sentiments Common in Several Nations.

Negative attitudes to GRT also lead to hate crime (Hall et al. 2014, James 2007). In Cornwall, James (2007) finds that over 90 percent of the GRT felt discriminated against and were threatened physically with 'spades and diggers' and told 'by a policeman that people like us should be put against a wall and shot as there was no place for people like us in society' (James 2019).[6]

At the time of writing, the Parliament is conducting an inquiry on the unequal condition of GRT, who are 'the most disadvantaged ethnic groups in the UK. On average, they have a shorter life expectancy than the rest of the population, poor educational outcomes and often face hostility and discrimination from others in society'.[7]

In spite of the institutional attempts to improve the relationship between these nomadic groups and settled society however, the contacts are mostly through heavy policing and space enforcement interventions by police forces. The degree of mistrust and hostility is still very high so that efforts to improve relationships end up making the racialization of Travellers and Gypsies even more acute while the provision of accommodation for them does not improve substantially. According to Mulcahy (2011), 'a logic of spatial regulation shapes the manner in which Travellers are policed in decisive ways. This operates against a backdrop of moral disdain towards Travellers which persistently constructs them as a criminogenic community and which gives rise to the over-policing and under-protection that characterizes their involvement with the criminal justice system' (p.321).

The meaning and history of the Travellers' transit site

The intersections between space and identity are filtered through the 'desire lines' from the title of Murray et al.'s (2007) book, or the aspirations to a different life that all the interviewees nurture. Space is interpreted as a complex notion that has a crucial impact on people's lives (Massey 2005). Citing Massey again (1992: 79), '[i]t's not that the interrelations between objects occur in space and time; it is those relations themselves that create/define space and time.' While this is the premise of the argument developed in this chapter, the discussion draws a distinction between the physicality of space and how this can act as a site of resistance in the first part; in the second part, the focus is on how space is discursively constructed as place by the Travellers during the interviews.

In Foucault's words, spaces are not void containers that can be filled with people and things; spaces result from and 'delineate' the web of relationships within which people live (Foucault 2008: 16). The Travellers' site where this study was conducted is a plot of land used originally by New Wave, hippie or New Travellers and tolerated by city residents. Always in service for the diverse and marginal, it is in itself a liminal space in being located on the margin of a motorway and at the end of a small path, invisible to the naked eye until one descends into the valley (Figures 5 and 6).

Figure 5   The transit site (personal photo).

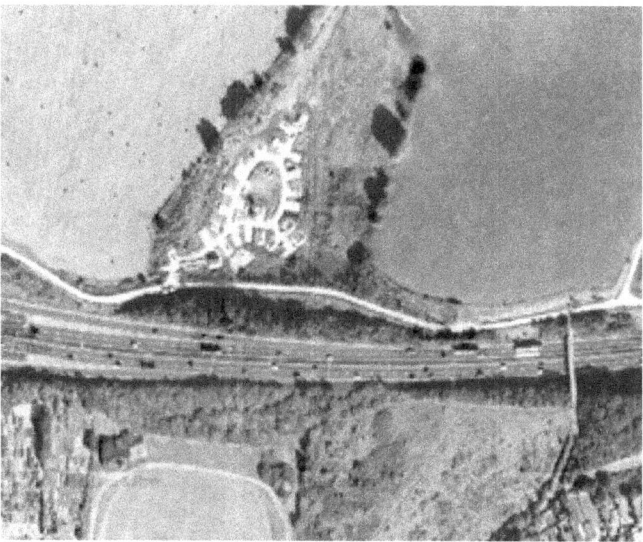

Figure 6   The site aerial view.[8]

Because of its physical invisibility, the site is a place in between places, a hybrid between stability and permanency, mobility and itinerancy, a space that is institutionalized because supported and serviced by the Council, while at the same time it is guarded off from citizens who may object to such an investment of public resources. A counter space for counter people, it is a liminal transit space where Travellers can station temporarily.

In the 1990s the site was inaugurated as a transit site for Gypsies and Travellers with twenty-three pitches 'through the Gypsy and Traveller Site Grants' (Salford University report 2014: 41). Two grants over ten years ensured electricity supply to the site through the building of an electrical substation, providing electricity posts for each individual pitch (See Figure 7). Pitches were available for a period of a maximum of twelve weeks at a rent of £60 per week in 2014. The households of English Gypsies or Romani and Irish Travellers would be eligible for the transit site according to the following criteria: 'need for accommodation; medical/special health needs; family or personal compatibility; previous known behaviour/references; and previous rent arrears' (Salford University report 2014: 41).

Figure 7 Electrical units at the site (personal photo).

A further word on the methodology

The interviews with Travellers were loosely structured but posed similar questions to all the respondents about their attachment to the space. The interviewees were given considerable leeway to take the exchange where they wanted. Ethnographic field notes were taken about the close and extended context around the caravans and with respect to the variety of events I witnessed outside the site, e.g. talks with various staff and volunteers, participation in Council events to sound out the local residents' attitude about the promised permanent site etc. Additional materials that informed this study were Travellers' magazines, TV documentaries and newspaper articles about GRT, Council reports and Council-commissioned surveys about the community.

The research fieldwork at the transit site was spread over three and a half years. Ten out of a total of sixteen interviews were included; they are the most significant covering the period from 2012 up to 2015 when the site was closed down in order for the new permanent camp to be built.

The analysis of space, part one: Physical space and affective place among Travellers

As mentioned earlier, this analytical section is split into two. The first part is devoted to an interpretation of the physical space, while the second returns to the main topic of the Travellers' discursive place.

The Travellers' transit site as spatial landscape

As discussed earlier, Travellers are widely perceived as a marginal, anti-social group by settled society in large part because of their nomadic lifestyle coupled with how they change urban and rural spaces from recognized recreational use to temporary residential sites viewed as untidy, unsanitary and generally unsightly through a land possession that generates new meanings. Lefebvre (in Cenzatti 2008: 80) refers to this contestation around the utilization of public land as *space of representation*.

Such space possession can be equalled to similar space disruptions like the 2010-12 occupation of Syntagma Square in Athens in response to the EU austerity measures, the use of a park in Milan or a bridge between skyscrapers in Hong Kong by Philippino maids on their free day (Cenzatti 2008: 7), the reinterpretation of space by the Spanish *Indignados* movement (Martin Rojo 2014) or the 2012 lying down as dead protest of the One in Nine Campaign as a form of resistance against the mainstream core of the Gay Pride in Johannesburg (Milani 2015).

Similarly, even though they are quickly evicted, through the very physical action of subverting the legally stipulated use of these public spaces, Travellers perform a heterotopia of difference and contestation to which society responds with such measures as the Public Place Protection Order.

Travellers' uncanonical use of space is not limited to the temporary appropriation of parks although this is the most apparent form of 'disobedience'. Life in caravans creates a dichotomy between the closeness in the trailer limited space and the openness of the outside area where people talk, children play and men plan their business. Such a dichotomy finds a response in the construction of a heterotopic space within the occupied area in the park, in itself a liminal locale vis-à-vis the rest of the urban centre; there the area around the trailers is marked by the often open door that ensures continuity between the inside of the caravan (the ultimate example of heterotopia, together with mobile homes, Palladino 2016: 25) and the open space outside. Women walking around in their nighties is evidence of such continuity.

Foucault refers to heterotopic spaces of deviation as spaces where dominant society allocates people 'whose behaviour is deviant in relation to the mean or required norm' (Foucault 2008: 16). However, such one-sided definition of heterotopia of deviance does not fit Travellers too well. Even with very limited power, with the crucial help of some dedicated charities (e.g. FFT), Travellers put pressure on institutions to deal with outcast and segregated communities like theirs. Local authorities therefore create Travellers' sites where this community can keep up with their traditional lifestyle in spite of mainstream society considering it deviant and unorthodox. The intersection therefore takes shape between a deviation allowed by the institutions in response to the one coming from the Travellers.

Once established that a Travellers' site can be read as a heterotopia of deviation, we can turn to the spatial consequences of the dynamic relation between local authorities and Travellers. Important transformations take place that need considering in this analysis. For example the spatial organization decided by the Council, albeit in collaboration with experts, may have been aimed to respect the Travellers' communitarian spirit and allow vicinity between caravans still preserving a degree of privacy, yet it realizes a form of deviance in itself.

In the case of the design of the transit site we are no longer dealing with the 'space of representation' discussed earlier that Travellers create when appropriating a park and subverting its use. This is a case of *spatial practice* (Cenzatti 2008) in that space is defined by the physical construction of individual bays or pitches bordered by massive man-cut cement boulders within which each caravan is parked. As can be seen in Figure 6, the Council-built transit site hosting about twenty pitches, is organized as a radius with the sanitary facilities on one side near the entrance and the security block. If compared with the random positioning of trailers that Travellers choose in the temporary occupation of parks (see Figure 7), the highly functional structured complex of the Council site appears to propose a radically different interpretation of space.

Deleuze and Guattari (2004) identify the two different configurations of *smooth* and *striated* space corresponding to the loose, 'free' and 'nomadic' space in opposition to the 'sedentary' and 'work-altered' space arranged along precise lines. A striated space can be best exemplified by the highway metaphor that regulates and facilitates the flow of vehicles moving between destinations (Nunes 1999); also 'in striated space, one closes off a surface and "allocates" it according to determinate intervals, assigned breaks; in the smooth, one "distributes" oneself in an open space, according to frequencies and in the course of one's crossings' (1999: 481). However, there is no permanent division between the two types of space that are in continuous state of flux: 'smooth place is constantly being translated, traversed into striated space; striated space is constantly being reversed, returned to a smooth space' (Deleuze and Guattari 2004: 552). This is evidenced by the Travellers transforming the site through the acquisition of additional mobile homes in the permanent site as will be discussed in the next chapter.

Figure 8 Caravans in temporary stay in a park.

A transformation occurred in the passage from the park to the serviced site. While the smooth space that Travellers adopt in parks and non-authorized sites is 'wind swept' and natural, the Council site is a striated space. In parks Travellers organize their space loosely with their trailers arranged along various lines and at various angles probably according to what family and friends they want to be close to, the time of their arrival at the park and the nature of the terrain (flat or hilly, soft or hard etc.); on the contrary, in the striated serviced site the space is regimented by the construction of separate bays where each trailer is orderly parked.

The choice of such a structure may have been dictated by an economic, rational exploitation of space rather than deliberate politics; however, considering the long gestation of the site, a politics of space cannot be dismissed as will become more relevant in the case of the later built permanent site for which the circular structure can be read as a 'container metaphor' (Hirst and Humpreys 2013: 1506) that aims to misunderstand space as a locale where things get done and which can be easily surveyed and controlled.

In the transit site the Council offers a service and aims to protect Travellers from unwanted others' intrusions (anyone entering the site needs to report to security) but the serviced rent-based (£100 per week at the time of the fieldwork) transit site is a striated space functioning as a punitive space that restricts and regulates Travellers' behaviour. Moreover, by creating the serviced site, the Council realizes a new heterotopia that deviates from the Travellers' aspired smooth space arrangement in parks. The two heterotopias, the Travellers' and the Council's, then clash to then merge as hypothesized by Deleuze and Guattari (2014).

In spite of the reading proposed here, all the interviewed Travellers showed loyalty to the Council Travellers' Liaison officers and trust in their ability and willingness to mediate on their behalf with the rest of the establishment (Jane. and there's lovely people. I mean the lady who runs this site is beautiful). Such positive attitude to the Council does not necessarily rule out Travellers' occasional dissatisfaction with the state of the facilities on the site.[9]

Part two: The discourse of desired place

How the physical geography of the Travellers' site impacts on the community's social life illustrates very well one of the basic premises of this study, namely, that the 'simultaneous coexistence of materially-embedded relations [...] makes the social and the spatial inextricably realise one in the other' (Hirst and Humphreys 2013: 1507).

The second part of this chapter explores how the Travellers in the transit site discursively constructed their place-identity together with a desire for an authentic ontological self. The two constructs of place-identity and desire are, therefore, associated and operationalized at the same time. While space is understood as constructed through the speakers' talk and as integral part of their personhood, desire is manifested through a wide range of affordances. The expression of desire goes well beyond the verbal articulation of it (desire is 'a primary force independent of linguistic expression' according to Whitehead 2002: 213), but linguistic ethnographers and discourse analysts can only trace desire in people's language choices and cannot follow the inner and hidden expression of desire.

As pointed out by Milani (2015), Kiesling (2011) offers a useful mediating position in the debate on desire and identity. In his analysis of interactions between men recruiting new members of a US college fraternity and a heterosexual couple at a bar, Kiesling proposes that desire can be realized as the speaker's 'involvement' with or, better, 'alignment' to an interlocutor. Such speaker's alignment is understood in Gumperz's sense of showing in the course of a conversation an 'observable' state of 'coordinated interaction, distinguished from mere copresence' (Gumperz 1982: 11 in Kiesling 2011:220). Kiesling's point is basically that a speaker's eagerness to empathize, albeit not necessarily agree, with an interlocutor is the result of a desire in one case to convince a new member to join the fraternity community and in the other to perform a particular gender identity. Following Kiesling's (2011) interactional study therefore, this second part of the chapter proposes ways to trace how desire is 'spoken' in the interviews with a number of women belonging to the travelling community.

The Travellers' attachment to the site is unquestionable and reflected in their sublimation of it as a space that totally fulfils their needs. In the following excerpt a woman constructs the transit site as a heterotopia in ways that are similar to what Martha did in the previous chapter; her terms of evaluation ('nothing to complain about, the nicest place') are clear and so is her appreciation of the space.

> *Excerpt 7*: Megan. it is good. Everything's really helpful ... kids ... schools
> and ... everything like *there's no things that I could complain about*
> Int. ah that's really good [to hear
> M.   [this place has everything

Int. ahm
M. this is a nice place, I've been travelling all my [life
Int   [have you
M. this is *the nicest place* I've think I've ever lived

Between the glorification of their space and the fear of losing it, these women's talk is framed within a clearly aspirational discourse. The conceptual construct of desire in a non-sexual key, understood as the longing that leads people's lives in various forms, helps characterize the construction of place as the discursive expression of an existential drive through which the speakers evoke a number of identities and attempt to associate themselves with a context of power and knowledge. Whitehead (2002) understands the concept of desire as 'unrest' (p. 32) or as the realization of what we do not but could have, in other words as the 'subjective passion', the 'urge' or 'drive' towards the future that hinges on a need to procure something in the present.

Mills reminds us how for Whitehead (1927/1960) an actual entity, a real self is 'desirous', in that it longs for fulfilment. In fact, '[i]f an entity did not desire, it would not seek- it would not experience, hence it simply would not be' (p. 215). From this perspective, therefore, desire is associated with and represents the essence of identity, which Whitehead defines as 'desiring production' (Mills 2003: 213). As identities do not operate in a vacuum, a desirous identity needs to be 'authenticated' (Bucholtz and Hall 2004) or recognized by others. This crucial concept of intersubjectivity and relationality refers to the ontological dimension of desire and implies that an act of desire can realize a 'performative' (Butler 1990) social act of identity. Following Whitehead, Cameron and Kulick's (2003) study of sexuality builds on the construct of desire as the 'continuous motivator' of subjects' actions and interactions within a spatial and temporal web of material and social relations (Whitehead 2002: 211). As they aspire to security, people 'constantly aim[s] at granting a stable and authentic position for the self' (Milani 2017: 411); to this effect they engage in acts of identity that can ensure a degree of 'ontological security' (Giddens 1991) as a stable mental condition that comes from experiencing one's life events as a continuity and results in a feeling of individual wholeness (Mitzen 2006: 342).

In the case of the interviewed travelling women a declaration of want such as 'We need ... education' not only indicates that these speakers have desires, it means that they have an active self able to identify a particular need and express it. In what follows it will be shown how by articulating such a desire constantly and insistently, the interviewees claim a specific continuity of the self and hence an 'ontological security' that is associated with a desired sense of dignity and respectability in a way that is very similar to what Ross (2005) finds to be the case among low-income communities in an estate in Western Cape. By such an ontological act, the women in Ross' study show how they are subjects with a will to power and a desire to be differentiated and liked, spatially and temporally, within the social web, thus proving their awareness of existing as individuals.

The following section is based on Kiesling's (2011) interpretation of desire and the linguistic expression of it. The discussion of desire however, it must be remembered, is situated within and associated with the consideration of space. The two constructs therefore are interpreted jointly as a way of observing how the interviewees in this study construct their identities.

As was mentioned earlier, the fact that the interviewees in this chapter are exclusively women cannot be overlooked. As a 'historically evolving and cultural construct' (Gajardo and Oteíza 2017: 143), subject to different representations in different contexts, among Travellers motherhood relies on a firm gender division. With few exceptions, women do not work, only tend to their children and housework (8 below), are often illiterate, while men are the breadwinners. Desire therefore needs to be understood within such a context.

> *Excerpt 8:* Lucy. and he's done, *he's done the work part . . .* and *I'd done the feeding and washing and the cleaning and the changing*
> Interviewer. and the babies @
> J. the babies @
> Int. and you got two right?
> J. me? seven, I got seven children
> Int. sorry?
> J. I got seven children. I was married at sixteen, I had four children by twenty . . . I'm forty one . . . but they're all grown up and then I had another one at forty which I didn't plan but it's the best thing that happened to me.

In spite of this, it is too simplistic to stereotype these women as passive and dependent. They are sometime single women who manage a whole family (three in my sample). Some seem to have an intermittent relation with their partners to not lose welfare support for single mothers (two in my sample). In other words, categorizing these women from a settled community's perspective does not seem to do them justice, therefore this chapter reflects on more subtle aspects of their female identity within the discursive context of liminality and on their roles within their nomadic community. The adoption of social constructionist perspective where gender is seen as realized through the interaction with others is the key feature of this approach (see Baxter 2008).

The expression of desire for space

In the women's talk very direct statements encode multiple desires for a future life on a permanent site. At a close look, however, these desires are vicarious because they are not directly aimed at the women but their children. The women Travellers live through and for their sons and daughters and in their name justify the aspiration to a permanent residence. The use of straightforward verbs of volition, if-clauses, direct irrealis moods and negative statements suggests the intensity of their longing. The noticeable repetition similarly adds to such a direct formulation.

i. *Verbs of volition and irrealis moods*

> *Excerpt 9:* Sheila ... like *I want her to have everything*, do you know what I mean? And *I want* ... like *I want* her *to have everything*, do you know what I mean? And *I want* to [overlapping conversation] to be able actually have a proper job not be like how we are, like the older ones.
> Int. Why, why do you say 'like we are'? You are kind of being negative about yourself.
> Sheila. No I mean like as ... don't ... can't do nothing, do you know what I mean?
> Int. Right.
> Sheila. Like you can't [inaudible] so you can't get a job. You [inaudible] and so you just stay at home [inaudible] I'm doing my kids.
> Int. Yes, yes.
> Sheila. Do you know what I mean which I obviously I enjoyed doing that.
> Int. Yes, I'm sure you do, yeah.
> Sheila. But *it would be nice* sometimes just to be able to do some for yourself as well.
> Int. Absolutely, yeah, yeah, yeah.
> Sheila. Do you know what I mean?
> Int. Absolutely, I agree with you.
> Sheila. *I would like* my little girl to have a job and *be normal.*
> Int. Yeah, normal.
> Sheila. Do you know what I mean?
> Int. Yes, yes, yeah.

A part from the insistence on direct forms of volition as 'want' and such irrealis moods as 'would like' and 'would be nice', this excerpt is revealing of how female Travellers can be upward mobile even within the boundaries of their community. Here the speaker establishes a clear hiatus between the older traditionalist Travellers and the modern ones who aspire to a better life with whom she wants to be associated. Worthy of note is also her use of 'normal' to describe a life not solely devoted to children (I'm doing my kids') but with a job. In the excerpt below the use of verbs of volition is associated once more with a permanent heterotopic space that will provide security and safety.

> *Excerpt 10:* Alicia. ... We *want* a home. We *want* a site, our kids is entitled to go to school like everyone else's. [...] Basically we *want* a site, we *want* a home. Yes, that's what I mean. [...] We've been promised the site for the last 20 year
> Interviewer. For a lot of years.
> Alicia. They're building it and they're not building it, they have the money, I can't see the problem. *They should just build it* if they're building it. *Just get their hopes* up every year and [inaudible] you know what I mean. *I want* a home. *I want* a daughter. *A gate to lock every night like everyone else, go to bed and go to sleep.*

ii. *If-clauses*

> *Excerpt 11:* Sheila. It's just really ... *it'd just be great if the site is done* and planning within our ... we got pass or whatever. Would you have something to look forward to, do you know what I mean? And *if they do get pass it will take like* a year or 18 months to build it. So you'd know for the past 18 months' time you'll have a home.

> *Excerpt 12:* Ruth. It's not worth it. Like having to fight constantly -- having to constantly say why you need to stay and constantly trying to get your point across, do you know what I mean. *Whereas if Johnny wasn't autistic I'd just travel.*
> Interviewer. Really?
> Ruth. I'd just go wherever it was that everyone has gone.
> Int. What about the education for the other kids?
> Ruth. They don't seem -- that doesn't really seem to come into it. You can't put them to school when you're getting sectioned off for camp and you've got to pick them up at 2 o'clock in the day or you might be out on the road until 11 or 12 o'clock at night trying to find the camp.

In the above cases, the if-clauses are associated with contrasting desires. While Sheila is still concentrated on the dream of a permanent site, Ruth's words express the desperation of a woman who has been struggling with a problematic child. Her hard words convey her tiredness of having to argue her case constantly to insensitive authorities to the point that she would be willing to give up the strenuous search for stability if her family situation allowed that.

Desire through negative propositions

In the women's talk, desire is also expressed indirectly by negative propositions implying the opposite of what the speaker is predicating. So, for example in (13) below the utterance 'I don't want to be thrown in a place for my children to smoke drugs and take drugs and drink' is an indirectly desirous proposition meaning 'I want a place for my children away from drugs and alcohol.' Similarly in (14) the speaker's admission that she 'couldn't do it' encodes her regret and desire to be able to read and write.

> *Excerpt 13:* Sue. I *don't want* to be thrown in a place for my children to smoke drugs and take drugs and drink. I *don't need* that so when we're travelling, when the kids were younger, if you booked into a camp site and there was people smoking dope, you can hook up, take your children [inaudible] a different direction. They *don't need* that [inaudible]. They *don't need* drugs. They *don't need* [inaudible] people. Do you know what I mean.
>
> *Excerpt 14:* Sheila. Like how nice here and her friends and they got play, like loads of stuffs that is really very, very interesting. You know, because I *couldn't do* it because I never went to school ...
> Int. You never went to school?
> Sheila. Do you know what I mean here, like a week here and a week there ...
> Int. Do you regret that? Do you regret that you didn't go to school?
> Sheila. Yeah of course I do. If you know what I mean? Because now I can't wait. Do you know what I mean? If I got [overlapping conversation] surgery, *or if I got to fill in forms, it's so embarrassing because I can't read.*

In this conversation, the desire is for a community that protects and safeguards children from the much-threatened excesses of settled society. This speaker's use of the passive voice 'being thrown' encodes her fear of being objectified to such degree that she becomes the recipient of the violent act of relegating into a negative space that will contaminate her children. In the latter excerpt on the contrary, desire is expressed indirectly through the regret of being illiterate and not self-sufficient.

Desire through topic insistence

This section is concerned with the interactional level of communication between the researcher and the interviewees following on from Kiesling's (2011) notion of engagement and affiliation between speakers as an expression of desire. As the excerpts below show, the interviewees take the interviewer's responses as a token of empathy and as an incentive to continue with their favourite topic, which is the necessity of a stable space. Repetition and topic insistence therefore encode the attempt to make the women's inner aspirations known to the interlocutor and hence are the expression of a strong longing. The stress on children's education conditional on spatial stability emerges in all the conversations with the women. In the exchange below a woman produces a crescendo of utterances extolling the positive values of her community, while the interviewer empathizes with her. Her topic insistence is clearly noticeable in her response to the researcher's input.

> *Excerpt 15:* Ruth. So the rest of our group are meeting up again at Christmas.
> Int. Yes, where you gonna meet?
> R. They're down in Salisbury, so we're gonna meet up with them but it's just a case of it's *very lonely,* and see like *being here now without them, it kind of shows you what it's gonna be like in a house.*
> Int. Yes, in a way, I understand.
> R. Do you know what I mean?
> Int. Yes.
> R. And it's like the kids now, *they have no one to play with* and they *are so used to having kids around.*
> Int. Yes, of course.
> R. Like you're *used to having all the nieces and nephews and cousins all here.*
> Int. So that's what I'm saying, in a community, yes you would have a community surrounding of friends etcetera, if this were a permanent site.
> R. Yeah, *if you had a permanent site.*
> Int. So yeah, *because otherwise it just continues the rotation of people* ... every three months.
> R. Yeah, so usually we used to get longer. Like our family we always got longer on here. We're here every winter for the past like five years, six years. We used to get the whole winter here and then it was only in the summer that you have to go and you really wouldn't mind that bit, do you know what I mean, but it's just a case of *now it's just getting harder and harder to stay somewhere,* and then of course as you said, *the education wise for the kids. Like my little girl, she's five, she can't even spell her name properly.*

Three themes emerge in the above excerpt: the community's custom of living together and sharing to avoid loneliness, the aspiration to have security in a site where communal life is possible, and finally education as a children's necessity. These three themes can only be achieved through spatial permanency. The woman's talk attests to her liminal condition. She is in-between stages of her existence, in a precarious situation in which the essence of her life, from community living to children's schooling, is predicated on a three months' stay. While this is her condition, she also constructs her place as liminal through her words. What characterizes her talk is how she supports her statements about her aspired living condition with interspersed small stories; in the first case, Travellers' communal spirit is made authentic by the insertion of a reference to her extended family ('Like you're used to having all the nieces and nephews and cousins all here'); while in the second, against the forced rotation in the site and the need for education, she provides the story of her still illiterate daughter ('Like my little girl, she's five, she can't even spell her name properly').

Similarly, the theme of communality in a heterotopic space of harmonious existence clearly emerges in another woman's talk.

> *Excerpt 16:* Alicia. *We are one family yeah. We're all of us together.* If I have problem, that *problem would be sorted out with my family*, yeah. And in my friends, they'll help. If any of my family has to go away, say for a funeral, we wouldn't think twice about bringing our family [inaudible]
> Int. Alright, so it's yeah. That's sweet, that's sweet. That's really nice. A lot of support.
> A. (. . .) *I would look after the kids better than I would my own.* Anyone of our family will do this. We don't have to be invited in for a cup of tea, we can walk in and out any time we want.
> Int. Alright. That's great. Absolutely great. Yeah.
> A. I wouldn't have to wait to be invited up there or up there. We can come in anytime. *If I have problem at 2:00 in the morning,* there's no hassle. *I can knock at any doors* and that problem will be sorted out. Vice versa, I do the same for them.

In the following excerpt the same speaker's practice of reiterating the topic is even more evident. The woman keeps expanding on her desire for stability and continuity and provides further support for her argument. Through the intense longing for her place and in a very accurate language, especially compared to that of the other women, Ruth constructs herself as a fighter against the insurmountable bloc of institutional insensitivity. The use of 'Oh well' that opens her animation (Goffman 1981) of the decision-makers' talk together with the repeated use of the generic pronoun 'they' ('But they feel like they can say whatever they want and treat you whatever way they want') conveys the speaker's perception of the authorities' aloofness. Such stance towards the institution is realized through 'a double-voiced discourse' (Baxter 2010) – in the form of direct quotes from the discourse of institutional people that 'add verisimilitude to the narrated event' (Moita-Lopes 2006: 301) – by which, Ruth harshly criticizes the Council staff's lack of understanding.

> *Excerpt 17:* Ruth. And it's like sometimes it just feels like *they don't give a damn about you, or your kids*. It's like (inaudible) they are perfect. (staff member name), I know for a fact, that (name again) could do anything for you.
> Int. Yeah, he's such a nice person and (another member of staff) as well, yeah.
> R. He really, really would and so would (same member of staff). But it feels like the ones higher up that don't know us, we're just a name on a paper. *It feels like they're judging your life and they're making the decisions* and *they don't realize how important the decision is that they're making,* for instance about me leaving, me having to leave here. They don't realize that the consequences of that is that Johnny [her disabled son] has to come out of school, he won't get speech therapy, he won't get the help he needs and he might lose his place like he did before, do you know what I mean? *They don't look at the consequences, it's just like, 'oh well they can't stay'.* And in reality they could because I've stayed here for two and half years before. So they try and say it's because of the planning permission, I don't care, the 12 weeks for planning permission, but yeah, I was on here for two and a half years, so why didn't the planning permission come into it then? Because Tom's specialist doctor got involved.
> Int. But I think things have changed.
> R. They haven't.
> Int. No?
> R. That happened, the new law came in two years ago and yet last year I came in in September and I didn't leave 'til the end of April and I left off my own accord. So, do you know what I mean?
> Int. Yeah.
> R. They try and tell you this like you're -- because obviously most travellers are uneducated. Unfortunately for them, I know everything about it because I read everything. *So as I turned around I said to them, do we a day, and they said they want to ban me off it, I said, you can't, there's no law to say that you are allowed to ban me off here for 12 months, it's a transit site.* Do you know what I mean? And if you ban me off, (inaudible) to camp out there so it doesn't make a difference to me. But of course it just feels like you're meant to just give up but unfortunately *I can't just give up*, so you know what I mean?

Int. Absolutely not, you shouldn't.
R. I have to fight for him.
Int. And you shouldn't, yeah.

Ruth's vocal condemnation of the authorities' dragged-out process of establishing the long-promised permanent site relies on the report of her own voice at official meetings. Interspersed with the small story of the exchange with a council staff about her disabled child, Ruth's plea for a space is intense. Yet it is not difficult to identify her satisfaction in producing a clever repost to the council officer, which contributes to her self-portrayal as an articulate and intelligent woman in contrast to the 'ignorant, rude' man. A series of oppositions, summarized under the term 'discrimination,' is created by this speaker: her thoughtfulness in opposition to the insensitive authorities, and the understanding Travellers Liaison Office staff versus the people 'higher up' who have the power to legislate but are unfamiliar with Travellers' harsh reality.

> *Excerpt 18:* Ruth. Like I said to them the other day at the meeting we had, it's not like saying that next year okay there could be a site built, or the year after okay there could be a site built, what about now. Do you know what I mean, what am I meant to do now? Why -- like I tried to get a house, *I went to the council to be told that having a son with a disability wasn't a privilege* and that I wasn't homeless because I have a caravan. Do you know what I mean, you get this kind of *discrimination* and it's a case of like well --
> Int. Yeah, absolutely. (. . .)
> R. But why would you say to somebody with a child with special needs, having a son with a disability is not a privilege? As I said to the man, 'have you got a kid with a disability? Because if you did *you would never under a million years think that it's some kind of a privilege.'*
> Int. Yes, yes.
> R. Do you know what I mean, that's just an ignorant, rude thing to turn around and say to somebody with a child with special needs. Do you know what I mean?
> Int. Yeah, yeah.
> R. But *they feel like they can say whatever they want and treat you whatever way they want.* And *I'm always polite, I'm very friendly*, and like with these boys [Travellers Liaison Office people], I know they're only doing their job. And as I said previously, I know [proper name] and the boys, if they could leave us here the whole time, they would and I know he would because he does whatever he can to help you. Do you know what I mean? And (proper name), is the exact same here, whatever he could do to help, he would do it for you. But it's just a case of, it feels like *the ones higher up*, is like –

Ruth illustrates the negative consequences of the authorities' decisions on her and her disabled son. As before, she supports her point with a small story of her much longer stay on the site in the past thanks to her son's doctor's intervention that circumvented the council's regulations. A member of her community at all effects, however, this Traveller is different in that she rises above the others. While Travellers are generally illiterate, this speaker can read and write; 'unfortunately' for the decision-makers, she is well informed and poses a challenge to them as she refutes their version of facts. Her resolution to have a place and be settled is unshakable even at the cost of accepting to temporarily live in a brick and mortar house.

The above excerpts show how the women Travellers articulate their desire for a space of their own. Together with language forms or words encoding their volition, the choice of topics and the semantic oppositions between what they aspire to and what they have to face in reality realize the sense of their space deprivation. Beyond these, one of the strategies they resort to is topic insistence, accompanied by small stories that provide personal illustration of the theme.

Desire through othering: Constructing the site as a fortress

During the fieldwork, the women were the only people willing to be interviewed and nearly the only people on the site while men were out working. Either engaged in domestic duties or, more rarely, chatting and smoking with friends, their role was that of their community's gate-keepers.

The emphasis on the communitarian dimension germane to Travellers' life is core to the women's construction of a heterotopic site as a safe fortress within which Travellers can live and defend themselves from the outside world. The site hosts only good things and is associated with the closing off to the permanent community (the 'country people' or 'Gorjas') accused of indulging in decadent habits and debauchery and hence negatively othered (Riggins 1997). In the excerpt below, the portrayal of the settled people is relentlessly pessimistic while Travellers are praised for 'not doing' not following the settled society's customs if they stick together in the safe harbour that Travellers' sites offer.

> *Excerpt 19:* Alicia. (talking about her son). He's married now with four kids. *He don't drink. He don't smoke. He earns a nice living.* I bring him up the way I thought he should. He understands that. *Now he is bringing his kids up the same way.* You know. So if you watch a crowd of strangers, you don't know what the kids are doing outside when they go out to play, don't know if they are smoking, if they are taking drugs, what they are doing.

> Int. Because I hear this all the time that for you ... um ... I mean that the settled community is dangerous you know because they drink, they smoke and always I keep hearing this. Is that what it is? Is that your worry?
> Alicia. *I know set up kids* [inaudible] *smoking and sleeping with boys down at the parks*. Our kids are not allowed to do that, do you know what I mean, our kids aren't allowed to go out to discos at five in the morning on their own. Our kids aren't allowed to walk alone at night, someone will be with them. Do you know what I mean? So just a different way of life.

As representatives of an 'intensive mothering' (Hays 1996) that locates the traditional model of motherhood at the core of feminine identity, these women insist on closing the doors to the outside world. The result of the deep distrust for country people is a heterotopia where everyone is self-disciplined and far from the settled community's feared abuses and where the women successfully raise their children to not drink, smoke or have pre-marital sex. Travellers' 'different way of life' therefore is safeguarded by both the women as policing guardians and the space where the community is protected and uncontaminated. Identity and place are therefore interconnected in the construction of the 'good mother' (Van Mieroop 2011) who knows what is best for her children and how to protect them.

Constructing the site as a heterotopia, however, necessitates not solely the distancing from settled people but also from the 'bad' Travellers whose behaviour is not consonant with the norms of good mobile citizenship.

> *Excerpt 20:* Alicia. We're the only family that's been around here in years and we're the only family that keeps this place clean. Because people came in here last Christmas and *they broke down that barrier,* they tied [inaudible possibly 'the security men'] into the shed and then people is going to be back again for Christmas.
> Other woman. And they'll get in.
> Alicia. And they will cut that barrier down.
> Other woman. And they'll get in.
> Alicia. And they will get in and *there is jack shit the council can do about*. They have it said already that that barrier is coming down.
> Other woman. So I can't understand.
> Alicia. So what we're thinking is if the five caravans was in, there's nobody else for them people to stay or wash.
> Interviewer. Yes, to stay absolutely yeah.
> Alicia. I told the council that they'd leave town, but if there's one caravan [inaudible] family in the village or in a [inaudible] or anything all of them people is coming. They all have settle plots in London. They all have yards. They all have houses. So it's

just for Christmas and they won't ... all they will be doing is leaving their caravans here because they will all be going on holidays and *they're rowdy people that love drinking and loves fighting and messing. Like our family is not like them.*
Int. No, I know.
Alicia. None of our family drinks or anything like that. Do you know what I'm saying? And they have it said that that barrier is getting cut down. The [inaudible] with the council couldn't get in. [...] They locked their security men into the shed. Like they don't give a fuck on what they do or what they don't do. Do you know what I'm saying? So, if the five plots was opened, well there would be nobody for them to say but *I told the council that two weeks ago.*

Alicia constructs the undesirable Travellers as 'rowdy' drinkers and disruptive fight lovers, being even more despicable because their needs are fake as they have their own homes. The 'they, them, their' in clear opposition to 'we, us, our' is reinforced by the speaker's statement that her family 'is not like them'. As in earlier cases, the result of the exclusion of both the settled society and undesiderable Travellers is that the interviewees construct their place as a safe haven where they and their families are screened and protected from evil. Within such a perfect heterotopia, the women feel entitled to explain the situation to the council and make recommendations, ('I told the council that two weeks ago').

These Travellers therefore construct an idea of decency and respectability similar to the ideational construct that Ross (2005) finds among people in an estate in Cape Town where 'ordentlikheid (decency, respectability) is concerned with appearances and with cementing reciprocal relationships' (p. 631). Similar to what Martha did in the previous chapter, these women parade a very positive self (Oliveira 1999) in their interaction with an interlocutor keen on learning about their community.

The thread therefore is the usual: desire to claim a positive identity as respectable individuals and mothers, which justifies the women's entitlement to a place where such 'ordentlikheid' can be achieved, and the construction of a heterotopia where these respectable people can lead the decent and rule-governed life they believe in.

Indirect expression of desire: Entitlement to the site

From the excerpts discussed so far, the vulnerable liminality of the women longing for a permanent site as a 'promised land' is apparent. At the time of the interviews, there was already a clear indication of the local authorities' willingness to provide a permanent site although the project was still stalled in a phase of consultation and discussion. The women were aware that not everyone would be allocated to the new site and the families would be chosen on the basis of their 'local connections'.[10]

This section therefore shows the women's insistence on their 'entitlement' to the permanent site in the name of their long-term sojourn in the area as Sheila does in the following excerpt.

> *Excerpt 22:* Sheila. Yeah, my people is would be like a Traveller community for years and years. And we've been travelling for years and years. It's been like ridiculous how long we've been travelling and *my family even before me would be in around (city name) ever since I can remember like I was a toddler when I came to Brighton with my mum and dad. We've been here ever since.* (...) we've been here years and years waiting for this permanent site.
> Interviewer. So it's been a long time huh?
> Sheila. Do you know what I mean like my little girl is like a toddler now and I've been waiting for this permanent site to be done. Do you know what I mean it is a lot of family problem that you like it's just really, *we are the residents of (city name) for years and years.*

Sheila asserts her consolidated Traveller identity through the explicit reference to 'my people' and then states her belonging to the area since she was a toddler. Her final ostensive declarative 'we are the residents of (name of city) for years and years' expresses the speaker's claim to her local identity. Similarly, in the excerpt below being mothers, the women abdicate their rights of residency to their children in the name of a pastoral duty of protection and safety.

> *Excerpt 23:* Melanie. I didn't come to Brighton yesterday, last month, last year. I came to Brighton 22 years ago. Do you know what I'm saying? And I think to myself if I have six kids, I think they have families now. *My kids are entitled to homes. They're English British.* They bring them love. All *immigrants* from all over the world they're bringing in and *they house them*. Do you get me?

In this woman's response space is the object of desire through the antagonizing of other groups that she argues receive a better treatment.

Travellers as planners: Desire through complaint

While the desirous discourse of place can be realized as (in)direct expression of a want often formulated through declarative acts, it can also be encoded in their dissatisfaction with the state of the site. In this case Travellers make suggestions to the authorities in the guise of 'guarantees' or pseudo 'commissive' speech acts by which, in Austin's and Searle's Speech Act Theory, speakers commit themselves to some future action through 'a firm promise that [they] will do something or that something will happen [and] a pledge that something will happen or that something is true' (Al-Bantany 2013: 26). As they have direct experience of the site, the women feel invested with the legitimate authority to propose improvements to it and in some instances criticize the local authorities for their decisions. By performing such acts, they show their insightfulness into the site design and make recommendations for future action that they are confident will be even of financial convenience. Such acts crucially realize an act of ontological security showing a stable mental condition and sense of wholeness by which the speakers abandon their identity as marginalized individuals who are not in charge of their life choices and instead claim an agentive identity as designers or planners of what could be a much better and more functional site.

> *Excerpt 24:* Sue. Do you know what I mean? That's not fair. *We're human beings like everyone else. We just want a chance.* We're not asking them to build us a castle. We don't need a castle. *We need a home. Basically, we need a home.* (...) what I meant... we need a home that we can call our own, it's our home. We can keep it clean. We can keep it.
> Int. And you will because you're so clean.
> Sue. Do you know what I mean? *We just want, we just want* a chance. I don't think it's very much to ask for. Do you know what I mean? House all of us... *It would cost millions to house us wouldn't it.* They're having houses for their own local people [inaudible] for me and my children and so as I said they have the money for the site, *they are only wasting time,* they are only wasting emptying bins, court orders here, court orders there. Do you know what I'm saying?

> *Excerpt 25:* Alicia. They're opening a pitch, I'll be honest with you, *they're only wasting council money.* They have an empty site that *should put people into it* and give £60 a week for it. Then they won't have to go to campsites, they won't be able to [inaudible] in paperwork. (...) And as we said *they would have an extra £60 a week per caravan.* So they will have to pay for the cesspit, but the way they're going [inaudible] bins removed and when anyone wants to come in [inaudible]. So *they're not doing themselves any favours* to be honest with them.

In the above excerpts Sue's and Alicia's propositions to alter the structure of the transit site and increase its functionality involve a change to a more clearly striated design in which more Travellers will be allowed in, fees will be increased and the result will be a reduction in the punitive measures local authorities take such as court orders. There is, in both women's words, a clear hinting at a deep division between them and the others where the latter are indirectly charged with making wrong decisions that cost tax-payers money ('they're only wasting council money'). On the contrary, Sue and Alicia know better ('that's what we're saying') and offer viable solutions. Therefore, similarly to what Martha was doing in the previous chapter, these women legitimate themselves as experts (Van Leuwen 2008) and construct their identity as far-sighting rational planners.

Conclusion

This chapter has focused on the second group of liminal people and continued the investigation of the discursive identity that space-deprived individuals construct in an interaction. Following a short account of the community and site history and a survey of the negative narrative surrounding mobile people, the analysis section was divided into two parts. The first one provided a context for the interpretation of the space-related discourse of the study's interviewees and discussed issues of space apportionment and design as allowances of the majoritarian society for this particular minority group. Following Lefebvre (1974/1984), the claim was that space reflects political and social forces. In the case of the transient community hosted in a temporary site, the choices that authorities made perpetuate a spatial discourse that privileges orderly or striated space, which may not be totally in line with the needs of the Travellers' mobile community. It was suggested that possibly this is due not to a deliberate political programme, rather to a perception and interpretation of space that centres on sedentarism and functionality even when authorities are dialoguing with groups who believe in different values.

The second part engaged with specific discourse issues showing how people who are deprived of a space to live talk about themselves and their dear ones and how they create an aspirational heterotopic place. Linguistic forms associated with the direct and indirect expression of desire such as verbs of volition and irrealis moods, if-clauses, thematic insistence were identified in the women's talk. The analysis of the desire constructed at discourse level together with the women's place-identities revealed that the women view the transit site as a heterotopic space that can assure them a secure and protected life away from the threatening world of mainstream society. Desire for place is discursively shaped as both entitlement when these Travellers emphasize their long-lived belonging to the area as well as complaint and recommendations to the authorities about a more functional management of the transient site and a more economical design of future spaces. Similar to the identity as competent planner that Martha invoked in the previous chapter, these powerless individuals attempt to construct themselves as having the inside knowledge that the institutions lack. They negotiate power through their discourse. Throughout the interviews the women portray themselves as the guardians of the site and the custodians of their children. Their insistence on the benefit of place permanency for their families and the construction of the Travellers' site as a fortress are a clear indication of how the discourse of isolation and marginalization produced by mainstream society along hegemonic lines has been internalized by them and how a response discourse is produced.

6

Irish Travellers: Mobility within immobility

Introduction: The nature of a stationary condition

The previous chapter discussed the place-identity construction of a group of Irish Travellers with respect to their social and geographical positioning in a transient nomadic site.

In July 2016, after two decades of waiting, central government funding (of £1.7 million) was made available to establish a permanent site comprising of twelve 'amenity blocks' each with an open-plan kitchen, bathroom, lounge/dining 'dayroom' without sleeping arrangements and a space for each individual family's car and caravan. The transit site continues to operate as before on the left of the site, which is therefore split into two sections. A small building in the middle of the encampment houses the offices of the local council's Travellers' Liaison Team and a room where various activities such as yoga and the girls' group and after-school homework club take place. The permanent pitches were allocated to Traveller families who had been regular transit site visitors. Each permanent site tenant signs a lease contract, and pays rent, council tax and utilities.

This chapter investigates the impact of this much longed permanent living space on the Travellers' identity discourse. All but two (Rita and Ivy) of the women interviewed at the new permanent site belonged to the original group of interviewees at the transit site. By reinterviewing the same women, therefore, it was possible to assess how their identity was impacted by the dramatic change in their lives (Ivy. It's changed everything about us. It has. Do you know? It has changed everything/ Elaine. Yeah, 27th of July. Int. Oh right. Was it? You remember that day. Elaine. Oh god, yeah. @) Waiting and counting). A detailed analysis of the women's talk reveals that this change led to the emergence of new place-related desires along with a stronger sense of individual agency.

Methodology

Lefebvre's conceptualization of space continues to inform this analysis that, following Low (2014), can be called 'engaged anthropology' (p. 14) in that it aims to bring to the fore issues of discrimination and exclusion that can be resolved by political praxis. In parallel with the previous one, this chapter combines the critical examination of the new physical space and its implications for the Travellers' community, with the consideration of how the construct of desire is still essential to understanding the women's heterotopic discursive construction and is still epistemologically rewarding to comprehend the community in its new condition of permanency.

This chapter follows the same methodology as the previous ones. As soon as I was informed by officers in the local council that the new site had reopened, I resumed my visits to the site. Successfully conducting the interviews was a long and laborious process and I had to negotiate with the women who were often too busy or distracted and unwilling to speak to me for any length of time. Also, while the interviewees were in a much better disposition now they were in permanent accommodation, I had lost my instrumental role as a person who could report the community's needs to the council; therefore, at times the women showed less interest in speaking to me. However, I somehow managed to capture their attention giving them the opportunity to tell me if there were still things that could be improved in the new arrangement. This luckily triggered good responses and above all succeeded in engaging the women in new conversations.

In addition to the interviews, I carefully recorded how the women Travellers were organizing their new living space, how they personalized it, what they were wearing, and how they related to one another and their family members and outsiders. Lots of work was still going on in the site and the families were making every effort to appropriate the new space by florally decorating it or arranging their children's playing structure (see Figures 9 and 10).

A total of thirteen women on the permanent site were interviewed. However, only seven were of good enough acoustic quality to be included in this chapter. Fortunately, except two, these women had been interviewed five years earlier at the transit site. In some cases, the women self-identified as they remembered me from the old camp. The interview excerpts tend to be long mainly because it was felt that textual context enables topics and discursive strategies to be more clearly identified.

Besides a focus on the contents and themes, the interview analysis focuses on the women's recurring lexical choices, their use of specific verb phrases indicating

Figure 9 Caring for the new site (personal photo).

Figure 10 Shrubs at the entrance to an amenity block (personal photo).

desire or suggesting evaluation and any other linguistic and pragmatic features that, by being repeated, showed a degree of salience and indicated the presence of a pattern.

The physical layout of the new site

Low claims that 'space and spatial relations yield insights into unacknowledged biases, prejudices and inequalities that frequently go unexamined' (2014: 34). The Travellers' new site, a liminal space in itself catering simultaneously for permanency and mobility, is not a neutral and unbiased space as will be discussed.

The previous chapter discussed two notions of spatiality: a loose or 'smooth' configuration in contrast to a 'striated' man-altered arrangement (Deleuze and Guattari 2004). The transit site was already a striated space while the new permanent site offers an even more structured geography of well-built semi-detached residences. Interestingly, the Travellers continue to call their new homes 'sheds' – a term that conjures up the provisional and mobile nature of wooden garden structures – which are arranged along each side of a semi-circular service road. Also, they continue to sleep in their caravans which are parked right outside their new homes.

> *Excerpt 1:* Elaine. We use our sheds for washing, cooking, cleaning, relaxing, watching TV. (pointing to the caravans) We're just really sleeping here before we used to live in these.

> *Excerpt 2:* Ivy. Now, the caravan is just for sleeping ... we live in here all day and we just sleep in the caravans.

Although tastefully designed (see Figure 11), the new site has none of the 'wind swept' character and natural spatiality typical of Travellers' traditional, non-authorized arrangements in fields and parks and looks like a suburban estate.

Striated spaces tend to be closed off or have allocated spatial intervals with specific functions, while people organize smooth space according to frequencies of use. As discussed earlier, the Travellers' interpretation of space changed to adapt to the transit site and was altered even more in the permanent site, which, in many respects, is the apotheosis of a rigidly structured space. While the overall design of the permanent site broadly replicates the spatial organization of the old transit camp, the space allocated to each family unit is significantly larger.

Figure 11 Artist impression of the permanent site.

During the interviews, the women expressed their satisfaction with the site layout despite the fact that they claimed that they did not have a major role in the planning process.

> *Excerpt 3:* Int. Did you have any ... did you contribute to designing this place? Did you have a voice? Could you say, 'We will like it this way.'
> Lucy. We did and we didn't.
> Int. Why?
> Lucy. They asked us what we.... (Overlapping background noise – woman talks to her son) Be quiet for a minute because I'm talking. They asked us what we thought we'd like. Um, because when they ... when they've done the plans for this, obviously, it was done by architects, so. (...)
> Int. Yeah, yeah. Of course, yes.
> Lucy. *So, when they have a plan for something, you can't really change the structure of things.*
> Int. No, of course not.
> Lucy. *But inside,* they asked us would we prefer a bath or a shower. We asked for a bath instead of a shower, well, they gave us both. And what else? The colouring.
> Int. Oh, all right.
> Lucy. The kitchens and that. *But apart from that, it was literally just done by the council.*

From these exchanges, it emerges that the women felt the council's plan could not be seriously challenged but generally evaluated the end result very positively as suggested by the excerpts below, which compare two similar moments in the fieldwork.

> *Excerpt 4:* (2017) Sheila. Oh, everything else about it is good. You've got a big garden, *sheds are lovely*. You've got everything here. You've got your electric, water, everything. *They couldn't have done a better job on the site to be honest.*
>
> *Excerpt 4a:* (2003) Sheila. I will have to heat up the water in a bucket because you can't bring the children into the *shower* because the block is *absolutely freezing*. (...) there's three toilets inside of it for all the children and all the adults.
>
> *Excerpt 5:* (2017) Int. So, how do you feel about this place now? What is it for you? How has your life changed?
> Elaine. Oh, it hasn't changed but it's a permanent place like, you know, *for life*.
> Int. For life, right.
> Elaine. It's for life really where your kids, kids go on and does their own things comes back with sees you. The only thing that's different here really, I think it's very peaceful, you know, very quiet. *A lovely view, the best.*
>
> *Excerpt 5a:* (2012) Elaine. but when you're in a caravan *you can open the windows* and you can open the doors, you can do whatever you want.
> Int. and you're kind of more at one with nature
> Elaine. yeah here you can *walk out of your door and hear the birds*.

Shelia appreciates the 'sheds' that can provide all she needs for her family and spares her from having to wash the children with buckets of warm water. Elaine praises the natural attractiveness of the new compound which is very much in line with her earlier statements in the transit site about wanting to live in harmony with nature.

Of particular interest is the extent to which the new site has impacted the degree of agency and advocacy among these liminal women and how this is encoded in their language.

Permanent but mobile: The Travellers' changed identities

The concept of liminality helps the understanding of the precarious nature of Travellers' hybrid situation as they continue to keep key aspects of their traditional life while adopting new living arrangements imposed on them by mainstream society. From being highly mobile, Travellers have now more or less morphed into a pseudo-sedentary group.

It took some time for the transformation in their living arrangements to be fully processed by the new site residents: 'It's just starting to sink in. Because when we first come on, you're still waiting, "Oh my god. How much time have I got here?" or "we're going to stay for the whole winter without getting moved." It hasn't really sunk in yet.'

In excerpt 6, for example, by listing the benefits of the new site, Shelia shows her appreciation for the amenities which most settled people take for granted. It is not simply the range of basic facilities that the new site offers, but the satisfaction of such basic needs as security of tenure, and, in particular, of being assured that one will not be evicted at a moment's notice.

> *Excerpt 6:* Int. So, now that (.) you are in this place, I would like to know how you feel about it.
> Sheila. It just changed our lives. (...) *Like, we've a bathroom, we've a cooker, a washing machine, things other people take for granted.*
> Int. I know!
> Sheila. Do you know what I mean?
> Int. I know, I know
> Sheila. So this, this is, (2.0) you just can't believe that you can close your door at night time, and *your Section 61 won't be on the door in the morning* and (...) we're paying our rent and our bills and we know what is ours, you know what I mean?

The refrain 'do you know what I mean?' which, at times, only functions as a back-channelling cue, here plausibly conveys Shelia's intention to make the significance of the new 'life changing' condition much clearer to the interviewer. Similarly, the inclusive pronoun 'you' referring to all the Travellers who are in exactly the same situation, also attempts to envelope the interlocutor in the now past tragic experience of the eviction order and suggests the speaker's still palpable incredulity at her changed situation. Finally, the possessive 'your' referring to Section 61 of the eviction law the Traveller sadly appropriates ('your' meaning 'our') indicates the repetitiveness of the enforcement order to which these Travellers were once subject.

Worthy of note is the fact that the new space occasionally allows the women to position themselves critically vis-à-vis their customs ('We didn't chose it [our life] ... We were brought up to that life ... just like settled people brought up in the house, we were brought up, we know nothing else) as (7) below suggests.

> *Excerpt 7:* Int. (...) what is the caravan still for you?
> Sheila. It's just a bedroom now.
> Int. So it's, your, your, is your heart in here or in the caravan?

Sheila. Here (pointing at the amenity room).
Int. Really?!
Sheila. Oh yeah, (.) oh I really love it (...)
Int. And, you don't realize what you're missing, (.) until you have it (...)
Sheila. People don't realize that it is *a horrible life*. Even *the young generation, they don't want it.* (...) *And I don't care what travellers say* (1.0) that will keep up the tradition. I can't see the tradition keeping up
Int. Really?
Sheila, No, not if they make homes (...)
Int. But you will stay here, you've had enough of that?
Sheila. *I've had enough, enough, enough, enough*. Do you know it's just, I don't know. It's just as I said we have everything in the one place. *Why move around a different place?* For what? Do you know what I mean?
Int. Absolutely
Sheila. I've been sleeping in a caravan all my life, *I don't want it*, do you know what I mean?

What stands out in Shelia's statements is her unconditional self-assurance and unequivocal show of agency. From the negative evaluation of Travellers' life to the emotional confession that she has had enough of that itinerant life, her talk is a clear condemnation of her tradition. This, incidentally, is a view shared by the two men I had a chance to talk to briefly in the transit site while I was interviewing their wives. One of them in particular was adamant that there is no future for the Travellers' community and soon their mobile way of life will be replaced by sedentarism. This, he explained, is due to the institutions putting pressure on Travellers to be settled and the young generations having less or no interest in the itinerant lifestyle.

Sheila's agency is manifested in her ability to make specific choices. Agents have a degree of control over the action they want to carry out and a choice over the behaviour related to that action (Enfield 2017). Shelia's decision to share her inner thoughts with her interlocutor and her choice of stylistic execution is both strong and daring.

Shelia's agentive voice is also supported by her 'accountability' and 'entitlement' (Enfield 2017: 6) to produce such statements. She can be held accountable for what she says as a Traveller with a long history of living in a Travellers' community. Similarly, she is entitled to express her views because she now has a sense of what mobile life is all about vis-à-vis the benefits of a settled existence. She may even feel an 'obligation' to speak up because she thinks that having a permanent secure accommodation is better for the young generation.

The utterance 'And I don't care what travellers say' followed by a short pause, is a distancing move from her group that shows her 'evaluative agency' (Kockelman 2017:19) as she chooses which feeling or desire to give reality to. Following her empowering stylistic choice, Shelia's self-construction as the augur of her community's demise becomes justified ('I can't see the tradition keeping up').

Such a critique of the nomadic tradition is interspersed with its persistent defence as in the case of Elaine who claims the new arrangement has not had any impact on her culture. With a monoglossic discourse that excludes any other alternatives, she emphasizes that her identity as a Traveller has not changed nor is it likely to in the future. The double negative, a frequent marker of these Travellers' language, here takes up the meaningful function of establishing the durability and persistence of traditions.

> *Excerpt 8:* Int. Okay, so you don't think, you're still who you are, who you were and nothing?=
> Elaine. =*Who I am is who I want to be for the rest of my life.*
> Int. That's fine. All right.
> Elaine. *I'm a Traveller and that's it.*
> Int. That's it and you normally have got . . . yeah.
> Elaine. *Can't do nothing about it, that's your culture* (. . .)
> Int. So has your attachment to the caravan changed? Do you still like it? Do you still . . . ?
> Elaine. I still love my caravan.
> Int. You love your caravan. @
> Elaine. I love my caravan.
> Int. Lovely caravan. @
> Elaine. Too lovely.

In this exchange, the choice of 'that's it', following the open declarative 'I'm a Traveller' also functions as a closure signalling Elaine does not want to discuss the matter any further, although this is later softened by the explanation that mobility is a cultural rather than a personal choice. As with the other women, the inclusive use of 'you' plausibly aims to portray the speaker's situation as inescapable and hence easier to understand to the interlocutor. Later on, the repetition of 'love' and 'lovely', although the result of a verbal negotiation with the interviewer, indexes the still affective relation the speaker has with what is left of her previous living arrangement.

The excerpt below further confirms Ivy's loyalty to a tradition of mobility in spite of the move to the permanent site.

Excerpt 9: Ivy. *I still feel like I'm a traveller*, obviously, *but I just feel like a settled person. I feel normal.* You know I feel safe now really that my kids *can go* to school and get an *education that I did never get.* You know and *they can do stuff* with their life because I'm settled now and *they can do* whatever they want to do with their life. Do you know what I mean? That *they can* actually go to school and go to college, *become* whatever … (…) You know, because *I would like for them* to actually make something of their life, to do something with themselves and actually get degrees, and do whatever *they wanted* to do.
Int. Yeah.
Ivy. Do you know what I mean? They'd be the *first ever travellers that could actually do something with their life*

The use of modals in Ivy's speech is an indication of how she feels empowered by the new site. Her children 'can' now do whatever they want with their lives and can be the 'first ever travellers' to be able to make choices. In her words, the new site only brings additions and opportunities without depriving her of her innate characteristics and ethnic customs. She is still a Traveller, yet she feels 'normal'. The term that occurs frequently in these interviewees (2013 Sheila 'I would like my little girl to have a job and be *normal*'; 2014 Alicia 'You got to mix with *normal* people whether you like it or you don't.') in both sites is complex in its meaning. 'Normal' is generally used to refer to behaviour that conforms to the norm and 'normality' is usually synonymous with 'conformity'. Normal, therefore, in the eyes of the women are the country people or gorjas. By contrast, Travellers are not 'normal', in fact they are an example of urban diversity in all senses. However, here Ivy's interpretation of 'normality' is associated with the notion of 'being able to do things' in particular 'being able to choose'. When in forced mobility, Travellers are not actors of their own life as they are subject to other people's decisions. Thus, for them, normality is the condition of having an important 'affordance' (to use Gibson's 2014 term) that comes with the new environment.

The expression of desire in the new space

The remainder of this chapter analyses how in the changed situation of 'striated' immobility, the women Travellers still construct discursively a desire for a heterotopic space.

Memory of previous desire

After they moved to the permanent site, the women reminisced their old life. In the following excerpt Shelia, a mature woman with many grandchildren, recalls how her daughter struggled through the winter months to provide safe and decent toilet facilities for her adult son.

> *Excerpt 10:* Sheila (...) even in the camp, love, my grandson over there, he's not little, he's at least twenty, and even they're having difficulties you know, (2.0) and in the winter, he's a big boy, and *she had to buy him a portable toilet for outside=*
> Int. Mhm, yeah =
> Sheila. *and a little screen around it. And I thought to myself 'you have no dignity at all'.*

Several words and phrases in this excerpt encode Shelia's feelings about the memory. Her insistence that her grandson is not a child ('he's not little, at least twenty, a big boy'), suggesting the memory of the humiliation is still painful, culminates in the speaker 'voicing' herself ('you have no dignity') in a bitter comment about the lack of respect Travellers suffer. The choice of direct self-address 'you' is particularly noticeable as it reflects the speaker's disembodiment that increases her already dramatic lack of decency and self-respect. Shelia's term of endearment, 'love', often used by older women in her community, plausibly invites the interlocutor to share the account of their ordeal.

Not surprisingly, often the memory of the desire for their own space is embedded within the narrative of their frequent evictions. The interviewees' insistence on this theme makes it one of the preferred tropes to construct the women's identities as guardians of their children and witnesses of the settled society's inexplicable cruelty. It is not simply the trope of the authoritarian order to leave the space they had temporarily occupied; rather, the emphasis is on the forceful and insensitive guise by which the order is carried out with repeated reference to the unexpected and unnecessary immediacy of the enforcement. The following excerpt from the interview with Alicia effectively conveys how her now realized desire of stability juxtaposes her present situation of security with her previous insecure and precarious existence.

> *Excerpt 11:* Alicia. Yeah, because *we've got a permanent address.* We know he can go today and I won't be in [inaudible] tonight. *I may be* in Littlehampton or wherever I moved to because of *getting moved on* and on. So, he knows when he goes where to come home to. Where, in the past, we put the kids to school.

We get a phone call, you have to leave. We'd have to get to the school, take the kids out. It could be any time of the day.

The women's realized desire for a space of their own hinges on the binary structure opposing 'now' versus' then' and the polarity between a past characterized by a longing for stable accommodation mixed with the memory of discomfort and the present satisfaction and fulfilment.

> *Excerpt 12:* Alicia. Yeah, that's it. We use a toilet. *Get some water from a tap instead of going to the garage.* There are a lot of ways that have changed. *Using the laundrette, we've got our own.* (…)
>
> *I don't have to share the showers. I don't have to share the toilet. I don't have to share the laundrette. I don't have to share anything.*

In conclusion, in these women's talk, the appreciation of the present situation is accompanied by the recall of the past frustrated desire for stability and comfort.

Agentive desires

Other features in the women's talk index their increased agency. In the following excerpt, for example, Shelia presents herself as a 'selecting' agent who 'evaluates instrumental acts in reference to values and, in particular, in reference to values that could be otherwise' (Kockelman 2017: 19). The permanent site offers the choice of staying or going, a choice that in the past was in the hands of the authorities not the women. Against this alternative, Shelia makes a conscious and informed choice, which she firmly asserts by her 'no' prefacing her negative statement 'I won't be leaving'.

> *Excerpt 13:* Sheila. This is permanent and you don't have to leave if you don't want to.
> Int. Okay, so would you plan to leave? Do you plan to …?
> Sheila. *No, I won't be leaving.*

In other cases, the agency the women now seem to have acquired is expressed through the tendency to criticize governmental policies. In the exchange below, Shelia feels entitled to call into question the offers of accommodation that the council makes to the Travellers.

> *Excerpt 14:* Sheila. No, no, they, they haven't accommodation for themselves, they haven't. They'll tell you that, they'll offer it, *but they have nothing.* Why's all the homeless people sleeping in the streets of Brighton? *They have no place for them*

The women's new sense of agency is a direct consequence of their new space and living arrangements. As Stack points out, '[p]laces need the action of people or selves to exist and have effect. The opposite is equally true selves cannot be formed and sustained or have effect without place' (2016: 215). The women's place-based agency or 'emplaced action' is 'a phenomenon in which [they] are involved instrumentally' (p. 215) which derives directly from their new relation with their permanent space. Since the Travellers now feel that they are entitled to express their views, their talks are punctuated with linguistic indicators suggesting a stronger sense of self. Deontic modals such as 'should' or 'would' are frequently used often in association with the personal and direct expression of evaluation ('I think').

Feeling she now has an 'identification with a place engendered by living in it' (Agnew and Duncan 1989: 2) and hence an entitlement to speak her mind, Elaine behaves as a reliable and accountable actor whose words can be trusted because she is experiencing the difficulties of the space by living in it.

> *Excerpt 15:* Elaine. *I would arranged, I would've made a path* for car park like for cars to be dropped and . . . .
> Int. Just away from- but don't you want to keep your cars and your trailers next to your house?
> Elaine. Oh yeah, the caravans is all right, your caravan, I'm going on about motors that you drive. The ones that's constant in and out. (. . .) You can park them in, because the big man will come down here. Like the fella who takes the bins. He can't get through because there's motors parked here and parked out there so when it tries to go the roundabout it's too wide to get around and then they said the kids from the transit side is hanging on to the back of these, back of these tip or whatever you call it, rubbish like, it'll cause an accident but you don't really know it's happened, so many kids are so stupid. (. . .) they *would* a *should've made* a park in there. *They should've made a park I think* so all the kids have something to do to occupy their mind, they won't be out along the street or along the road. (. . .) Yeah, so they'll occupy . . . their brain is occupied. So, when they are bored of sitting and doing nothing they do get bored of it, don't they? But if there's park . . . *they should've made a park down the bottom actually for the kids.* We have a lot of small kids there.
> Int. Yeah that would've been really nice.
> Elaine. *Swings, slides* like the round you bend in, like *climbing things*, things that you climb up. (. . .) But I think *they should've closed up* the transit site, all that is being left, it's *awkward really* because this is the permanent site and that's the transit site. *I think they should've made* a different way in, *have higher fences* so look at the back of the caravans on there at the back, if you know what I mean.

Besides the repeated use of deontic 'should', what is also noticeable in Elaine's talk is the construction of an urban 'enclavization' triggered by fear and desire for security (Davis 1990 and 1992, Low 2001) usually associated with people living in gated communities. In order to secure the safety and wellbeing of her new space and in the name of her love for it, Elaine uses a discourse of 'territorial defensiveness' by proposing to 'exclude' the transit site to protect the permanent one. The evaluative judgement 'it's awkward really' justifies her dissatisfaction with a single entry to both sites (a concern shared by all the interviewees) and her plea for two separate paths, if the permanent and transit sites really have to co-exist side by side. Once again, the personalized suggestions realized by 'I think' 'I would've made' are a token of her affective bond with the new space and her achieved agency that entitle her to criticize the existing design and express her desire for a different spatial organization that guarantees safety as in a gated community (Low 2014: 153). This is integral to the discursive construction of a different and new heterotopia that coincides with a place solely for the good Travellers, fenced off to the others. The terms of the new heterotopia, easily identifiable in many women's talks, are imbued with the newly found agency that the permanent space has bestowed on the interviewees (I'll tell you the truth, love I, to be honest (…) I think it is ridiculous (…) There should be, and, *it should be blocked off*/ How would I change it? I'd start by putting a fence the whole way around).

The women's newly acquired emplaced agency contributes to a more forceful and, at times, emphatic construction of desire than was the case at the transit site (Elaine: '*I did wanted* a proper wooden fencing, but you could get green wooden fencing, the same colour as the grass so there's green rising from them'/ Ivy. The council *has to provide* a school bus (…) Do you know what I mean? And, it … if there's no footpath, *they have to provide* a school bus, which we ain't got a footpath).

The last excerpt in this section in sync with the critical attitude to the institutions of the previous ones is revealing of the Travellers' dreams of a perfect space based on their free choice.

> *Excerpt 16:* Ivonne. They could build [inaudible] so a lot of travellers has went and bought. Now, *I'm not saying that you should let them buy a field* and turn it into 50 because we wouldn't want I wouldn't want to go in and live with 50.
> Int. No.
> Ivonne. No, to be … no way.
> Int. No. How many is the maximum? (Laughter)
> Ivonne. Twenty.

Int. Oh, really?
Other woman. It all depends=
Ivonne. =on the company. You see, you have to think that everyone has kids, everyone has big family. Some people are strict. Some people isn't. It's in every community. Some people let their kids go wild.
OW. And, your kids can get mixed up bad.
Ivonne. Bad . . . and, there's bad in travellers just like there is in every community.
Int. Yeah, of course, yeah.
Ivonne. But, I'm not saying that you should let them buy a field and that they should be allowed to put 500 trailers in it, but for families that did buy it and they want one place on its own or a couple or (overlapping conversation) *they should*. When they can lift the licence to build [inaudible] homes in greenbelt, they should live sometimes they should make it a little bit easier. Then, *if they can't afford to build sites, well then, let the families maybe buy a piece for themselves and let them settle on it.*

Punctuated as usual by deontic modals, Ivonne's talk is a plea for the right of Travellers to have a free choice of space. She wants to be able to decide which Travellers to cohabit with rather than that decision be made by others. Furthermore, Ivonne is campaigning for Travellers to have the freedom to buy a piece of land and settle on it and for the law on greenbelt areas to become more relaxed, especially if the council has no resources to build more new sites. Once again, what this woman aspires to is autonomy and self-management together with freedom of choice which she expresses in a much stronger voice than in the past transit site.

Desire as challenge

Lahlou (2017: 226) defines agency as the capacity of a subject who has the determination ('a representation of a specific desired final state') to reach a goal. According to this definition, therefore, the women Travellers have reached the final objective of a permanent space and, therefore, now have a 'material agency' through access to material resources and 'control over affordances' (Lahou 2017: 226). However, according to Lahlou, such a condition is not sufficient to grant people full agency. These women still need the capacity and freedom to access such resources in the way that they think is best suitable. Thus, beyond a material agency, they need to develop an 'embodied agency' (p.226) consisting of education, experience, mental configurations, memory and more that is recognized by mainstream society and institutions. As such, they have not yet reached an 'institutional agency' and still remain liminals suspended between a state of acquired and another of still-pending agency. The following excerpt illustrates the type of struggle in which the Travelling women engage with the council ranging from small material requests to core issues including the education of their children (in later excerpts).

> *Excerpt 17:* Elaine. I was going to put a little bit of fence along there and *you're not allowed, you have to get* it from the council, *you have to get permission* [inaudible]. If it's your own place, like a council house, they're allowed to put a shed in the back of it.
> Int. But I see lots of people who have these sheds.
> Elaine. *I'm not allowed* to have a shed
> Int. Oh really?
> Eaine. You know what they said? They'll bring the court to set up the sheds.
> Int. But I mean there are other people who had sheds.
> Elaine. Yeah, I know but I asked for one shed, *no*.
> Other woman. You can have plastic sheds
> Int. Yeah, oh you wanted a brick=
> Elaine. =No, *I wanted* a wooden shed to put all my things inside of it.
> Int. Yeah, why not?
> Elaine. *They said no, you can't have one.* The council said no.
> Int. How do you feel about this?
> Elaine. A bit stupid really. (...) But it's not bothering me, don't get me wrong but the only thing I *wanted, I wanted* to put a little fence along here. Like something like Leslie's wooden fencing with a little gate so when you have your tables and chairs and you could leave these two doors open, you *could lock that door, put a little fence* and play around, whereas ... because that's what the [inaudible] really, the barbeque on top of your concrete.

Through the marked use of 'want' contrasting with 'not allowed' and 'have to' and conveying the still on-going struggle of these women with the council's decisions, Elaine expresses a desire for security and safety, as indexed by her aspiration to establish borders. Moreover, it is noticeable how she reports on her struggle for what she wanted, the shed and the fence, which she verbalizes in a more elaborate way than the council's blunt 'no'. Such a monolithic reply from the authorities is associated with the Council's statement 'They'll bring the court to set up the sheds', which is constructed as absurd by her preparatory question 'You know what they said?' In short, by these discursive strategies, Elaine constructs her requests as logical and rational against the resolute and irrational response of the authorities that would be ready to engage in laborious legal procedures to negate the right to the very small things that the women need in what now is their own space.

While fences and garden sheds can be considered minor requests (although they are not devoid of symbolic value), Traveller children's education is a more intractable problem for both the Travellers themselves and the relevant public authorities. Travellers appreciate the importance of education for their children but, in general, they believe that only basic literacy and numeracy skills need to be acquired. At the secondary school level, most Travellers only want their children to attend single-sex schools. Underlying this preference is a deeper concern about the corrupting influence of mainstream secondary education which is seen as a threat to the traditional values and beliefs of the Traveller community. Traveller parents strongly believe that boys and especially girls learn too much and too early about things they do not need to know about until later in life. This is particularly the case with regard to sex education. Most mothers strongly resist sending their girls to school much beyond their early adolescence. Local education authorities, on the other hand, have a legal duty to ensure that children attend school up until the statutory school leaving age of 16.

The following excerpt exemplifies the Travellers' distrust of the public educational system still in the name of the maternal function of raising morally shielded children (Fuller 2004, Molina 2006).

Excerpt 18: Rita. No, we haven't got problems in our school where the small kids is going.
Int. Right.
Rita. But *they* want the big kids to go to high school, but *we don't want them. We want them* in an all-girls school. *We would send* the girls but we want all-girls school. *We would send* them, yeah. (...)
Int. Yeah, of course.
Rita. *We wouldn't send* them to a ...
Int. Okay, a mixed school, yeah.
Rita ... boys and girls, yeah. Because there's big 16-year-old boys, 17-year-old, they smoke, they like.... (...) Oh, *we said* they [Inaudible] *we'll do it. We'll get a tutor. Nope, they want to set it.*
Int. Because that's the law, right?
Rita. Yeah, *they want* to set it. But *I've never heard* of it before.
Int. Mm-hmm. Right. So, how do you feel about this? You feel that ...? How do you feel about ...? Are you angry? Are you worried?
Rita. Yeah, yes. Yeah. Because when *they're coming down* for meetings and then it's ... you got this place built to put *your girls* to high school. *We didn't get* this

built, um, to put *our girls* to high school. *We didn't*. But that's what *they* keep telling us. Do you know what I mean? *They* keep telling us that.(...) *We didn't ... they* didn't build this so our girls could go to high school. *We, uh, we want to send* them to high school, *we will send* them to high school, *but it has* to be an all-girls school *or* give them home tutoring. *We said* we were willing to pay for home tutoring and show them the proof. *Nope, they want* to set that.

Rita's struggle to acquire an embodied agency is apparent in this excerpt. Her argument is unequivocal. Punctuated by a persistent opposition between 'we' and 'they' that constructs an insurmountable separation between the Travellers and the settled world, her talk represents irreverently the response of the Council as illogical and unsympathetic by the nearly rhyming repetition of 'no' and 'nope'. Her several 'wants' juxtaposed to the council's 'wants' reflect the strained relations between her community and the authorities. Rita is not devoid of embodied agency in as much as she can convincingly support her arguments; her talk also conveys self-confidence as she constructs herself as an accountable speaker when she refutes the point put forward by the Council that education is mandatory by rebutting 'But, I've never heard of it before'. However, in the settled mainstream world where education is interpreted in a particular way and where alternatives are limited (Montessori, Buddhist schools etc.), her lack of institutional agency serves to perpetuate her liminal position.

Another delicate issue is the position of the council office right in the middle of the site. Empowered with a greater sense of agency, the women Travellers strongly express their objections to the siting of this office.

Excerpt 19: Ivy. Yeah, but they don't really come down here anymore. They ought up to be up there in their shed, in *their little hut thing*. So, if you had a problem, you could walk up to them if you want to.
Excerpt 20: Elaine. *I'd get rid of it*, one or the other and *make a park there for the kids* and a park there for *more things to get parked in*.

The following excerpt contains a delicate piece of information that Ruth shared with the interviewer.

Excerpt 21: Ruth. To be honest, since (clears throat) *since we're brought here*, I don't mind you coming in here chatting to me. I honestly don't.
Int. Thank you.
Ruth. But you ... here, you've constantly got people here at your door, do you know? *I know they're only trying to help*.
Int. Yeah.

Ruth. But you feel constantly like there's someone here, 'Oh, [inaudible] wants to speak to you about this, and [Inaudible] wants to speak to you about that.' (. . .) um, the council and the health visitors and school (. . .) You've constantly got people. *I know they're only trying to help*, but sometimes you don't need the help.
Int. Yeah, yeah, yeah. I understand that.
Ruth. And they're still there constantly, do you know? Like here *you constantly feel like you're getting watched.*
Int. Yes. That's so interesting. I understand completely what you say.
Ruth. *You constantly feel like you're getting watched and every. . . . There's always people there just . . . just observing your life to be honest. Do you know what I mean?* (. . .) And we got a letter the other day, 'There's a meeting in the shed. I would like you to come.' I went to it anyway because I get, I feel bad if I don't go even if I don't want to go. I really don't want to go and it's tormenting me. I'll still go because . . .
Int. You're great. @
Ruth. I don't want to I don't want you know. [unintelligible] And I sit there and I'm probably not even listening to a word anyone's saying but I just sit there out of . . . .
Int. Yeah, courtesy or duty in a way.
Ruth. Yeah, yeah. But it gets *quite aggravating sometimes. Do you know what I mean?*

As an articulate and thoughtful respondent, Ruth laments her lack of independent space within the site which, again, is symptomatic of the still limited institutional agency of the women Travellers.

The charge of this excerpt is powerful. Ruth clearly says the Travellers did not make the decision to move to a permanent site but 'were brought' there. This revelatory statement summarizes the essence of Travellers' life that they do not choose but is in the hands of dominant hegemonic groups. In the space that even with the best of intentions she 'was brought to live'. Ruth feels she is being watched, while her life is being monitored by the Council, which she says, is 'aggravating' at times. The use of the repeated phrase 'I don't want to' indexes the woman's visceral desire for a space that is independent and uncontrolled. The relevance of Foucault's (1975) notion of 'surveillance' is evident here and it is not difficult to understand how the Travellers can interpret what the council is doing, albeit in good faith, as a form of disciplinary power or even a policing strategy to control and regulate their lives. The women Travellers are, therefore, reacting to being monitored and watched, which in some cases may produce information against them.

After careful consideration, I decided to share Ruth's concerns with the council's Traveller Liaison team who welcomed this feedback and agreed that a 'lighter touch' would be more productive.

Conclusion

This chapter has investigated the new identities of a small group of Irish Travelling women after they had moved to a permanent site. At last, they had a secure place of their own where they could raise their children and grant them a 'normal' life.

The move to a permanent site transformed their lives in a number of ways. Firstly, being able to enjoy much greater security and stability, significantly changed their sense of self and self-confidence. Their appreciation for the new space was accompanied by the expectation that lives would change for the better. This despite the fact that the permanent site was an imposed socially constructed striated topography.

Secondly, the new living arrangement markedly increased the women's material agency. However, their levels of embodied agency and institutional agency (especially with respect to the local state) have not improved enough for them to escape from their liminal state. The new permanent site still remains, therefore, a heterotopia that interrupts 'the apparent continuity and normality of ordinary everyday space […] and inject[s] alterity into the sameness, the commonplace, the topicality of everyday society' (Dehaene and De Cauter 2008: 4). However, the permanent site acts as a space of mediation between the liminal alterity of the Travellers and their newly acquired voice and agency since it allows the women to continue to lead their lives in harmony with their mobile traditions while granting them the opportunity to lead normal existences with a degree of freedom of choice.

The new site is also a mediating place in that it merges the exclusion from the mainstream society and protection from inside the community; the Traveller women now declare their sense of safety within the new space which distances them from the threatening moral code of settled citizens which they reject; at the same time, they aspire to protect themselves even more by building further boundaries between themselves and those transient Travellers who are now dissimilar from them.

7

Rough Sleepers: 'Homeless is what I am, not who I am.' Rough sleeping as a liminal condition not the essence of being

Introduction

This chapter is a case study of the discourse of place-identity among a group of individuals who attend a day centre for the Street Homeless or Rough Sleepers in a coastal town in Southern England.

As with the two other liminal groups in this study, the existence of Street Homeless and Rough Sleepers in particular, challenges the ethos and logic of mainstream society. While less apparent than in the past, homelessness is now a very visible and dramatic reality in most urban centres. According to Shelter,

> [t]he latest government figures estimate that there are 459 people sleeping rough on any given night in England. Of these, nearly 50 per cent sleep rough in London. A report for the Office of Deputy Prime Minister, however, has acknowledged that the number of people sleeping rough over the course of a year is at least ten times higher than the snapshot on any given night provided by the street counts.[1]

Estimating the number of Homeless people is notoriously difficult. In part, this is because there are various forms of homelessness. According to Shelter, since 1998 the number of Street Homeless has decreased by one third. The *Economist* (18 Aug 2018) quotes the official number of Rough Sleepers in England as about 4,700 on any autumn night in 2017, and up from 1,800 in 2010, while others put the total at 8,000.

The average age of death for those who sleep rough is forty-three. Many are the social causes of homelessness, from the lack of affordable housing, to unemployment. People may end up on the street when they leave prison or care homes. Former soldiers are also prone to becoming Rough Sleepers. Trauma, domestic violence and mental health issues are some of the other frequent causes of homelessness. Street homelessness can take different shapes; it can be: i. transitional or temporary, for those individuals who end up on the street in between housing situations; ii. episodic, when people get in and out of homelessness; and iii. chronic, if homelessness becomes permanent. 'The chronically homeless are overrepresented in cross-sectional investigations, yet many more people experience transitional and episodic homelessness, given the higher turnover rates' (Barrett et al. 2010: 502). Finally, in terms of demographics, children make a bigger percentage of the Rough Sleepers population than they did before as do women and families (often female-headed) (Barrett et al. 2010: 503).

Societal perceptions of homelessness

Attitudes to street homelessness vary and although some people are sympathetic, many others believe Street Homeless are responsible for their own unfortunate condition. They are not just considered an eyesore disturbing the aesthetics of city centres, which is consistent with the commodification of urban landscapes (see Figure 12); they function as a dystopic narrative to neoliberalism in that they point to the failure of that overall economic and social system. In the narratives of the men and women interviewed for this study, this perception is dramatically apparent. People who live on the street are also a reminder that there are other ways of living beyond the settled and individualistic existence which characterizes conventional

Figure 12 Street Homelessness in the town centre (personal photo).

society. The interviewees' talks occasionally allude to a desire to break away from a structured routine or refer to their inability to endure an existence in a profit-orientated society. In short, Rough Sleepers and Street Homeless are an indirect challenge to what society advertises as a desirable life based on residence permanency, stable occupation and ownership of material goods.

Fundamentally, homelessness is 'a spatial phenomenon'; a homeless person is someone without their own space, 'dis-placed or out-of-place' (Wardhaugh 1996: 704). Farrington and Robinson (1999) lament the lack of a precise definition of the homelessness. The term means 'being without a home' but many more interpretations exist beyond that, and homelessness can be better defined as the absence of a secure and satisfactory domicile (p. 175). For example, during the period of my fieldwork at the day centre, one of the clients was a young man who had a place although it was too derelict to use it other than as a shed to spend the night in when it was really cold; during the day, he would roam the streets and use the public facilities in the city centre that his accommodation could not provide. Rough sleeping is defined by the Government as

> people sleeping, or bedded down, in the open air (such as on the streets, or in doorways, parks or bus shelters); people in buildings or other places not designed for habitation (such as barns, sheds, car parks, cars, derelict boats, stations, or 'bashes'). [...] Street homelessness is a much wider term than rough sleeping, taking into account the street lifestyles of some people who may not actually sleep on the streets. Street homeless people are those who routinely find themselves on the streets during the day with nowhere to go at night. Some will end up sleeping outside, or in a derelict or other building not designed for human habitation, perhaps for long periods. Others will sleep at a friend's for a very short time, or stay in a hostel, night-shelter or squat, or spend nights in prison or hospital.'[2]

This chapter adopts the terms used by the Homeless charity Shelter of 'street homelessness' (henceforth SH) and 'rough sleeping' (RS). As in the previous chapters, as people-indicating nouns these labels are capitalized.

Homelessness, rough sleeping or sofa surfing is not simply linked to lack or space insecurity; it involves losing 'sense of identity, self-worth and self-efficacy' (Boydell et al. 2000: 26), which, in most cases, leads to mental issues including fragmented psychosocial personalities.

This chapter is not a socio-political exploration of the causes of homelessness, which continues to be an 'unresolved' debate (Mostowska 2013: 1126) nor is it an attempt to propose possible solutions. Rather, as with the other two groups in this study, the chapter analyses the relationship between identity and space among these unsettled, uprooted and liminal individuals as realized through their language during the interviews conducted in the day centre by two researchers over a period of slightly more than two years.

The title of this chapter echoes the study by Parsell (2010) 'Homeless is what I am, not who I am' and, slightly more indirectly, the earlier study by Osborne (2002) 'I may be homeless, but not helpless'. While Osborne discusses the benefits and drawbacks of an identification with the identity of homelessness and how this relates to self-esteem, Parsell warns us about the shortcomings of studies of homelessness that, addressing it as a discrete and unique area of inquiry, tend to reify the phenomenon and obscure its relation to society. He points out that the literature on the Homeless is inherently flawed in that, by treating them as a standalone social category comprised of undistinguished and undistinguishable individuals, deprives them of their unique identity.

Given the prevailing consensus among sociologists, social psychologists and anthropologists that identity results from an individual's experiences and exposures to the world, it is understandable how the literature has considered individuals in a condition of homelessness as people with that and only that identity. However, relatively little attention has been given to establishing 'what exactly a 'homeless identity' is, and whether people labelled homeless actually have personal identities as 'homeless people' (Parsell 2010: 182). Crucially, an excessive emphasis on homelessness as a condition that characterizes some individuals may obliterate or obscure the things housed people actually share with RS (Parsell 2019: 185). To obviate this limitation, this chapter focuses on how a small number of RS describe themselves and their daily routine, and the speech modalities they use in doing so. The discussion emphasizes both the abnormality and normality of their lives. Clearly, the absence of a permanent living space strongly shapes these people's identity along with their daily routines. From this perspective, therefore, their behaviour is not normative and generalizable to other individuals in this situation. However, in terms of their desire for a space to live, their verbal responses to stimuli, the way they narrate or not narrate their past, the ability to self-reflect, their social and occupational aspirations and the desire for a recognized membership in a group, they are very much like housed people.

As liminal individuals, SH share many of the key characteristics of the other two liminal groups in this study. By contrast, however, their situation is, in key respects, more fluid and less permanent than for instance Travellers' due to an intense desire forchange.

Research on homelessness

Most of the literature recognizes that SH and RS are denied access to socially significant roles and, not being financially secure and independent, are excluded from most opportunities for self-development (Park and Crocker 2005, Snow and Anderson 1987, Juhila 2004 among others). Following the seminal study by Snow and Anderson (1987), subsequent research has graphically shown how poverty and deprivation among the SH profoundly challenges their existence and overall well-being. However, at the same time, SH do not accept passively a devalued sense of self-worth.

In most neoliberal societies, people who sleep rough are commonly viewed as social pariahs and unworthy scroungers most of whom are responsible for their own condition (Takahashi et al. 2002, Juhila 2004). Social devaluation triggers discrimination and leads to punitive and often aggressive behaviour towards them. For example, Trimingham's (2015) interview-based study chronicles the 'gruesome details' of hate crimes and other violent behaviour inflicted on SH. In a study based on interviews with twenty-nine SH in Bristol and conversations with eight of them about photographs of places of their choice, Cloke et al. (2008) similarly highlight SH's struggle even in supposedly welcoming places as hostels ('This is my first hostel in my life I've been in and never again! This is a nightmare. I hate it' 2008: 248).

The relation between identity and space is a key topic in the research literature on the SH and RS. The classic separation between a private, safe space and a potentially dangerous, public space among domiciled people ceases to apply to RS as their spaces are always uncertain and unsafe. A more functional difference proposed in the literature is between 'prime' and 'marginal' spaces (Duncan 1983, Snow and Anderson 1993, Wardhaugh 2017). This derives from the idea that cities are controlled by different 'host' groups that organize space and differentiate between productive or leisure areas opposed to others where the unwanted tend to be confined. The distinction goes beyond permanent or temporary ownership usually associated with private and public spaces and refers to the more crucial issue of the value that settled communities ascribe to particular areas. Thus, prime spaces are used for residential, commercial or recreational purposes or are those that have the symbolic function of indexing order. Marginal spaces, on the contrary, are those that have been ceded to the Unhoused or any other outcast groups (Wardhaugh 1996: 704).

This division, originally proposed by Duncan (1983), has been challenged by studies showing how marginal people negotiate their use of prime spaces often as part of efforts to refute their stigmatized identity. Most research highlights the regulatory control of spaces to which SH are subjected and their resistance to and negotiation of society's controlled geographies. SH can use multiple public spaces such as beach lockers (Wolch and Rowe 1992 in Cloke et al. 2008), shop doorways (Smith 1993 in Locke et al. 2008), railways, and airports (Hopper 1991 in Cloke et al. 2008). Casey et al. show how women openly 'challeng[e] the boundaries laid down for them and carv[e] out a space in the public realm' (2008: 905) by for instance occupying spaces accessible to all at strategic times (often disappearing when the day breaks).

Homeless women are less visible than men, women tend to 'blend in by adopting [the] *expected behaviour*' (Casey et al. 2008: 906, emphasis in the original) associated with other users' in a given context. They favour McDonald's (Casey et al. 20087) or libraries (reading a book while recharging their phone, or napping while listening to a CD in a music booth) where they can disguise their homeless state and defy the law of social oblivion (Sheehan 2010). According to the traditional literature, women's geographies challenge their choice and consumption of public spaces by restricting them once more to the margin of homelessness (Wardhaugh 1999). However, Casey et al. (2008) challenge this view by showing that nearly two-thirds of the female participants in their study occupied uncontested public spaces as a 'form of resistance' to their exclusion and exercised their right to exist in those areas (p. 904). Women may operate in cahoots with public space gate keepers. For example, in a study by Casey et al. (2008: 907) a Homeless woman was allowed to sleep on the steps of a museum (as long as she left in the early morning) since her presence actually deterred other unwanted people such as graffiti artists or people loitering outside the museum entrance and engaging in anti-social behaviour such as littering. While this particular case is more similar to the service that Martha the squatter claimed her crew offered to abandoned buildings, in this chapter the case of a speaker reporting on sleeping rough close to a police station is an example of an accepted form of deviance.

In conclusion, most research highlights the space regulation to which SH are subjected and their resistance to and negotiation of society's controlled geographies. Similarly, while some studies emphasize the loss of self-worth among RS and their vulnerability (Deutsche 1990), others stress their tenacity and ability to cope and their capacity to construct strong social networks (Ruddick 1990). Even in cities that offer high service provision, many RS try hard to not be corralled into institutional marginal spaces preferring instead to find their own ways to eat, sleep, earn and socialize (Cloke et al. 2008).

Psychology studies concentrate on the different mental challenges and processes associated with short- and long-term homelessness (see Farrington and Robinson 1999). While the short-term (less than two years) RS tend to refuse to acknowledge their condition, long-term RS seem to be more accepting of it and, being resourceful, use fewer services. Most studies insist on the need to go beyond a rationalist response to homelessness and highlight the role of 'affect' and 'emotion' among SH (Cloke et al. 2008). Such a consideration has an impact on the choice of restorative activities that, rather than conventional options such as vocational training, can more directly encourage self-confidence and self-worth among the Homeless (see Iveson and Cornish 2016). In line with the other chapters, this study does not understand SH and RS as people in a permanent state, rather as liminal individuals in transition between a limiting problematic past and a desired future.

Most of the interview-based qualitative studies of SH tend to emphasize how identity is continually changing and evolving within the experience of homelessness. RS resist their loss of self with different coping mechanisms that associate with or disassociate them from the general homeless population and locate their identity construction in the past, present and future. In particular, Boydell (2000) recommends that more studies highlight the resilience and strength of SH in the belief that these positive features can be capitalized on by practitioners to encourage RS to escape their condition.

Public discourses on homelessness

Media reporting

As with the other two liminal groups, the public discourse on homelessness is often very negative. At times, newspaper articles convey an almost visceral feeling of hate towards RS. Devereux (2005) pinpoints the following list of shortcomings in the media coverage of the Homeless.

> (i) a failure to adequately explain what homelessness is; ii) a seeming reluctance to focus on the structural causes of homelessness; (iii) the use of stereotypes which narrowly define, homogenize, stigmatize, exoticize and infantilize homeless people; (iv) an overemphasis on charity as being the most appropriate (and inevitable) response to homelessness; (v) a focus on the 'heroic' acts of homelessness activists or celebrities such as footballers, media personalities and rock stars 'doing their bit' for the homeless; (vi) persistent source bias – i.e. an

over-reliance on the views of state and NGO spokespersons, as opposed to the lived experiences of the homeless themselves (see Devereux, 1998); (vii) a failure to engage critically with the politically powerful as to their role and responsibility in resolving homelessness in the longer-term; and (viii) a distinct lack of reflexivity on the part of journalists on the likely impact of media reporting on homelessness on public perceptions and the actions (or not) of policy makers (p. 263).

In this light, therefore, homelessness appears 'inevitable' and the real reasons behind it, from the closure of psychiatric hospitals to an increasingly deregulated housing market, are obscured. In the present heightened neo-liberal era, negative media reporting on homelessness has noticeably increased. The frequent reports of begging 'scams' by individuals who are not actually homeless is a prime example. Devereux also refers to the emergence of a discourse of 'disgust' which covers all poor and outcast groups in society.

Individual views on homelessness

The following discussion moves from the macro media representation of the homeless to the micro views of ordinary citizens. This is done by analysing the written comments of average individuals, which are stored in the Mass Observation Archive in Brighton, UK. The 'observers' are ordinary people of all ages, gender, class and to a degree ethnicity living throughout the UK, who respond to 'directives' or theme-based invitations to write diaries or letters about their reflections on specific topics. The 2015-2017 directive on 'Homelessness' contains a total of 178 responses.

The observers had to answer a variety of questions such as 'has there ever been a time when you have been without a permanent home?', or 'have you ever faced the threat of homelessness or experienced homelessness?' Other questions asked them what they thought are the causes of Homelessness or invited them to reflect on governmental policies for example, 'the Government is currently debating a new law to prevent people becoming homeless. If the law goes ahead in its current format, it will place a duty on local authorities to help eligible people at risk of homelessness to secure accommodation. We would like your thoughts on this policy'. Not surprisingly, these questions elicited a variety of different responses.

The question about the observers' own experience of Homelessness triggered statements accompanied by emotional language: 'Thank God, I've never been homeless', 'I honestly don't know what I would do if I became homeless!' or 'No direct link to homelessness (touching wood)'.

The observers' diaries on homelessness reflect how the average person feels about the dramatic and increasingly worsening situation of people living on the street in the UK. Often the writer's stance towards homelessness emerges through narratives as in the following account by a trained counsellor that centres on an experience of discrimination and bigotry (excerpt 1) and a more positive report of generosity (excerpt 2):

> *Excerpt 1:* One guy had two dogs with him and he told me that he and his girlfriend have been living in a tent. He told me that he despairs that people assume he's drunk and a drug user, in fact as we were speaking, a group of women passed and he asked for spare change. One woman, drunk and clutching a can of lager and a cigarette, shouted: 'I'm not giving it to you (as) you'll only spend it on booze and drugs'.

> *Excerpt 2:* 'The other week I went for coffee with a friend and I must've passed five or six homeless people on the way to the coffee shop. While we were in there it began to belt down with rain and outside the window (I saw) a guy in drenched clothes and tattered sleeping bag. It was heart-warming to see a well-to-do looking lady give him an umbrella, and another (illegible) (after?) gave him £10 which seemed to bring him to tears. I felt really sorry for him as he was cold and shaking.'

Both narratives show how people's response to Homelessness varies from the typical belief that Homeless are drug addicts to the Dickensian scene of the street dweller moved to tears by the generosity of his benefactors.

Searching the corpus of the responses for concordance of the lemma 'help' reveals further attitudes to homelessness. Some comments are positive and empathetic.

> *Excerpt 3:* I am warm and loved and I should *help* others/It makes me feel good to *help*/I do what I can to *help* these organisations/I must try to *help* those with no home to go to/Perhaps education, support for addicts, offenders, job seekers or those with mental and physical health problems would *help* reduce homelessness.

However, others are quite negative.

> *Excerpt 4:* Do I feel that I should do anything to help? *In my case the answer is no*/ As a shy introverted individual, *I do avoid the homeless in much the same way that I avoid any other interactions with strangers.* I would love to*help*, but my confidence holds me back./ I have to admit to being a bit sceptical about food banks. Whilst it would be demeaning to ask for proof of need, I can"t help feeling

that not all those who benefit from them are in need of a *handout of free food*/ If I see someone homeless on the street, *I don''t go out of my way to help. If someone asks for money, I do ignore them because I'm not convinced they are genuine.*

Other people look to government and institutions to solve the problem:

Excerpt 5: There should be *more government help* with shelters and rehabilitation schemes/local *authorities should* offer *help* to all homeless/To further *help councils should* provide access to education, having a safe space to interact and participate in positive activity I think would *help* with the isolation of being homeless).

Similarly, concordances for 'money' highlight differing positioning among the observers.

Excerpt 6: I'm *wary about giving money* as I'd rather not finance someone with drugs or alcohol/I used to give *money* directly to people, but feel a bit *uncomfortable* about it. It's not for me to say how people should spend *money* I give them, but I don't want them to use it on anything that may be *contributing to the problem* they already have (like drink or drugs), so would rather give it to an agency or registered charity./It's all very well for the government to dictate local authorities should house homeless people but *where is the money coming from?* Liverpool council is one of the *least well-funded*, and is in huge debt due to previous administrations and because we keep electing shysters who rob us blind./If someone asks for *money I do ignore* them because I'm not convinced they are genuine./I *won't give money* to beggars. I feel that too many of them are crooks, taking *money under false pretences*, they're not homeless at all. The others only want to waste money on cigarettes, dog food and even *expensive* Costa coffee, which they all seem to have.

Some comments contain small narratives reflecting on the human aspect of the problem of Homelessness while others are more directly political.

Excerpt 7: I saw a homeless person sheltering near the lifts to a car park in town. I gave him *some money* and we had a bit of a chat. He looked at my son and said I wish I could start again.

Excerpt 8: There are so many *empty buildings* in this country. Even in my home town of Scarborough there are buildings that are empty, why are we not using them to *help homeless people*, especially in winter?

In conclusion, the responses reveal a variegated scenario; therefore, although the homelessness diarists are not necessarily a fully representative sample of the

British population, the directive provides useful insights into popular perceptions and attitudes towards homelessness.

Methodology

The RS interviewees attended a day centre for the Homeless centrally located in a seaside town in southern England. Open daily, except Sunday, the centre also provides emergency night accommodation in winter when the temperature drops below zero. It has shower and toilet facilities, comfortable seating areas and a library with desktop computers. It offers breakfast and lunch, medical support, and a number of activities (writing, drama, drawing, painting workshops, yoga, singing) all of which are run by volunteers.

I was introduced to the day centre by a friend[3] who had been a volunteer there for a number of years. I took considerable time to explain my research goals and related activities to the managing staff. Such a vetting procedure was necessary, I was told, in order that the research did not compromise the individual integrity and privacy of the centre clients as had happened on a number of previous occasions.

In line with notion of 'standpoint epistemology', the interviews were aimed to give a voice, against more hegemonic accounts, to the RS who do not usually have that 'vantage point' or the 'epistemic privilege' to be heard (Rolin 2006 among many others). The interviews, between thirty and forty minutes in duration, were conducted by myself and my friend. They were unstructured, to give total freedom to the interviewee to take the lead.

As interviewers, we justified our investigation of the lives of RS as a strong personal interest in this alternative existence. In general, everyone was happy to share their thoughts and reflections on their lives.

Our interviewing styles were slightly different in that I was more inclined than my friend to follow-up on comments made by interviewees. However, this did not fundamentally prejudice the comparability of our separate conversations. Interview consent was obtained orally as we believed it would have been off-putting and even disrespectful to ask for written approval which could also have disrupted the friendly atmosphere that we had managed to create at the centre and that made the conversations relatively natural. The interviews were later transcribed in full for the analysis.

The RS interviewees were selected mainly according to their willingness to participate. They were mostly individuals with whom the researchers had developed a degree of closeness. Exceptionally, the clients did not want their interviews to be recorded. In this case, in front of them, I used the recorder to rephrase in my own voice their statements or took notes to ensure their desire for privacy was respected.

Alcohol and other drugs are very often used by RS as an escape from their desperate existences (or is the cause of their homelessness). Their common usage is also a way of creating community membership (see Parsell 2014 and Mostowska 2013), although this has been denied by other speakers in later interviews (May 2020). However, this study avoids a specific focus on alcohol and substance use because most of the people interviewed were momentarily 'clean' or were not heavy substance users and, more importantly, because it was felt that dwelling on negative topics of this kind could result in 'othering' RS as 'pathological' subjects and reproducing a conventional and stereotyped view (Parsell 2014). The prime concern was with revealing the identities that RS construct when the opportunity of engaging with a sympathetic outsider is presented to them.

Twelve out of a total eighteen interviews were included in the study with equal numbers of female and male respondents. Apart from one individual, my friend interviewed the male and I interviewed the female clients. Since I have had more experience with and was more at ease with female interviewees, I felt that this would encourage more openness and frankness in our discussions.

The liminal identities of Rough Sleepers

Following on from Ruddick's (1990) view of RS as people who respond creatively to the spatial imposition of mainstream society, this discussion focuses on the identities that the Homeless respondents evoked discursively in response to their condition.

The institutional approach to homelessness tends to be generic and indiscriminate. For example, a female respondent who did not want to be recorded, complained that, often for economic reasons, RS are not listened to and their problems are not sufficiently taken into account. She commented that RS are invariably encouraged to return to their 'home towns' where they have 'local connections', which fails to recognize the very reasons why they left in the first place. While revealing something about the speaker's own history, such comments also indicate the ability of RS to critique official policy and reflect a degree of personal agency.

The general discursive patterns of the interviews are analyzed by identifying salient themes and linguistic indicators. As always, the speakers' identities are not viewed as reflecting 'some pre-existing social reality', but as creating one in situ that reflects an engagement not just with 'social and geographical space, but also [with] history, and [...] time' (Kramer, 2014: 1).

The following discussion is based on a number of distinct identity categorizations of the RS interviewees' personas beyond the stereotypes that society attaches to them.

Heroic identities

The term 'heroic identity' is used to describe those RS respondents who presented themselves as past high achievers. Identities engage with space but also time; this is particularly true in the case of RS who, on the one hand, have an extremely complex relationship with space, while, on the other, are situated in time as they have gone from one existential past situation to a totally different one in the present. The Bakhtinean (2002) notion of the chronotope in which space and time intersect in the construction of personhood is, therefore, essential for any interpretation of what these individuals are creating through their words.

The relationship with the past among the RS has been analysed in detail. Usually, the recovered past is seen as a time about which they are proud, especially when this is juxtaposed with the present. For Boydell et al. (2000), the present means a loss of address and identity, while the past is synonymous with control and agency. Although many of the studies on the Homeless are based on a considerable number of individuals (Boydell et al., for example, consider 300 adult shelter users in Toronto, Canada), there is a tendency to overgeneralize how RS feel about their past.

The day centre interviewees showed very complex and variegated relationship with their pasts. These are both positive and negative including, of course, the particular time when they became Homeless. The category of 'heroic identity' allows, therefore, for a greater degree of flexibility by providing the opportunity to reflect on their selfhood as being situated in the past as well as in the present.

In the interviewees' talk, heroic identity is generally indexed by an emphasis on the self that can be in the past, present or future, positive or negative. For example, the following excerpt from Andrew's interview contains thirty-four instances of '*I'm*' that refer to a variety of situations from 'I'm in court this month' by which the speaker simply reports on a future obligation that is marking his life in a short period of time, to such admissions as 'I'm addicted to spice' that amounts to a confession of his frailty. In other instances, more directly related to the past, Andrew self-indexes his heroic persona, even though dramatic mistakes ruined his life and reduced him to his current condition.

> *Excerpt 8:* Andrew. ... my life history is um I had um a plastering company called (company's name) and (other company's name) and *thirty five guys worked for me* and thirty five guys subbies I had three members of permanent staff then *I set up another company* (name of other company) which specializes in underfloor heating you know so *then I went into the line of drug dealing,* which is *not a good thing* to do, do you know what I mean *but I've lived the life style of a multi-millionaire lifestyle. I lost three kilos of pure cocaine from Peru,* the issue that one has is because of the- I was um on the way down from, from the north of England where the majority of the work was and I had a substance called ayahuasca now ayahuasca is *the strongest known drug* known to man or woman, it's found in the Amazon rain forests and it's a tree bark. *I don't know much about what I'm going to say next* but I had it. And you're supposed to, you're supposed to carry out five simple instructions like you know um go to the toilet er don't drink water there's five to undertake and um I didn't carry out the full five and as a result *I has two brain aneurysms, two brain bleeds, a coma for three months, I died twice in theatre and I've got a twenty-thousand pound graphite rod here in my neck,* which you can see there. *I had two of the best brain surgeons in Europe work on me. I had twenty members of staff also work on me* do you know what I mean and and and as a result I um thank them with my heart because I'm here because because because of them I'm here do you know what I mean.

Through the use of numbers, Andrew constructs a heterotopic reality in which he is powerful and has social salience: thirty-five people working for him, three kilos of pure cocaine, two aneurysms, two bleeds, a coma for three months, double death, a £20,000 graphite rod, two of the best brain surgeons, and twenty members of staff. The emphasis is not on the particular negative or positive evaluation of his past events (although there is an admission that going into 'the line' of drug dealing, as if it were a particular line of business, was not a right choice); rather, the attempt is to show he was able to embark on big plans that attested to his ability to have a place in society, no matter whether for condemnation or praise. Besides the presence of numbers, the concentration on the self is a strong indicator of the speaker's attempt to construct a heroic identity as in the case of '*I had*' and '*I had ... on me*'. The lack of space that damages a person's sense of self, therefore, in this case engenders a desire to appear capable, socially incisive, meaningful and, above all, visible in a variety of ways. Such desire is further supported by the speaker's declared eagerness to be included in the book that the male interviewer (Philip) describes as a possible output of his conversations with the day centre clients, 'Will I be in it? Do you promise me?' 'Yeah I'm in a book, yeah. Yeah, dad, I've made it.' In other words, the possibility of being mentioned in a book ensures that degree of visibility the speaker does not have due to his lack of a domicile.

This participant's heroic identity is also associated with a macho language (ballocks, balls) through which, on the one hand, Andrew prides himself while, on the other, he admits defeat. By this, the speaker's surrender to Ayahuasca acquires the meaning of an inevitable loss against an invincible force.

> *Excerpt 9:* Andrew. Which makes me slightly er fucked off do you know what I mean but, at the end of the day, I've had all the drugs in my life time that I've had through cocaine through the ayahuasca that'll kill me through all the different smokes and stuff all the different weeds and lalalala and the LSD lalala this this spice is the one that's *got me by the bollocks man really got me by the balls* um and um yeah @ *fucking hell man* the memory but without memory you're fucked do you know what I mean seriously you might as well seriously forget it do you know what I mean.

The past as recounted by this participant and others is not necessarily, therefore, a source of pride as some of the literature claims (Boydell et al. 2000: 30) but a desire to show a visible identity that seems to have evaporated in the on-going reality of homelessness.

The past as the time when the speakers had their own space is often not a good memory even if it is associated with a productive and socially functioning identity. For John, for example, the past meant a lot of money but also dissatisfaction with his job and life in general.

> *Excerpt 10:* Int. What was your trade? John. I was a steel fixer, shuttering joiner all that kind of stuff, ganger man. Massive money. Seven eight hundred pound a week in your pocket. *Middle of nowhere, so you had nowhere to go.*

In other narratives, however, the speakers construct themselves as reacting strongly to their condition of homelessness and display a determination to show a strong inner self as part of their heroism. This is the case of Marie who repeats in her interview: 'I'm very strong. I'm a very, very strong woman. And, I've learned to stand up for myself'.

> *Excerpt 11:* Marie. *I'm strong. I stand up to these guys. I don't take shit from anyone.* I'm like, do you know who I am? I'm South African, I'm passionate.... And, *I had a little break down* and I ended up homeless in London, yeah. Quit

> my job, *I was a franchise manager* of (company's name) in London. Really good job because my background is fitness and health and personal training.
> Int. Oh, ok
> Marie. I did that in Dubai, Qatar, *all over the world. Opened gyms for Richard Branson* like.... [...] *I did* a YouTube video, *I've done* a march for the homeless in London, *I've written* to the queen.
> Int. Yeah ... you were saying that the other day, yeah.
> Marie. *I've built* a web page where [...] as a woman on the street you're exposed to all sorts of vulnerabilities, obviously. *I was almost trafficked* once by a Romanian man. *I've been asked* by members of the public, males, do you want to make quick buck, give me a blow, all this stuff, yeah.

The main feature in this excerpt is again its enumerative nature. Marie starts with a list of adjectives that describe her, e.g. strong, passionate, to then continue with an inventory of achievements. Even the events in which she describes herself as a victim or recipient of some unwanted invitation are presented as part of her enumeration and contribute to her self-portrait as a strong and capable woman in spite of the difficulties she has to face on the street. Similarly, the reference to the break down that led to her being homeless is defined as 'small' and minimized in juxtaposition to the catalogue of achievements she reports to the interviewer.

The letter to the Queen story continues to further advertise the speaker's entrepreneurial persona.

> *Excerpt 12.* Marie. *I wrote to the Queen and I said* ... because my family is from Scottish Royalty, right. And we have a castle in Scotland called (name) and the movie The Queen was shot in our castle. So, there's a link between the royal family and our family. [...] But, they've sold it now. [...] So, I'm from ... I know it sounds ... I'm from good bloodline, yeah. I've got good education. My uncle went to school with Charles, there's a lot of links. You know that Harry does work in Africa? *So, when I wrote to the Queen I said, Your Majesty, you have the right to address issues of the poor. These people have served your country in the army, navy and all these things, they've ended up homeless, there's no support.*

The direct quotation from her own letter to the monarch introduces the persuasive argument Marie constructs to obtain the Queen's support for ex-service men who, after fighting for their country, have become homeless. The choice of the word 'right' rather than 'duty' related to addressing 'issues of the poor' is similarly strategic in its being a delicate reminder for the Queen that she needs to think about the poor, rather than a forceful intimation that the monarch may be disregarding a major social problem. By making the choice of telling the interviewer about her letter to the Queen, Marie is picturing herself as a resourceful and creative narrator. She is also distancing herself from the anonymous group of homeless people by presenting herself as a special individual able to reach out. The letter-narrative is, therefore, a strategy which she deploys in order to cope with her 'negative social identity'. Tajfel and Turner (1979) conjecture that when members of a low status group find themselves in a situation in which positive social identity and high social esteem are not possible, they try to remedy the situation in various ways. For example, they can change group membership (social mobility), alter the social structure of society (social change) or resort to social creativity. In the case of Marie who reinvents herself in a very different way from the ordinary RS, this involves 'seeking[ing] new bases for comparison giving more favourable outcomes either by changing the dimension for comparison or by switching the comparison group' (Tajfel and Turner 1979 in Farrington and Robinson 1999: 177).

The most notable point in Marie's talk is that her heroic identity is not limited to the recollection of her past since, in spite of her extremely difficult situation, she talks about her present accomplishments in a proactive way as a rescuer, a donor, a saviour, a sensitive helper and natural social worker. Marie's heterotopia is, therefore, similar to squatter Martha's, where she sees herself as an entrepreneur with innovative solutions for the capitalist world. In a similar vein, Marie constructs a positive 'spatial self' (Schwartz and Halegoua 2015) by reporting on a number of physical activities through which she performs aspects of her identity to her interlocutor. She describes herself as a benefactor for people in a similar and worse situations. The repetition of 'blessed' further underlines Marie's agency who admits to acting for her own benefit ('I get a real sense of satisfaction'). Similarly, the use of direct quotations from her own and others' speech contributes to an identity construction that is highly performative, punctuated as it is, by a series of actions in which the speaker is the main protagonist.

> *Excerpt 12:* Marie. *What's really exciting with this whole thing with having been homeless* is that it's *taught me a lot about life* and I was quiet ... not materialistic, but I loved my designer clothes and now I mean I've got money come in. I went and I gave, blessed this guy with 20 pounds and he's like, '*oh my gosh I need new guitar strings thank you so much*'. I put 60 pounds under the church door, I've blessed another guy with 30 pounds and I went and I helped a lot of people when I have clothes, too much clothes, I give them away. I give me food to help people and I love it. I get a real sense of satisfaction. The other day there was a girl on the street, right, 18 year old girl, pissed and I said '*where are*

you sleeping tonight?' 'Oh I don't know'. I took her, I paid for her, I snuck her into the backpackers. First night, second night bought her breakfast, spoke to her mom, paid for her for two nights in a backpackers'. She was sleeping with all these men in the backpackers', selling herself for drugs and now she's in a hostel.

The construction of Marie's heroic identity is directly related to her accounts of both the past and present. While deprived of a home and a sense of dignity and selfhood, she adopts a positive, reassuring and accepting discourse (for example, '[homelessness] taught me a lot about life'). These small narratives in which the speakers are the triumphant protagonists index the desire to redress a lack of place by establishing a resilient persona that survives disheartening adversities.

Discursive heroism can be achieved also by omissions and by silencing references to traumatic events that have contributed to destabilizing the speakers' life. For example, Jude spends the first three-quarters of her interview constructing a positive representation of her present life and only when she has done this does she turn to the more tragic aspects of her life. She talks optimistically of her rough sleeping arrangement in a tent close to a police station with police officers regularly checking on her.

> Excerpt 13: And we, um. *On the police station where the police cars are parked we stay there*. At the moment, we've got a tent and it was our first night in the tent last night. So, we're actually out of (the town) for the weekend.
> Int. Right, right.
> Jude. That'll be quite nice. Umm, but apart from that that's where we are. *It's not too bad there, we're safe* there cos there's police cameras and everything on us.
> Int. And, you don't get hassled by the police or anything?
> Jude. No, they know me, so *they know me by my name* and they know me so they actually they *come and check up on me*. [...] Sometimes, they'll try and wake me up if I'm asleep and they'll call me and go -- just to *check see that I'm OK* ...

Like Marie, Jude insists that she is not afraid of living on the street.

> Excerpt 14: Jude. I *don't feel unsafe*. Um, ninety per cent of the time *I feel safe*. Obviously, there's that risk. Things happening in the the street but I think because I'm female a lot of people won't start with me or they won't, I think, do you know what I mean?'

She maintains that the homeless are a community. As she puts it, 'we're all like a little street family'. She portrays herself as a strong person who is happy and capable of handling street life and in fact protecting her partner.

Excerpt 15: Jude. *I'm like his little pit bull beside him.* He'll be snoring and *I'm like keeping guard.* [...] *I was alright on my own I'd had lots of nights on the street on my own* but it was easier to find places to crash when you're on your own ... The way I look at it is, there are people worse off ... I always try and make myself feel better. I think there's a lot of people could be worse. I could be on drugs or I could be on me own or you know, and I'm not, *at least I've got a clear head on me while I'm on the street.* And, I'm not alone.

Jude's desire for a place is still strong.

Excerpt 16: Jude. I want to try and get just a studio flat. That's be perfect. That's be ideal. *Don't need a room. Just a matchbox will do.* @@ Anything with a roof over our heads [...] I'd be happy with anything. But, it'd have to be out of (town), which I don't mind. [...] Cos it's so expensive in (town).

Only after forty-nine turns and, in response to the interviewer's question, 'How did you lose your place?' does Jude reveal her drama.

Excerpt 17: Jude. Um, *they kind of sort of fucked me over really.* And, they're very clever at it to turn it on to you so it's your fault and you've made yourself
Int. Made yourself homeless?
Jude. Yeah. They used that one on me. *Basically, I lost my children,* um 2014 *I lost my children* and you know so they (.) 2015=
Int. = What, they took them into care?
Jude. Yeah, *they took them off me*, my mental health. *I just weren't coping no more* and, um, I was diagnosed with a few mental health problems. *They used that against me* quite a lot, um, but when I lost my children, um, my money got stopped for my children which is fair enough but because I'd never been in that situation before *I didn't understand* all the like certain things never been in that before. It was the first time *they took the kids off me* so but, um, because my children's money got stopped my housing benefit got stopped but *I didn't know* and the first I got a letter and actually *they done the same thing to a friend of mine* really recently they're doing it to her now, um, I got a letter saying I owed eight hundred something pounds and I wasn't like receiving any money, um, *I wasn't even eating* I was having to keep going to people's for dinner and stuff like that cos *I didn't have no money* and so, yeah, I was so how do you expect me to pay this I can't even afford to feed myself, eight hundred something pound but it went up each week, obviously it got more and more and more and they took me to court and *they took my house off me* so they did kind of it feels like *they have fucked me over* and now it's I've appealed it a few times with (name of trust) they helped me but the *council are really hard* ones to when they've made their mind up on that that's it. Feels like they do it

deliberately though. Because I was supposed to be downsizing, that was the original plan.

Memories are always reconstructions which are continuously transformed as they are (re)told and '[n]arrative is a recursive organization of data; that is, its components may be embedded successively at various micro- and macro levels' (Branigan 1992: 18). The tragic story of the loss of her children is embedded within the more positive narrative of Jude's street resistance and only crops up at a later time when she is prompted. Jude is not being insincere in her account and what is relevant is how she chooses to order the events as 'what people believe happened is often as important as what really happened' (Hall 2009).

Jude's narrative of her children's traumatic removal, which she attributes to her mental issues, is accompanied by the repeated occurrences of negative utterances (Didn't understand/Wasn't eating) underscoring her inability to cope as a mother ('I just weren't coping no more'). She does not, however, indulge in recrimination but maintains her heroic identity by justifying both the loss of her children ('Yeah, *they took them off me*, my mental health. *I just weren't coping no more*') and welfare benefits ('My money got stopped for my children *which is fair enough*').

Heroic identities are constructed by the interviewees regardless of their gender, age or length of time on the street. Discursive heroism refers both to a past about which the interviewees do not necessarily feel proud and a future whereby the speakers project their aspirations to redress the personal shortcomings which led to them becoming homeless.

Propositive identities

Propositive identities are discursively constructed by those interviewees who make projections into the future and propose a humane social heterotopia. In general, in this case study the male interviewees were more timid about the possibility of change than the female respondents who exhibited much greater determination to sort out their lives. The following excerpt from the interview with Neil is an example of such male hesitancy about the possibility of change.

> *Excerpt 18:* Neil. But, deep in the back of me mind, I knew that *I've got to change*. I can't just sit around doing this for the rest of my life. *I've got to get on and do something*. More positive a routine and, you know, there's other things I could be doing (.) volunteering, trying to help other people maybe, I don't

know. But, I've got this mind set *I can't help other people* unless I've got to help meself and get meself to a certain position, place first before I can do anything else for other people in a way.

The repetition of the epistemic modal 'I've got to' which functions as a moral imperative is particularly noticeable. By contrast, Marie strongly evokes another identity, revolving about her transformative desire to construct a heterotopic future that sums up all her ethical and socialistic aspirations.

Excerpt 19: Marie. About my homeless shelters that *I want to build*, 200 shelters. *I've got a webpage* called (name) and it ... it means to harvest in African. So, what we want to do is *we want to have* [inaudible] like an allotment, a gym, hairdressers, podiatrists, councillors, a safe place for women on the streets who have been homeless, been abused. *We'll let them stay there* for three months, empower each other through the skills they have, so one might be a painter, whatever and we'll say, who wants to do painting? So that gives them a sense of purpose and like any plant or tree you need to nurture it, don't you? So it's like human beings, you need to ... the right environment, the right sort of whatever. *I've got a charity event coming up that I'm doing in* (street name). The drag queens are doing *a show for me*.
Int. Oh, wow.
Jude. Yeah. And the proceeds are going to go to that. *I've written to the council, I've been seeing housing offices, I'm applying to do my social work degree this year.*

The repetitive use of 'I've' referring to what the speaker has done in combination with the emphasis on what some people (the drag queens) are doing for her indexes her desire to show how she has not been defeated by street homelessness and that she is able to discursively invoke a businesswoman's identity. The choice of 'we', whether synonymous with the first person singular or actually referring to the people who contribute to her project, also adds to the strength of the proposition the speaker puts forward.

The positive outlook that Marie expresses, to which some literature refers as 'fantasy' (Eberle 2017) is the result of her perception of the present not as a permanent state but only as a stage of transition in her life. Some scholars associate such a positive thinking with the young female gender and use this element of constructive agency to defy the general thrust of the literature on homelessness that mainly views RS as hopeless and hapless individuals. This study's interviews confirm that many of the SH show discursive resilience towards rough sleeping and often positively portray their experience in their own unique heterotopia.

Loner identities

As noted above, many RS highlighted the existence of a strong community spirit among their group. This is similar to squatter Martha's 'squamily' or the happy squatter family where liminal people construct a homely heterotopia outside the traditional canons of settled society. Home is not a physical space, rather it equates with the friendship and the support which people in similar conditions can offer.

Listening closely to the conversations of the clients as they entered and left the day centre was particularly revealing. For example, a client who had just walked out of the centre informed two others about to walk in that a friend had been brutally attacked the night before and was in hospital. The need to share with others this dramatic news indexed that the existence of most of the day centre clients and other users of the city services is embedded in a community of practice that replaces permanent people's family relations. The street becomes, therefore, the place where this community comes to life and develops in the more or less safe corners it can offer especially during the night. In the following excerpt, Sam describes in a very matter of fact way his sleeping arrangements with the same accuracy of detail that would be used to describe one's bedroom.

> *Excerpt 19:* Sam. In this car park. It's absolutely fine, *it's good for me actually because it shows where I was, where I am now and where I don't want to go back to.* I used to sleep in an underground car park off (street name) under the tower block, used to be a few people in there but I used to sleep, there was a fire cupboard for the hose reel and stuff like that but that was all broken. It was all you know, the door was kicked off, so used to sleep in there *either me on my own or a couple of other people,* freezing cold.

In stark contrast to the resilient and positive identities of some RS interviewees, are the voices of despair and negativity of others. For example, in (20) below, Peter is very open about his feelings of loneliness and fear. For him, being homeless is a dramatic, 'frustrating' and little more than a 'survival' experience even after many years on the street.

> *Excerpt 20:* Peter. I was sleeping in all kinds of different places. *Just feel alone, you feel alone, you feel frightened* I've been in the streets on and off for a good fifteen years and it doesn't matter how long you're on the streets for you've always got to watch your back you've always got to keep your wits about you so you know so it's frightening and *it's survival er um it's frustrating* it's you get by the way you're treated by some people some people's as good as gold there's

some lovely people out there but but there's some horrible people out there as well *I've been kicked I've been punched I've been weed on* everything by people it's not nice but there are some lovely people about but um yeah when you know I've been in a doorway and *someone's run over and booted me* you know on the way home from a club or something like that and and you know it just you know *you just don't want to be around anymore. You just don't want to be around anymore, you know you want to give up.* you've had enough you know [...] *I've tried to do myself in a couple of times,* years ago you know but as I got older I don't know why I don't know *I suppose I stopped trying.*

In Peter's narrative as usual, it is not solely the content that matters but the form too. The interactional positioning is, therefore, crucial to understanding how Peter is constructing himself. By offering a narrative in the second person, he could be intending to generalize his experience as when he states that 'when you are ill, everything seems very difficult'. At the same time, Peter may be using 'you' to solicit the interviewer's involvement in his narrative and his sympathetic position towards his experience. Following his description of the appallingly difficult lives of RS, the 'you' prepares the ground for the dramatic admission that, this time in the first person, he tried to commit suicide many times. The even more dramatic assertion that, in his old age, Peter stopped trying is then presented as a further failure as if the speaker had lost the energy and perseverance to reach his goal, however negative and self-annihilating this was.

Margaret is another example of an interviewee who constructs a solitary, excluded and deliberately outcast persona. She is a transsexual woman who had pitched her tent in the country and whose life revolved around her two cats. Because of her sexual identity, Margaret has been totally cut-off by her family and other close friends. Nonetheless, she is a happy loner who refuses support from anyone. Accordingly, Margaret chooses to refer to her friends' lack of consonance with her rather than the way round; the fact that her family and friends do not accept her new identity is their problem, not hers.

> *Excerpt 21:* Int. So you don't have a network that can support you, you know, family, friends . . .?
> Margaret. well, you know what I mean, well because I'm trans, my friend, my mum and dad—well, my mum is dead but my dad doesn't talk to me anymore.
> Int. oh, really?
> Margaret. *Friends don't really fit in* that much to be honest with you. I mean I know a lot of people in (city name) but *I would never ask them for their help.*
> Int. why not?
> Margaret. because . . . 'cause I just, *I stand up for myself @ thank you very much . . .*

Int. I like that. @) I really like that. Yeah . . .
Margaret. *I don't want their help, ain't it. I'm alright.*

Margaret desires her own place to be in a natural setting, 'I'm going for the stars', which is behind her architectural design of her home, for which she relies on her previous building experience ('I've already built a deck'). Some RS don't feel disempowered by their living conditions; on the contrary, homelessness fuels their creativity and resourcefulness (see 23 below). Worthy of note is Margaret's expert play with 'the stars' presented as the natural scenario where she plans to live and later used as a metaphor for all the things she can possibly aspire to in life.

> *Excerpt 22:* Margaret. *I'm gonna, I've already built a deck* so, and then off the deck, *I'll build* something to cook on, get some roofing in, do you know what I mean? I don't know. *I'm going to do that*, yeah. Set it up for the winter so I can stay out this winter, pretty comfortable and warm.
> Int. Uh-hmm, uh-hmm.
> Margaret. Do you know, just in case they haven't found me somewhere with the cats. Just go for it from there really. *I'm going for the stars to be honest with you. I'm going for the fucking lot* and I ask about—
> *Excerpt 23:.* Margaret. So, as soon as you find a place that I can have the kittens then I'll go back inside but until then, *I'm just learning aren't I? I'm learning new things* . . . [. . .] I've got a perfect excuse to learn haven't I? And I *don't really need any money* for the next year do I because I'm learning guitar so I'm doing my guitar lessons at St Luke's. You know what I mean? I do my singing. *I do my writing and that will all come together won't it?).*

Margaret portrays herself as a liminal person in the process of transforming her life and devising a heterotopic place for her that will be free of limitations, boundaries, and normativity which she will share only with her cats. Other RS interviewees, such as Neil, also highlight their exclusive and separate lives as a strategy to maintain their distance away from some other individuals who they feel may have a negative influence on them.

> *Excerpt 24:* Neil. My problem with being homeless though is *I tend to drag meself away from everything, I go off on my own* since I left (town name). *I pulled meself away from all the drinkers* and all the people that I just, live on the street, *don't use centres.*

Neil also emphasizes how his choice of a solitary existence ensures he has a healthy life away from substance use and alcohol.

Excerpt 25: Neil. I'm in there cos I've got CCC TV camera on me twenty-four hours a day
Int. Keep you safe.
Neil. *I don't drink, don't take drugs. Go round on me own.* I do a bit of begging like for money. Like I don't ask just sit there on me sleeping bag. Just sit there, people give me food cups of tea outside MacDonald's, sometimes I sit outside Subway. I used to sit down on the seafront last year, begging, but it's so cold down there at night so yeah um then you get other homeless people come up asking you for money but you don't give em that. It's alright in 'ere but like I say when I'm outside *I just keep meself to meself* but a lot of people, all the people know me in here so I'm alright *I just keep meself* cos I'm sixty-two I was on the streets last year I'm on the streets again now. [. . .] *The best thing* is when you're on the street *is just keep yourself to yourself,* if a fight breaks out with another homeless bloke you're not going to butt in, *it's none of your business is it?*

The self-confessed sinner

Some of the male interviewees offered reflections on themselves or their past life that resembled a confession, in terms of a discourse of self-disclosure associated with the admission of culpability or sinfulness. In such an attempt to revisit the past and interrogate themselves, they construct their identity as people able to analyse their life and admit their past mistakes.

Confessions are speech acts which 'require explicit and factual recall of past events perceived as wrong according to some set of recognized norms shared by the parties involved' (Archer and Parry 2019: 592). For some scholars (e.g. Briggs 1997 520) a confession 'consists of a narrative, a representation of a segment of social life in such a way as to create a series of sequentially ordered events'. Research on confessions has mostly developed in the field of forensic linguistics and focused on distinguishing false from real and truthful accounts (Villar et al 2013), and on celebrities' confessions in the media (Archer and Parry 2019) in which the mitigation and extenuation have a strong role in reducing the person's responsibility.

In the confessions by RS a different factor is at play. What the speakers decide to share with the interviewer is their choice of elements they think are useful and relevant in constructing their identity at that particular moment. Beyond the issue of truthfulness and sincerity, therefore, what is of interest is how these individuals construct themselves as 'sinners' and tell their story of damage. The following excerpts from the interviews in which the speakers produce spontaneous confessions are in fact small narratives in which the RS acquire a degree of centrality and agency.

Excerpt 26: Peter. I mean I had family living in (town) but they used to see me sitting in doorways *because it was so difficult for them* to see me like that they didn't used to approach me, *they blanked me* basically because *it hurt them so much*. And that was quite a big thing for me because I should be on the streets freezing cold and thinking they only live up the road, you know. But the thing is they would let me stay there occasionally but we'd fall out you know *I'd get drunk and they wouldn't let me in because I'd be drunk and stuff like that*. So it's not like they didn't try with me but *I would always burn me bridges* you know 'cause I *was a heroin addict* as well. So *I probably steal* coppers you know pounds or whatever out of their pound jar. You know stuff like that that I'd say was little stuff like that you know to them you know you're thieving aren't you so *the trust went out the window. I was angry with them because they wouldn't help me* although *they tried* and I see now they *tried many times*. But I just you know *burned me bridges and abused the trust that they gave me*.

Peter's account offers a delicate balance between the role his family has played towards him and his own responsibility in addressing his homelessness and addiction. Through a Bakhtinian polyglossic construction (Martin and White 2005) the interviewer is provided with two perspectives, Peter's as opposed to his relatives'. The account sways between what Peter imagines his relatives feel when they see him sitting in doorways ('hurt them so much') and the admission of his own responsibility for his antisocial behaviour in 'I'd get drunk and stuff'. Therefore 'they blanked me', an accusation of cruelty on the part of people who knew how much Peter needed help, is softened by his admission of his family's diminished responsibilities. Similarly, the fact that they would not let him into their house is counteracted by his other admission of his drunken disruptiveness. The result is Peter's admission of guilt: he portrays himself as the only one responsible for his own misery as a heroin addict, a drunkard, a thief ruining the little trust his family put in him. He repeatedly 'burns bridges' (the expression appears twice) and destroys any attempt from other people to save him. Only on one occasion does Peter admit to being angry. This reference to his 'negative' humanity is the only instance of direct perspective on his situation, immediately tempered by the concession that 'they tried many times'.

A confession is powerful if it is simple, instinctive and showing reflexivity; in other words, if is not just as a self-disclosure but an effective admission of sinfulness (Tell 2009: 3) as in the following by Neil.

Excerpt 27: Neil. And I just can't get me head clear or straight. I mean I'm good at pretending that's my problem a *great bloody pretender pretending that everything's hunky dory and I'm dead happy* but I am happy in a way but I'm not, I'm very, very. *I'm just good at pretending* I think. *Which is not nice.* [..] the crack cocaine. It's making me funny with people I mean I've never had a go at anyone I was in (name of day centre) *the other day and I had a go at someone* because he asked me for a roll up and because I'd been *picking up butts*, you know *butts*, I says 'haven't you got the fucking strength to pick up your own *cigarette butts*' and it's not like me I'll just go yeah have one I won't even think about it I'll think about it but I won't say anything. It's like when I go in there now I'm everyone's butt collector. They'll all walk in with not a rollup but I've got a cigarette. 'Give us some your butts'. What the fuck you know and I think it's the crack that's making me angry and *snappy at everyone*. So I'm finding myself *a bit snappy* at the moment being rude only when confronted though with it and just *snapping back* at people I think that's down to the crack so at the moment Phil yes I'm using that I'm back on that and I'm pinning it as well and so so I'm stuck there. I've got to stop that.

Neil points his finger at the culprit of his malaise, crack cocaine, which is illustrated by the small narrative of how he snapped at other homeless people when they asked him for a roll up. While such a request is usually a token of friendship both on the part of the asker and the giver (especially within the homeless community), here Neil perceives it as a negative face threat (Brown and Levinson 1987) and an episode of exploitation to which he 'snaps' aggressively.

Within the interviews, confessions were uttered only by male RS who seem to take the interactional opportunity to reconsider their past life. In Steven's narrative below, for instance, the emphasis is on what he has missed in terms of the help offered to him by some good-hearted people. The sense of guilt he experiences and the accompanying emotion are visible in his conclusive crying.

> *Excerpt 28:* Steven. *The police officer offered his service* er he was engaged and er his er fiancé was a nurse at (place name) so *he offered to help me* out of er work hours sort of thing off duty same with his er missis came round to me house not every night couple of days a week popped round *helped me gave me* a bit of medication cooked for me I remember they cooked for me a couple of times in me own kitchen *especially one day* they came round they cooked a meal for me they sat down we sat down together we eat it together watched TV so like *respect* because a lot of *people like me probably don't have no respect* for a lot of government figures particularly police they're a lot of them probably see them

as bullies and this that and the other which most of them probably are corrupt but you know what *respect* to that police officer
Int. Yes, absolutely.
Steven. *he went out of his way to help someone* that he thought needed his help and I did and yet him and his missis helped me. And yeah *respect* to them. I got off it I moved away from Stockport for a while went down to Blackpool lived down there for a year. Came back to Stockport started dabbling in the drugs again er ended up getting arrested one day and funnily enough the desk sergeant that was on was the copper that helped me that day
Int. Oh
Steven. he asked me he said 'how are you doing are you still off the drugs?' and do you know what? I didn't want to tell him but I had to I told him that now I'm dabbling again I disappeared for a bit came back started to dabble again don't want to so I told him the truth that I was doing it again he was disappointed but *he offered to help again do you know what I mean* (*crying*).

In his narrative, Steven shows the difficulty of his relation with the officer by indirectly referring to the negative 'othering' of government figures by people in his condition. His claim is supported by an elaboration: policemen can be 'bullies' and 'corrupt'. This policeman and his 'missis', however, are different as they went out of their way so they were worthy of his respect, a word occurring four times in Steven's confession. The narrative is visibly split into two sections expressing temporality in different ways. The first section exhibits a degree of balance in presenting the events and thus along Labovian lines (Labov and Waletzky 1997) works as an 'orientation', till the 'complication' when Steven is arrested due to his renewed substance abuse. The second section heightens Steven's remorse for slipping into his old habit and failing his benefactor's trust when he accidentally encounters him again.

The last excerpt below is the climax of Steven's crude self-accusation when he calls himself 'ignorant', 'arrogant' and 'wrong'. The conclusive utterance is summative of his admission of guilt as Steven sees himself as the only one responsible for not getting an occupation, being evicted and ending up on the street.

Excerpt 29: Steven. I was trying to run round and trying to get a job but couldn't get a job probably didn't get the job because probably because I was so stressed I was probably *ignorant or arrogant* at the interviews I was probably like trying *to bully the boss* into giving me a job or something. Hence the reason why I probably *failed every interview* never got a job 'cos I was coming across *wrong* they probably seen it that I was *desperate* I didn't care about the job I only cared about the money and that's probably why I *never got the jobs* in the six months and I eventually *got evicted* and *this is where I am now on the streets*.

Conclusion

Some general conclusions can be drawn from this case study. Firstly, RS are most certainly not 'cultural or political dupes', seeking only to survive within the prevailing socio-spatial order' (Cloke et al. 2008: 244).) Rather, they 'exercise choices' by drawing on their individual and collective creativity (ibid.) in their responses to the interlocutor. Viewing RS as a static and permanently damaged group, therefore, fails to capture the wide diversity of individuals in this liminal group. This small collection of interviews suggests a rich diversity of relations with a missing space and a discursive construction of very different identities even within the same interview (as in the case of Marie). While for some the interaction with a sympathetic interviewer is an opportunity to show a heroic and powerful self, or construct themselves as propositive and aspirational Homeless exiters (Farrington and Robinson 1999), others claim less positive but more self-reflexive identities.

As in the previous chapters, the analysis of the RS interviews showed once more that language is a form of social practice and a cultural resource embedded in social relations. Words are not neutral, rather they reflect the speaker's experience and their view of the world. They do not relay information uni-directionally because meaning is co-constructed through the linguistic choices the speakers make; the interviewees discursively create who they are and some give shape to their desire for a different future in which life is fairer. Within such a social-constructionist view of identity, the concept of liminality has proved epistemologically useful in that it has helped us to view RS as transient people (Stephen 2010: 458) who are on a trajectory that from the past develops towards an albeit still uncertain future and whose identities are fluid and variable like any others'.

The SH in this study continually display their 'agency' in terms of 'a socio-culturally mediated capacity to act' (Ahearn 2010: 28) that does not have an ontological existence but emerges in the given context and is understood within the process of production and reception. By constructing themselves as self-confessed sinners rather than heroes, or loners rather than planners, the speakers behave as both 'actors' that is rule-governed persons, and 'agents', that is people capable of changing the world.

In general, the interviews show how the reality represented by RS does not only reflect a 'bipolar' distribution of power between the wealthy and the poor; in certain key respects, it also undercuts the ideology of post-industrial cities and challenges the meaning systems according to which people in neo-liberalism interpret their lives. The words of these speakers reveal the complex universe made of aspiration and dreams, past recollections punctuated by pride and guilt that space-deprived people create in their attempt to survive the dramatic marginalization of which they are victims.

8

Conclusions

Pulling the threads together

This study has focused on the impact that the lack of living space has on the way liminal individuals invoke their identities through discourse in the interactional situation of the interview. While post-modern research on identity is replete with studies of this kind, this is the first effort to bring together three types of people who suffer from a particular type of social fragility as they live on the English domestic limen. As such, this book is an attempt to 'give[ing] voice to otherwise muted groups' (Atkinson and Delamont 2006: 166) whom society ignores and relegates to invisibility. The words of these groups can be defined as 'diverse' if one takes 'diversity' to mean out of the norm, whatever that norm is. Certainly, this study's interviewees are out of the hegemonic social canon because, first and foremost, they occupy alternative spaces in society. Nor is this simply a useful metaphor as is most graphically exemplified by the actual living spaces of Squatters, Rough Sleepers and Travellers. The very existence of these people unsettles mainstream society because, it has been argued, they are visible proof of the lack of integration of many individuals in the post-industrial capitalist system.

The core questions that have guided this research are: How do people who live outside the norm and occupy marginal, unstable, threatened, in a word liminal spaces, construct their personhood if they are to talk to a sympathetic interlocutor? What things do they choose to discuss? What episodes of their life will they want to recall? What words do they use to describe them? In short, how do they portray themselves? Although all the participants are severely affected by material and psychological deprivation, this study reveals a wide variety of identity constructions among them and generally an ability to reflect on their condition, recall the past critically and project ahead. These questions have been answered by following an interactional sociolinguistic approach within linguistic ethnography (Gumperz 1999), that pays attention within the interview to 'the efforts individuals make to get other people to recognise their feelings, perceptions, interests etc' (Rampton 2007: 3). In line with the recent 'reconfiguring of approaches within sociolinguistics and increasing attention to social and cultural dimensions of language' (Tusting and Maybin 2007: 576), the study's methodological framework effectively combines linguistic ethnography and the analytic tools of Critical Discourse Analysis, especially in terms of how speakers' linguistic choices echo hegemonic discourses of exclusion (McNamara 2019). The combination of linguistics and ethnography 'brings finely-tuned methods for analysing text together with the more open, reflexive social orientation of ethnographic methods, which offer analytic purchase on the related social practices and structures' (Rampton et al. 2004 in Tusting and Maybin 2007: 576). In so doing, the study's methodology responds to 'the lack of explicit articulation of a political position for linguistic ethnography' (Tusting and Maybin 2007: 580) by relying on the clear critical engagement of CDA. This eclectic disciplinary combination 'ties ethnography down' and 'opens linguistics up' thus providing tangible language evidence for the analysis while not overlooking the crucial element of 'reflexivity and participation' and the 'ineradicable role that the researcher's personal subjectivity plays throughout the research process' (Rampton et al. 2004: 3).

The study has been able to draw on recent ethnographic and sociolinguistic research that relates place to a dynamic dimension against the contexts of mobility and migration. Place is, therefore, no longer conceptualized as stationary and permanent, but as fluid and above all de-territorialized. While place loses its essentialist and sedentary component, more and more it is approached from an anti-essentialist 'progressive' view (Massey 1985 and 1992). Relation to place, however, is more complex than the simple opposition between rooted home and rootless movement and the discursive construction of place reflects the tensions between an aspiration for security and the contestation of a master narrative or hegemonic discourse of permanency.

The critical discourse approach to place and identity has a series of theoretical implications. Firstly, the participants are treated as subjects who construct their identities against a background of society's narratives understood 'not [as] a synonym for a single story, but rather [as] a system of stories with shared elements that assume a variety of expressions through space and time' (Halverson et al. 2013: 315). Narrative refers, therefore, to culturally constructed modes of interpretation of social phenomena and 'grand narratives' (Lyotard 1984). As such, the analysis of mainstream society's discourses around the three case study groups is central to understanding the individuals' identity construction. Secondly, discourse is central to any post-modern analysis of identity. Therefore, the study has used traditional critical discourse analysis techniques to interpret the interviewees' talks from an attention to the lexis, occasionally through concordance programmes, to a focus on the processes and the choice of modals, expressions of evaluation and other linguistic indicators or the stance expressed by each speaker, together with indirect and implied meanings. The attention to the form and content of the speakers' contribution is justified by an understanding of the close albeit complex relation between identity and '[l]anguage [that] not only reflects who we are but, in some sense, it is who we are' (Llamas and Watt 2012, p. xv).

Finally, the participants' identity construction has been interpreted against the context of the interview understood as a particular speech act that allows people to project their special self. Following Eckert and McConnell-Ginet, it is not just the right to take a turn that determines a speaker's contribution. 'The effect of one's verbal activity depends, among other things, on one's apparent legitimacy to engage in that activity' (2013: 91). As an illustration, the words of an epidemiologist are more likely to be heeded than those of an MP during an epidemic due to their authoritativeness and expertise. Similarly, during the interviews, a shift of interactional dynamics occurred. The narratives of the three sets of liminal individuals acquired strong legitimacy while, as a researcher, I slowly moved from a position of power as the person who was asking questions and had a plan of action, to a listener eager to learn from the legitimate speakers about their cause and experience or even theories about life as in the case of Martha who opened up to me the world of ecoliving.

The specific social-constructionist approach that underpins this study has approached social identity as locally situated and discursively constructed and has highlighted the extent to which it is a multiple, dynamic, negotiated and intersubjective phenomenon. As a performative achievement, personhood is continuously redefined through verbal and, crucially, non-verbal communication. Martha's choice to be interviewed in a particular section of the squat proved an important point and was part of her identity construction; similarly, the Travellers' invitation to show me the inside of their trailers and their insistence on cleaning even during the interview or the Rough Sleepers' show of their relation to and control of their dogs are as meaningful as their narratives are.

While the interview is the dominant methodology in qualitative ethnographic research, this study shows just how important it is to take into account the researcher's roles, responsibilities and covert influences. By rejecting the notion of neutrality, it is possible to take an approach that is grounded in cultural and epistemological relativism. From this perspective, the interview is not seen as a resource through which to obtain the 'truth' but, rather, as the forum and tool for the construction of particular and locally situated identities co-created by the parties involved that will be different from others invoked in different contexts. The study interviews demonstrate just how much the choice to tell particular events and facts or to omit and postpone painful references is integral to the construction of the speaker's personal story. This choice, however, is not neutral or absolute but entirely dependent on the speakers' perception of the interviewer's expectations.

By analysing an individual's emotional relation to space or spatialization, the study reveals how the three types of liminal interviewees evoke different subject positions and thus construct different ways of being a person. To these particular individuals, space, in general a scarce and valuable resource, is an instrument of power enjoyed by only entitled members of that mainstream society from which they are excluded; therefore, liminal individuals occupy a 'neglected' spatiality (Amin and Thrift 2002) that is continually elusive and negated. As a consequence, the interviewees discursively construct identities that strongly encode an idealized rather than a realistic positioning to space. In spite of the differences between them, the study's participants share a desire for agency and control through the creation of a heterotopic space in which their exclusion is resolved. This imaginary realization compensates for their needs while also fulfils the function of contesting the social norms of settled society.

Similar to the interviewees' imaginary constructions, liminality is not only physical and social, but also and especially discursive. It is the response to society that relegates these people to a segregated space to avoid their interference with the politics of productivity and sedentarism. However, the study's interviewees portrayed themselves as caught between a past that is unresolved and a future that cannot be achieved. It is through this tension between the two chronological dimensions that their discursive liminality is manifested.

The study's theoretical constructs of desire and heterotopia

The ideological constructs adopted in this study were based on the conviction that they can provide a more nuanced understanding of the discourses of individual need. Far more so than 'normal' individuals, the study shows how liminal individuals with deficit identities who are in a suspended and transitional state, discursively create a reality of projections and imaginary plans to survive their present deprivation. In this context the choice of desires as the discursive articulation of constant aspirations and longing, whether realized directly by verbs of volition, irrealis moods or indirect and implied meaning constructions, has proved to be a useful conceptual tool for the interpretation of what the study's participants are missing: for Martha, the Squatter, this is the creation of alternative but still profitable living solutions although still markedly different from the conventional corporatist ethos; for Travellers Ruth, Elaine and Rita, it is the control of one's life away from the council's influence, the freedom to have one's own garden shed and a choice about where and if your child is educated; for the Rough Sleepers, Jude and Margaret, it is being allowed to be re-united with her children and the recovery of one's dignity beyond rejection. These diverse desires are responses to the lack of social citizenship that is associated with space deprivation.

The Foucauldian construct of heterotopia adopted in this study is the physical space in between spaces into which these liminals are relegated by a society that wants to make them invisible through obliging them to skulk in shop doorways or disguise themselves at MacDonald's or at libraries for the RS, blend their presence with the natural landscape for Travellers and Gypsies or hide behind boarded up windows for squatters. Heterotopia is also a discursive construction of rejection and aspiration that characterizes the talk of these individuals. Having distinguished between geographical and material space and emotional and discursive place, the heterotopic reality constructed by the interviewees is a locale of safety, dignity and self-recognition. The heterotopia conjured up by the Squatter contests the capitalist system by proposing self-sufficient communes, but it is also a heterotopia that compensates for her missing family relations. Her crew and squamily satisfy her emotional needs. In a not dissimilar way, the Travellers construct a heterotopia of deviance by pursuing their aspiration to mobility but also by constructing their community as a pure and morally disciplined fortress protected against the decadent mores of settled society. The heterotopic dream persists even when they have achieved a much more dignified permanent space in that they project into a future where they will be able to make their own choices and manage their own life independently and completely autonomously from the service-providing settled society. Finally, the Rough Sleepers construct similar heterotopias of freedom from need, dignity, occupation and normality.

The study reveals that, while there are many common traits between these liminal heterotopias, important differences also exist. Squatter Martha's heterotopia of deviation and transgression alternates with a heterotopia of illusion and compensation, both of which are discernible through the language she uses to refer to her site and her corporate and self-defence frames. As she talks about her squat, Martha portrays herself as an individual living in a 'realm of pure possibility', projects an exit from her condition of suspension and plans her 'final stable resolution of [her] ambiguity' (Turner 1974: 233). She does so by creating a heterotopia that endows her with a strong degree of agency as ecological entrepreneur. Her identity construction expresses her desire to reinvent traditional society's structures devoid of patriarchal connotations and compensate for or justify her social marginalization.

A degree of similarity was identified in the heterotopia constructed by Martha and some of the RS through a desire to exit the neo-liberal system with plans involving alternative ways of living beyond society's norms. However, while some of the Rough Sleepers expressed a longing to escape mainstream neo-liberal society, most of them invoked different kinds of identities with often a weaker sense of desire. It seems that their more painful and taxing liminality stymies their capacity to dream and project into a less dramatic future.

Among the Travellers, the study reveals that their heterotopia is an alternation between the aspiration to have their own space and their political critiques of mainly national and local state institutions. Their aspiration to 'ordentlikheid' (decency, respectability) (Ross 2005: 631) and a recognized agency are other constant tropes in the talk. Despite significant improvements, their liminality coupled with their desire for more autonomy and agency has persisted in the permanent site.

In the study's interviews frequent is the reference to 'normal' even though the individuals who use the term are highly liminal and live, therefore, largely outside society's canons of normalcy. For the women Travellers, their 'normal' reality is being able to access the benefits from key services, yet at the same time they want to remain largely apart from this reality. Although not every speaker explicitly uses the word normal, the outside mainstream society is very present in their talk, both as a reality to condemn and escape from and a condition to revisit and reinterpret in a different and more positive way. Normalcy is constructed as a threat in the case of the female RS who lives alone with her cats escaping society's condemnation of her sexuality; alternatively, it is constructed as pressure to reach high levels of wealth in the narrative of the male RS who entered the drug world to increase his income. Similarly, the elaborate heterotopic projects that Martha, the Squatter, designs are a clear indication of her aspiration to embrace normalcy at least partially. Martha politically contests the productive circuit while at the same time she proposes a different and healthy reality in which squatters are socially reintegrated. Similarly, the Travellers' talk of safe gates, fences and other strategies to protect their households are comparable to the mainstream society's construction of gated communities. Thus, normalcy is contested but at the same time aspired to. This aspirational aspect of the participants' identities adds further to their liminal *in fieri* status. Their relegation to interstitial spaces is, therefore, not simply material and social but more crucially it is conceptual as they are pursuing an alternative way of living while still struggling to escape from pressures from mainstream society to conform and aspiring to a different normalcy. The study highlights the extent to which these three liminal sets of individuals are caught in a tragic conundrum: while their lives are in many ways a testimony to the shortcomings of neoliberal capitalist society, at the same time, their very existence 'undercuts the very ideology of the post-industrial city itself' (Mair 1986: 244) and, as such, they constitute a political charge; however, this charge is not fully realized as, in their talk, these liminal individuals still feel the pressure, at least partially, to have dealings with mainstream society and become 'normal'. And, this is where their tragic condition lies.

Two key theoretical premises of this study are that space is both a discursively constructed entity and a physical reality and that any space is shaped by political and social forces. By focusing on both striated (i.e. orderly) and smooth (i.e. free) spaces, the study highlights the hegemonic use of space among liminal groups. In the case of the transient Travellers, in particular, their situation perpetuated a spatial discourse that privileged striated space, which was not in line with the needs of their mobile community. Harvey (1990) quotes Bourdieu stating that '[e]very established order tends to produce the naturalization of its own arbitrariness'; out of the normalizing mechanisms put into place by society comes the construction of limits and rules, the so called 'sense of reality' which is 'the basis of the most ineradicable adherence to the established order' (p. 268). The study demonstrates how the physical spaces occupied by the three liminal groups are not uncontested realities and how liminal individuals engage in a continuous negotiation with mainstream spatiality. While the case of Squatters is self-explanatory, with regards to RS a similar tension is evident in the refusal of some people to be housed even during the 2020 Covid-19 epidemic crisis. Accepting the Council's allocation to a particular part of town in the company of unknown people is a move not everyone is ready to make and some still prefer to live in a tent in a corner of a local park. The case of Gypsies and Travellers is also indicative of a spatial negotiation. They are accommodated in such striated spaces as Council sites but transform them according to their needs. From 2016 when the permanent site where this study was conducted opened and the time of writing, much has changed. Many Travellers have acquired massive, three or four room mobile homes which they have positioned in the space adjoining the amenity room built for them by the Council. From being striated and other-constructed, therefore, their space has now become more personalized and smooth organized as is according to their real growing needs.

A reflection on the methodology of a study with a social justice lens

How this study started and shaped up was discussed in the opening chapter while further details about the methodology were provided in the relevant chapter with the specifics of each group's data collection in the analysis sections. The researcher's complex positioning vis-à-vis the study has been commented on together with the impact their own concerns, shaped by their particular life histories, have on the formulation of the research questions and the approach. Furthermore, a study like the present one expresses a political commitment as confirmed by Tusting and Maybin (2007: 580), '[t]o date, much work associated with linguistic ethnography has been associated with broadly critical commitments'. In light of this, the side taken in the study is deliberately not objective but critical.

There is no easy recipe for a study like the present that comes from a social interest in the lives of those who do not belong and this investigation could not have been carried out had it not been accompanied by a strong commitment to these people. Echoing Cameron et al. (1993), this ethnographic study was one that 'worked *on, for, and with*' the people. The balance between an academic and a social focus was very delicate in this study. Working with the three sets of individuals discussed here meant caring about their condition and attempting to improve it. Obtaining the vetting of the council and working in collaboration with their staff was a necessary condition. Interviewing the Travelling women, however, was only just a tile in the mosaic, that was accompanied throughout the fieldwork by a number of community engagements such as educational activities for the Travelling children, gatherings for the Travelling community at large, or public workshops for the public to raise people's awareness. It also meant working in conjunction with those charities that are very close to the Travellers and have a preferred entry in the community like Friends Family and Travellers. Without these contacts and connections, this study would not have been possible.

The very same applies to the SH. Working as a volunteer in different forms was essential to the study, from distributing meals during the Covid-19 pandemic to provisionally housed individuals, offering engaging activities to the day centre clients, spending time in the centre just to establish a relation with the people and staff in it. Once again some of the interviews' observations were shared in many of the activities organized to sensitize the public to the issue of homelessness. In particular, a series of creative and self-reflective workshops for the clients of the same day centre where the study was conducted including acting, drawing, light physical exercise, writing for about two months was particularly successful. Run by community-engagement theatre company RAPT, the project consisted of a series of activities, which were filmed and which, as a participant, I observed ethnographically (Piazza in preparation). During the course of weeks and months, the participants opened up to tell small stories about themselves and invoked various identities within the context of the space and time we spent together. On that occasion, more interviews were collected, which were facilitated by the rapport established with the day centre clients. Activities and projects like the one described here therefore, on the one hand, can be realized only after engaging in research with these liminal people and understanding their aspirations and needs; on the other hand, they can provide non-intrusive and participatory ways to collect data that limit the risk of objectifying these individuals and aim to treat them with respect and equality.

Throughout many years some funding was made available by my institution (University of Sussex) to carry out social work with this study's liminal individuals in the belief that this would have an impact on their condition and public perceptions. In some cases, this was achieved as the council for instance changed their approach to allow more autonomy to the Travellers, while in the case of the SH the attempt to provide intellectually stimulating rather than solely vocational activities was very much in line with the policy of the day centre. Collecting the words of Martha, the Squatter, was laborious and I am very thankful to a friend, who had been a squatter himself, who introduced me to her. However, as I said in the relevant chapter, Squatters are people in a transient condition who are not too difficult to approach. Lingering outside an occupied space and starting a conversation with one of the people was an opportunity that presented itself after I had interviewed Martha and that could have led to further conversations with other squatters. In a completely different scenario, some years ago on a beach in Sicily I managed to connect with an itinerant immigrant vendor and through him to some others to whom I talked during their lunch break. In conclusion, a balance between tenacity and braveness is necessary and very often people are not reluctant to talk if approached with kindness and respect.

This study has its obvious shortcomings. The two most obvious ones are the relatively small number of interviewees and limited interview sites. However, this was never intended to be a thorough and exhaustive investigation; rather, the much more modest aim was to penetrate the inscrutable world of these liminal people whose lives are so little known and understood and, in so doing, open a small window on their existence. To this extent, the study does reveal the complexities and contradictions of the lives of liminal people.

As discussed, even classifying these individuals as 'groups' is potentially problematic in that it risks imposing a societal classification that reifies marginalization and prevents seeing the participants as unique individuals. The study further reinforces, therefore, concerns and doubts about the role of the researcher in undertaking decisions that can impact the data analysis.

A follow-up study would be very worthwhile. Extending the data base and collecting a more substantial corpus of interviews would be the first step forward. However, this study shows that conventional questionnaires and surveys and other more traditional data collection methods are unlikely to be useful given the sensitivity of the topic and the basic ethical issues that need to be addressed in research of this kind.

In conclusion, an imperfect research like the present one involves risky and intrinsically unethical decisions therefore I hope the readers who approach this book will bear these thoughts in mind and appreciate the overall goal of the study.

Notes

1 Introduction

1 http://www.qcc.cuny.edu/diversity/definition.html, accessed 29/12/2019.
2 Cf. Channel 4 *Dispatches* controversial documentary, 'The Truth about Traveller Crime' aired in April 2020 was responded to with a threat of legal action on the part of activists who claimed the programme 'set the community back by decades' and made it even more vulnerable to hate crime. Jasmine Andersson *The Independent* https://inews.co.uk/news/channel-4-dispatches-gypsy-documentary-has-set-community-back-decades-campaigners-2541751.

2 Theoretical framework

1 Butler and Fitzgerald's (2010) study of a family meal showing that identities are made 'operative in and through the moment-by-moment organization of specific sequences of action' (p. 2462) is one of many examples.
2 Cf. Rowles' (1983) research with the elderly residents of an Appalachian community or Bonauto et al.'s (1996) study on the correlation between place attachment and favourable perception of space among many others.
3 See for instance the interesting chapter on Paris as a collective representation by Milgram and Jodelet in Gieseking.

3 Methodology

1 Point in parentheses: (.) indicates a micro-pause of less than two tenths of a second,
Numbers in parentheses: (.) audible pause within utterances < 0.2 seconds,
(0.9) audible pause > 0.2 sec, with duration,
@ indicates laughter,
(Other non-verbal information is in brackets),
[inaudible] refers to indistinguishable or uncertain words,
(. . .) indicates deliberately missing text,
Square brackets: [ ] within a turn indicates the point where overlap occurs,

Equals sign = identifies a 'latching' or lack of interval between utterances,
Full colons:: denote an extension in the vowel or consonant sound,
CAPITALS indicate specific emphasis and change in volume,
Smaller fonts indicate softer volume,
^ indicates noticeable rising intonation,
ᵛ indicates noticeable falling intonation,
Italicised word indicate relevant words or phrases.

2 My thanks go to my friend Philip Morgan with whom it was very rewarding to work and whose enthusiasm in the cause of the Homeless inspired me.

4 Locating the transient self in a transient heterotopia: Squatting as an affective and entrepreneurial proposition

1 http://www.thesite.org/housing/your-place/squatting-7971.html accessed 12/06/16.
2 Do It Yourself, the British tradition of doing house repairs without resorting to professionals.
3 There are no exact and reliable figures on the numbers of squatters in the UK. Some estimates put it at around 20,000.
4 Camelot HQ squatted https://www.squatter.org.uk/ accessed 07/02/2017.
5 Following Toolan's (1997) use of COBUILD.
6 Stuart's Ted Talk 17 Sept 2012 https://www.youtube.com/watch?v=cWC_zDdF74s.
7 Wortham (2001) identifies linguistic and pragmatic elements indexing the various levels of positioning.
8 This is a quick procedural ruling of Her Majesty's Court Service whereby if an order is made, anybody occupying some premises without consent must leave them within twenty-four hours or they will commit a criminal offence.

5 'We don't need a castle. We need a home.' Desire for place in a Travellers' transit site

1 In spite of the etymology and the specific meaning of the word Gypsy and Travellers, the interchangeable use of the two terms is noticeable even among Travellers' themselves. The following extract from an interview with an English Romany woman is a good example.

Interviewer. Right. So, what do you call yourself? Because you're not a Traveller.
  What do you- I mean tell me about this definition.
English Gypsy. We're an English Gypsy.
Int. You're an English gypsy. Is it because you're not Irish?
EG. Because we're not Irish.

> Int. So wouldn't you call yourself English Traveller?
> EG. Yeah, we are . . . we are still a Traveller Gypsy all the same.
> Int. All the same, okay.
> EG. But just we're English and they're Irish.

2   As in the previous chapter, all names are pseudonyms.
3   https://www.nuj.org.uk/documents/briefing-gypsies-roma-and-irish-travellers-in-the-media/.
4   https://www.bbc.co.uk/news/av/education-47828886/my-kids-were-called-trailer-trash accessed 07/04/2019.
5   https://www.equalityhumanrights.com/sites/default/files/is-england-fairer-2016-most-disadvantaged-groups-gypsies-travellers-roma.pdf.
6   Paper delivered at Gypsy, Traveller and Roma history month Conference Brighton (20 June 2019).
7   https://www.parliament.uk/business/committees/committees-a-z/commons-select/women-and-equalities-committee/inquiries/parliament-2017/inequalities-faced-by-gypsy-roma-and-traveller-communities-17-19.
8   https://www.google.co.uk/search?q=map+of+horsdean+travellers+site&source=lnms&tbm=isch&sa=X&ved=0ahUKEwjwk-a0-_3SAhVlIcAKHXbzAq8Q_AUIBygC&biw=670&bih=406&dpr=1.25#spf=1 accessed 30/3/17.
9   The reading of space that I propose here doesn't express a critique of the Council staff to whom I am truly indebted for their generous assistance and support during my years of study of the Travellers' community. I am reading spatial organization against the institutional context in which it is embedded, in the belief that the vision of space that such institutions, as the Council, reflect simply belongs to a cultural tradition of space interpretation.
10 In legal terms, this means that a person, who has resided at least six of the last twelve months in a particular location, has been employed, has family relations or has special circumstances is entitled to the Local Authorities' housing support in that area. Therefore, on the very basis of the extended stay in the city, Travellers can claim entitlement to a space in the planned permanent site.

7 Rough Sleepers: 'Homeless is what I am, not who I am.' Rough sleeping as a liminal condition not the essence of being

1   https://england.shelter.org.uk/__data/assets/pdf_file/0011/48458/Factsheet_Street_Homelessness_Aug_2006.pdf.
2   Shelter factsheet at Shelterhttps://england.shelter.org.uk/__data/assets/pdf_file/0011/48458/Factsheet_Street_Homelessness_Aug_2006.pdf accessed 31/12/2019.
3   Philip Morgan.

References

'A Briefing: Gypsies, Roma and Irish Travellers in the media', 2012, https://www.nuj.org.uk/documents/briefing-gypsies-roma-and-irish-travellers-in-the-media

Adams, P. (2017), 'Place and extended agency, in N. Enfield and P. Kockelman (eds.), *Distributed Agency*, 213–220, Oxford: Oxford University Press.

Agha, A. (2007), *Language and Social Relations*, Cambridge: Cambridge University Press.

Agnew, J. and Duncan, J. eds. (1989) *The Power of Place: Bringing Together Geographical and Sociological Imaginations*, Oxford/New York: Routledge.

Ahearn, L. (2010), 'Agency and language', in J. Jaspers et al. (eds.), *Society and Language Use*, 28–48, Amsterdam/Philadelphia: John Benjamins.

Al-Bantany, N. (2013), The use of commissive speech acts and its politeness implication: A case of Banten Gubernatorial candidate debate', *Passage*, 1(2): 21–34.

Allweil, Y. and Kallus, R. (2008), 'Public-space heterotopias. Heterotopias of masculinity along the Tel Aviv shoreline', in Allweil, Y. and R. Kallus (eds.), *Public-space heterotopias. Heterotopia and the city: public space in a postcivil society*, 191–201, Milton Park, England: Routledge.

Amin, A. and Thrift, N. (2002), *Cities: Re-imagining the Urban*, Cambridge: Polity Press.

Anfara, V. (1997), 'Urban schools and liminality', *National Forum of Teacher Education Journal*, retrieved from http://www.nationalforum.com/Electronic%20Journal%20Volumes/Anafara,%20Jr.%20Vincent%20A%20Urban%20Schools%20and%20Liminality.pdf. (02/01/2020)

Appadurai, A. (2013), 'The Future as Cultural Fact: Essays on the Global Condition', *Rassegna Italiana di Sociologia*, 4: 649–650.

Archer, W. and Parry, R. (2019), 'Blame attributions and mitigated confessions: The discursive construction of guilty admissions in celebrity TV confessionals', *Discourse and Communication,* 13(6): 591–611.

Atkinson, P. and Delamont, S. (2006), 'Rescuing narrative from qualitative research', *Narrative Inquiry* 16(1): 164–172.

Auer, P. (2005), 'A postscript: Code-switching and social identity', *Journal of Pragmatics* 37(3): 403–410.

Bakhtin, M. (1981), *The Dialogic Imagination: Four Essays*, in M. Holquist, (ed) Austin, TX: University of Texas Press.

Bakhtin, M. (2002), 'Forms of Time and of the Chronotope in the Novel: Notes toward a Historical Poetics, 1937–38', in M. Holquist (ed), *The Dialogic Imagination*, 84–254, Austin: University of Texas Press.

Bamberg, M. (1997), 'Positioning between structure and performance', *Journal of Narrative and Life History*, 7: 335–342.

Bamberg, M. (2004), 'Talk, small stories, and adolescent identities' *Human Development*, 47: 366–369.

Bamberg, M. and Andrews, M. (2004), *Considering counter-narratives: Narrating, Resisting, Making Sense*, Amsterdam/Philadelphia: John Benjamins.

Bamberg, M. and Georgakopoulou, A. (2008), 'Small stories as a new perspective in narrative and identity analysis', *Text & Talk*, 28(3): 377–396.

Barrett et al. (2010), 'The New Homelessness Revisited', *Annual Review of Sociology*, 36: 501–521.

Bauman, R. (1986), *Story, Performance, and Event: Contextual Studies of Oral Narrative*, Cambridge: Cambridge University Press.

Baxter, J. (2008), 'Is it all tough talking at the top? A poststructuralist analysis of the construction of speaker identities of British business leaders within interview narratives', *Gender and Language* 1 (3): 197–222.

Beck, U. (1992), *The Risk Society: Towards a New Modernity*, London: SAGE.

Bednarek, M. and Caple, H. (2014), 'Why do news values matter? Towards a new methodological framework for analysing news discourse in Critical Discourse Analysis and beyond', *Discourse & Society*, 25(2): 135–158.

Bednarek, M. and Caple, H. (2017), *The Discourse of News Values*, Oxford: Oxford University Press.

Benwell, B. (2011), 'Masculine identity and identification as ethnomethodological phenomena: revisiting Cameron and Kulick', *Gend. Lang*, 5: 187–210.

Benwell, B. and Stokoe, E. (2006), *Discourse and Identity*, Edinburgh: Edinburgh University Press.

Berger, P. L. and Luckmann, T. ([1966]1991), *The Social Construction of Reality: A Treatise in the Sociology of Knowledge*, London: Penguin.

Bermudez, J. L. (2016), *Understanding 'I'*, Oxford: Oxford University Press.

Bernstein, B. (1964), 'Elaborated and Restricted Codes: Their Social Origins and Some Consequences', *American Anthropologist Part 2*: *The Ethnography of Communication*, 66(6): 55–69.

Bettis, P. (1996), 'Urban students, liminality, and the postindustrial context', *Sociology of Education*, 69(2): 105–125.

Biber, D. (1993), 'Representativeness in corpus design', *Literary and Linguistic Computing*. 8(4): 243–157.

Billig, M. (1997), 'The Dialogic Unconscious: Psychoanalysis, Discursive Psychology and the Nature of Repression', *British Journal of Social Psychology*, 36, 139–159.

Block, D. (2015), 'Researching language and identity', in B. Paltridge and A. Phakiti (eds.), *Research Methods in Applied Linguistics*, 527–540, London: Bloomsbury.

Blommaert, J. (2005), *Discourse*, Cambridge: Cambridge University Press.

Blommaert, J. (2001), 'Investigating narrative inequality: African asylum seekers' stories in Belgium', *Discourse & Society*, 12(4): 413–449.

Blommaert, J. (2013) *Ethnography, Superdiversity and Linguistic Landscapes: Chronicles of Complexity*, Bristol: Multilingual Matters.

Blommaert, J. (2015), 'Chronotopes, scales, and complexity in the study of language in society', *Annual Review of Anthropology*, 44: 105–16.

Blommaert, J. and Jie, D. (2010), *Ethnographic Fieldwork: A Beginner's Guide*, Bristol: Multilingual Matters.

Blommaert, J. and Rampton, B. (2011), 'Language and superdiversity', *Diversities*. 13(2): 1–21.

Blommaert, J. et al. (2000), 'Spaces of multilingualism', *Language & Communication,* 25: 197–216.

Bloom, J. (1990), 'The relationship of social support and health', *Social Science & Medicine*, 30(5): 635–637.

Boccagni, P. (2015), '(Super)diversity and the migration–social work nexus: a new lens on the field of access and inclusion?', *Journal Ethnic and Racial Studies,* 38(4): 608–620.

Bonautio, M. et al. (1996), 'Identity processes and environmental threat: The effects of nationalism and local identity upon perception of beach pollution', *Journal of Community and Applied Social Psychology*, 6: 157–175.

Bourdieu, P. (1977), 'Symbolic Power', *Critique of Anthropology,* 13–14 (summer): 77–85.

Boydell, K. (2000), 'Narratives of identity: Re-presentation of self in people who are homeless', *Qualitative Health Research*, 10(1): 26–38.

Boyer, C. (2008), 'The many mirrors of Foucault and their architectural reflections', in M. Dehaene and L. De Cauter (eds.), *Heterotopia and the City: Public Space in a Postcivil Society,* 53–75, London and New York: Routledge.

Branigan, E. (1992), *Narrative Comprehension and Film*, London, England: Routledge.

Breakwell, G. (1986), *Coping with Threatened Identities,* London: Psychology Press.

Brenmer, L. (2010), *Writing the City into being: Essays on Johannesburg, 1998–2008*, Johannesburg: Fourthwall Books.

Brewer, M. and Gardner, W. (1996), 'Who Is This "We"? Levels of Collective Identity and Self Representations', *Journal of Personality and Social Psychology,* 71(1), 83–93.

Briggs, C. (1997), 'Notes on a "confession" on the construction of gender, sexuality, and violence in an infanticide case', *Pragmatics*, 7(4): 519–546.

Brown, P. and Levinson, S. (1987), *Politeness: Some Universals in Language Usage,* Cambridge: Cambridge University Press.

Bucholtz, M. and Hall, K. (2004), 'Language and identity', in A. Duranti (ed), *A Companion to Linguistic Anthropology*, 369–394, Malden, MA: Blackwell.

Bucholtz, M. and Hall, K. (2005), 'Identity and interaction: A sociocultural linguistic approach', *Discourse studies*, 7(4–5): 585–614.

Butler, J. (1987), *Subjects of Desire: Hegelian Reflections in Twentieth-century France*, New York: Columbia University Press.

Butler, J. (1990), *Gender Trouble. Feminism and the Subversion of Identity*, New York: Routledge Press.

Butler, W. and Fitzgerald, R. (2010), 'Membership-in-action: Operative identities in a family meal', *Journal of Pragmatics,* 42: 2462–2474.
Cameron, D. and Kulick, D. (2003), *Language and Sexuality,* Cambridge, UK: Cambridge University Press.
Cameron, D., Frazer, E., Harvey, P., Rampton, B. and Richardson, K. (1993), 'Ethics, advocacy and empowerment: Issues of method in researching language', *Language and Communication,* 13(2): 145–162.
Canakis, C. (2015), 'The desire for identity and the identity of desire: Language, gender, and sexuality in the Greek context', *Gender and Language,* 9(1): 59–81.
Capps, L. and Ochs, E. (1995), *Constructing Panic. The Discourse of Agorophobia,* Cambridge, Mass/London: Harvard University Press.
Casey, R. (2007), 'Resistance and identity: homeless women's use of use of public spaces', *People, Place & Policy Online,* 1/2: 90–97.
Casey, R. et al. (2008), 'Homeless Women in Public Spaces: Strategies of Resistance', *Housing Studies,* 23(6): 899–916.
Cattaneo, C. and Martinez, M. (2014), 'Squatting as an alternative to capitalism, an introduction', in Cattaneo, C. and Martinez, M. (eds.), *The Squatters' Movement in Europe. Commons and Autonomy as Alternatives to Capitalism,* 1–25 London/New York: Pluto Press.
Cenzatti, M. (2008), 'Heterotopias of difference', in M. Dehaene and L. De Cauter (eds.), *Heterotopia and the City – Urban Theory and the Transformations of Public Space,* 1–13, Oxford, UK/Cambridge, MA: Blackwell.
Cloke, P. et al. (2008), 'Performativity and affect in the homeless city', *Environment and Planning D: Society and Space,* 26: 241–263.
Cogo, A. (2012), 'ELF and super-diversity: A case study of ELF multilingual practices from a business context', *Journal of English as a Lingua Franca* 1/2: 287–313.
Cook-Sather, A. (2006), 'Newly betwixt and between: revising liminality in the context of a teacher preparation program', *Anthropology and Education Quarterly,* 37: 110–127.
Copland, F. and Creese, A. (2015), *Linguistic Ethnography: Collecting, Analysing and Presenting Data,* Los Angeles/London: Sage.
Costas, J. (2013), 'Problematizing mobility: A metaphor of stickiness, non-places and the kinetic elite' *Organization Studies,* 2013, 0(0): 1–19.
Crang, M. (2002), 'Qualitative methods: the new orthodoxy?', *Progress in Human Geography,* 26(5): 647–655.
Creasap, K. (2012), 'Social Movement Scenes: Place-Based Politics and Everyday Resistance', *Sociology Compass* 6(2) 182–191.
Creese, A. (2008), 'Linguistic Ethnography', in K. A. King and N. H. Hornberger (eds.), *Encyclopedia of Language and Education, Volume 10: Research Methods in Language and Education,* 229–241, New York: Springer.
Creese, A. and Blackledge, A. (2016), 'A linguistic ethnography of identity: Adopting a heteroglossic frame' in S. Preece, S. (ed), *The Routledge Handbook of Language and Identity,* 272–288, London: Routledge.

Cresswell, T. (2006), 'The right to mobility: the production of mobility in the courtroom', *Antipode*, 735–754.

Crul, M. (2016), 'Super-diversity vs. assimilation: how complex diversity in majority-minority cities challenges the assumptions of assimilation', *Journal of Ethnic and Migration Studies*, 42(1): 54–68.

Czarniawska, B. and Mazza, C. (2003), 'Consulting as a liminal space', *Human Relations*, 56(3): 267–290.

Davies, B. and Harré, R. (1990), 'Positioning: The discursive production of selves', *Journal for the theory of social behaviour*, 20(1): 43–63.

Davis, M. (1990), *City of Quartz: Excavating the Future in Los Angeles*, London/New York: Verso.

Davis, M. (1992), 'Fortress Los Angeles: The Militarization of Urban Space', in M. Sorkin (ed), *Variations on a Theme Park*, 154–180, New York: Noonday Press.

De Fina, A. (2003), *Identity in Narrative: A Study of Immigrant Discourse*, Amsterdam/Philadelphia: John Benjamins.

De Fina, A. (2009a), 'Narratives in interview – The case of accounts. For an interactional approach to narrative genres', *Narrative Inquiry*, 19:2 (2009): 233–258.

De Fina, A. (2009b), 'From space to spatialization in narrative studies', in J. Collins et al. (eds.), *Globalization and language in contact, scale migration and communicative practices*, 109–129, Harrisburg, PA: Continuum.

De Fina, A. (2015), 'Narrative and identities', in De Fina, A. and Georgakopoulou, A. (eds.), *The Handbook of Narrative Analysis*, 351–368, London: Blackwell.

De Fina, A. (2019), 'Discourse and Identity', in C. A. Chapelle (ed) *The Encyclopedia of Applied Linguistics*, 1–8, Hoboken, N. J.: John Wiley & Sons.

De Fina, A. and Georgakopoulou, A. (2008), 'Analysing narratives as practices', *Qualitative Research*, 8(3): 379–387.

De Fina, A. and Georgakopoulou, A. (2011), *Analyzing Narrative: Discourse and Sociolinguistic Perspectives*, Cambridge: Cambridge University Press.

De Fina, A. and S. Perrino, S. (2017), 'Introduction: Interviews vs "natural" contexts: A false dilemma', *Language in Society*, 40(1): 1–11.

Dee, E.T.C., (2013), 'Moving towards Criminalisation and Then What? Examining Dominant Discourses on Squatting in England', in Squatting Europe Kollective (eds.), *Squatting in Europe: Radical Spaces*, 247–267, Urban Struggles. Wivenhoe: Minor Compositions.

Dee, E.T.C. and Debelle. G. (2015), 'Examining mainstream media discourses on the squatters' movements in Barcelona and London', *Interface 7 (1): 117–143*.

Dehaene, M. and De Cauter, L. (2008), 'Heterotopia in a postcivil society', in M. Dehaene and L. De Cauter (eds.), *Heterotopia and the City: Public space in a Postcivil Society*, 3–9, Oxon: Routledge.

Dehaene, M. and De Cauter, L. eds. (2008), *Heterotopia and the City: Public Space in a Postcivil Society*, Oxon: Routledge.

Deleuze and Guattari (1988/2016), *A Thousand Plateaus: Capitalism and Schizophrenia*. Minnesota: University of Minnesota Press.

Denzin, N. and Lincoln, Y. (2011), *The SAGE Handbook of Qualitative Research*, London: Sage.

Deppermann, A. (2013), 'Editorial: Positioning in Narrative Interaction', in M. Bamberg (ed), *Narrative Inquiry*, 1–15, Amsterdam: John Benjamins.

Deutsche, R. (1990), 'Architecture of the evicted', *Strategies*, 3: 159–184.

Devereux, E. (2005), 'Thinking outside the charity box: media coverage of homelessness', *European Journal of Homelessness*, 9(2): 261–273.

Dixon J. and Durrheim K. (2000), 'Displacing place-identity: A discursive approach to locating self and other', *British Journal of Social Psychology*, 39: 27–44.

Dörnyei, Z. (2007), *Research methods in applied linguistics: Quantitative, qualitative and mixed methodologies*, Oxford: Oxford University Press.

Doron, P. (2008), '"…those marvellous empty zones on the edge of our cities": heterotopia and the "dead zone"', in M. Dehaene and L. De Cauter (eds.), *Heterotopia and the City*, 203–214, London/New York: Routledge.

Du Bois, J. (2007), 'The stance triangle', in R. Englebretson (ed), *Stancetaking in Discourse: Subjectivity, Evaluation, Interaction*, 139–182, Amsterdam/Philadelphia: John Benjamins.

Duncan, J. S. (2005/1983), 'Men without property: the tramp's classification and use of urban space', in Lin, J. and Mele, C. (eds.), *The Urban Sociology Reader*, 164–172, London, Routledge.

Duran Eppler, E. and Codó, E. (2016), 'Challenges for language and identity researchers in the collection and transcription of spoken interaction', in S. Preece (ed), *The Routledge Handbook of Language and Identity*, 304–319, London: Routledge.

Eberle, J. (2017), 'Narrative, desire, ontological security, transgression: fantasy as a factor in international politics', *Journal of International Relations and Development*, https://doi.org/10.1057/s41268-017-0104-2.

Eckert, P. and McConnell-Ginet, S. (2013), *Language and Gender*, Cambridge: Cambridge University Press.

Edwards, D. and Stokoe, E. (2004), 'Discursive psychology, focus group interviews, and participants' categories', *British Journal of Developmental Psychology*, 22: 499–507.

Edwards, J. (2009), *Language and Identity*, Cambridge: Cambridge University Press.

Enfield, N. (2017), 'Elements of agency', in N. Enfield and P. Kockelman (eds.), *Distributed Agency*, 3–8, Oxford: Oxford University Press.

Fairclough, N. (2010), *Critical Discourse Analysis: The Critical Study of Language*, Harlow: Longman.

Farrington, A. and Robinson, W. P. (1999), 'Homelessness and strategies of identity maintenance: A participant observation study', *Journal of Community and Applied Social Psychology*, 9(3): 175–194.

Feagin, C. (2006), 'Entering the Community: Fieldwork', in J. K. Chambers, P. Trudgill, and N. Schilling-Estes (eds.), *The Handbook of Language Variation and Change* 20–39, Malden, MA: Blackwell.

Feagin, J. R. (2006), *Systemic racism: A theory of oppression*, New York: Routledge.
Forsyth, D. (2014), *Group Dynamics Belmont*, CA: Wadsworth Cengage Learning.
Foucault, M. ([1966/7] 1986), 'Of Other Spaces', *Diacritics*, 16:1 (1986): 22–7.
Foucault, M. (1975), *Discipline and Punish*, New York: Vintage.
Foucault, M. (2008/1967), 'Of other spaces' (L. De Cauter & M. Dehaene, Trans.), in M. Dehaene and De Cauter (eds.), *Heterotopia and the City: Public Space in a Postcivil Society*, 13–29, New York, NY: Routledge, (original work published 1967).
Fox, A. (1992), 'The Jukebox of History: Narratives of Loss and Desire in the Discourse of Country Music', *Popular Music*, 11(1): 53–72.
Fox Tree, J. and Schrock, J. (2002), 'Basic meanings of you know and I mean', *Journal of Pragmatics*, 34: 727–747.
Frankfurt, H. (2010), *On Truth*, London: Pimlico.
Freeland, N. (2002), 'The Politics of Dirt in "Mary Barton" and "Ruth"', *Studies in English Literature, 1500–1900* 42(4), 799–818.
Freeman, M. (1998), 'Mythical time, historical time, and the narrative fabric of the self', *Narrative Inquiry*, 8(1): 27–50.
Freeman, M. (2019), 'Narrative as a Mode of Understanding Method, Theory, Praxis', in A. De Fina and A. Georgakopoulou (eds.), *The Handbook of Narrative Analysis*, 21–37, Hoboken, N.J.: John Wiley & Sons.
Fuller, N. (2004), 'Identidades en tránsito: femineidad y masculinidad en el Perú actual [Identities in transit: femininity and masculinity in current Peru]' in: Fuller, N. (ed), *Jerarquías en Jaque: Los estudios de género en el área andina*, 189–220, Lima: Red para el Desarrollo de las Ciencias Sociales en el Perú.
Gajardo, C. and Oteíza, T. (2017), 'The ideological construction of mother identity in the discourse of four women of the lower socio-economic group from Santiago, Chile', *Discourse & Society*, 28(2): 142–161.
Garkinkel, H. (1967), *Studies in Ethnomethodology*, Englewood Cliffs, NJ: Prentice-Hall.
Garsten, C. (1999), 'Betwixt and between: Temporary employees as liminal subjects in flexible organizations', *Organization Studies*, 20(4): 601–617.
Gee, J.P. (2005), *An Introduction to Discourse Analysis*, New York/London: Routledge.
Georgakopoulou, A. (2003), 'Looking back when looking ahead: Adolescents' identity management in narrative practices', in J. Androutsopoulos and A. Georgakopoulou (eds.), *Discourse Constructions of Youth Identities*, 75–91, Amsterdam/Philadelphia: John Benjamins.
Georgakopoulou, A. (2006), 'Thinking big with small stories in narrative and identity analysis', *Narrative Inquiry*, 16: 129–137.
Georgakopoulou, A. (2007), *Small Stories, Interaction and Identities*, Amsterdam/Philadelphia: Johns Benjamins.
Georgalou, M. (2017), *Discourse and Identity in Facebook*, London/New York: Bloomsbury.
Gibson, J. (2014), 'The theory of affordances' in J. J Gieseking et al. (eds.), *The People, Place and Space Reader*, 56–60, New York/London: Routledge.

Giddens, A. (1991), *Modernity and Self-Identity: Self and Society in the Late Modern Age*, Stanford, CA: Stanford University Press.
Gieryn, T. (2000), 'A space for place in sociology', *Annual Review of Sociology*, 26: 463–496.
Goffman, E. ([1963] 1986), *Stigma: Notes on the Management of Spoiled Identity*, New York/London/Toronto: Simon & Schuster Inc.
Goffman, E. (1967), *Interaction Ritual: Essays on Face-to-face Behavior*, Chicago: Aldine.
Goffman, E. (1981), *Forms of Talk*, Philadelphia: University of Pennsylvania Press.
Gramsci, A. (1971), *Selections from the Prison Notebooks*, translated and edited by Q. Hoare and G. Nowell Smith, New York: International Publishers.
Gumperz, J. (1982), *Discourse Strategies*, Cambridge: Cambridge University Press.
Gumperz, J. (1999), 'On interactional sociolinguistic method', in S. Srikant Sarangi and C. Roberts (eds.), *Talk, Work and Institutional Order*, 453–472, Berlin: Mouton de Gruyter.
Hall, K. and Bucholtz, M. (2012), *Gender Articulated: Language and the Socially Constructed Self*, New York/London: Routledge.
Hall, L. (2009), 'Looking for answers: Striking the right balance', *National Oral History Association New Zealand Journal*, 21: 1–11.
Hall, N. et al. eds. (2014), *The Routledge International Handbook on Hate Crime*, London: Routledge.
Hall, S. (1996), 'Introduction. Who needs identity?', in S. Hall and P. du Gay (eds.), *Questions of Cultural Identity*, 15–30, London: Sage.
Hall, S. (1997), 'The work of representation', in S. Hall (ed), *Representation: Cultural Representations and Signifying Practices*, 13–64, London: Sage.
Halverson, J. et al. (2013), 'Mediated Martyrs of the Arab Spring: New Media, Civil Religion, and Narrative in Tunisia and Egypt', *Journal of Communication*, 63: 312–332.
Harvey, D. (1990), 'Flexible accumulation through urbanization: reflections on "postmodernism" in the American city', *Theater, Theatricality, and Architecture*, Perspecta, 26: 251–272.
Harvey, D. (2005), 'Spacetime and the world', in J. Gieseking et al. (eds.) (2014), *The People, Place, and Space Reader*, 12–16, London: Routledge.
Hays, S. (1996), *The Cultural Contradictions of Motherhood*, New Haven, CT: Yale University Press
Heigham, J. and Croker, R. (2009), *Qualitative Research in Applied Linguistics: A Practical Introduction*, Houndmills, Basingstoke/New York: Palgrave.
Hester, R. (2000), *Social Control of New Age Travellers*, PhD, University of Birmingham.
Hester, S. and Eglin, P. (1997), *Culture in action: Studies in membership categorization analysis*, Washington, DC: International Institute of Studies in Ethnomethodology and Conversation Analysis and University Press of America.

Hirst, A. and Humphreys, M. (2013), 'Putting power in its place: the centrality of edgelands', *Organization studies*, 34 (10): 1505–1527.

Hocking, B. et al. (2019), 'Place-identity and urban policy: Sharing leisure spaces in the "post-conflict" city', in R. Piazza (ed), *Discourses of Identity in Liminal Places and Spaces*, 166–192, London/New York: Routledge.

Hopper, K. (1991), 'Symptoms, survival and the redefinition of public space: a feasibility study of homeless people at a metropolitan airport', *Urban Anthropology*, 20: 155–175.

Hoskins, G. and Maddern J. F. (2011), 'Immigration stations: the regulation and commemoration of mobility at Angel Island, San Francisco and Ellis Island, New York', *Geographies of Mobilities* file:///C:/Users/Roberta/Downloads/Immigration_Stations_the_regulation_and%20(2).pdf.

Hult, F. (2014), 'Drive-thru linguistic landscaping: Constructing a linguistically dominant place in a bilingual space', *International Journal of Bilingualism*, 18(5): 507–523.

Human Rights Commission report 2016, https://www.equalityhumanrights.com/sites/default/files/is-england-fairer-2016-most-disadvantaged-groups-gypsies-travellers-roma.pdf

Hunziker, M. et al. (2007), 'Space and Place – Two Aspects of the Human-landscape Relationship' in F. Kienast, O. Wildi and S. Ghosh (eds.), *A Changing World. Challenges for Landscape Research*, 47–62, Dordrecht: Springer.

Hutchby, I. and Wooffitt, R. (2008), *Conversational Analysis*, Oxford: Polity Press.

Irving, A. and Young, T. (2004), '"Perpetual liminality": Re-readings of subjectivity and diversity in clinical social work classrooms', *Smith College Studies in Social Work* (Pedagogy and Diversity special issue) 74(2): 213–227.

Islam, A. (2017) 'Constructing narratives through story telling: A study of refugees in Estonia', *Anthropological Notebooks*, 23 (2): 67–81.

Iveson, M. and Cornish, F. (2016), 'Re-building bridges: homeless people's views on the role of vocational and educational activities in their everyday lives', *Journal of Community and Applied Social Psychology*, 26: 253–267.

James, Z. (2007), 'Policing marginal spaces: controlling Gypsies and Travellers', *Criminology & Criminal Justice*, 7: 367–89.

Jenks, C. (2011), *Transcribing Talk and Interaction: Issues in the Representation of Communication Data*, Amsterdam/Philadelphia: John Benjamins.

Johnstone, B. (2016), 'Enregisterment: How linguistic items become linked with ways of speaking', *Lang Linguist Compass,* 10: 632–643.

Johnstone, B. Andrus, J. and Danielson, A. (2006), 'Mobility, Indexicality, and the Enregisterment of "Pittsburghese"', *Journal of English Linguistics*, 34(2): 77–104.

Johnstone, B. and Kielsling, S. (2008), 'Indexicality and experience: Exploring the meanings of /aw/-monophthogization in Pittsburgh', *Journal of Sociolinguistics*, 12(1): 5–33.

Johnstone, B. (2004), 'Place, globalization, and linguistic variation'. In Fought, C. (ed) *Sociolinguistic Variation*. 65–83, Oxford: Oxford University Press.

Jones, T. and Newburn, T. (2001), *Widening Access: Improving Police Relations with Hard to Reach Groups*, London: Home Office.

Joseph, J. (2004), *Language and Identity*, Houndmills, Basingstoke: Palgrave.

Juhila, K. (2004), 'Talking Back to Stigmatized Identities: Negotiation of Culturally Dominant Categorizations in Interviews with Shelter Residents', *Qualitative Social Work*, 3(3): 259–275.

Kabachnik, P. (2009), 'To choose, fix, or ignore culture? The cultural politics of Gypsy and Traveler mobility in England', *Social and Cultural Geography*, 10, No (4): 461–479.

Kabachnik, P. (2012), 'Nomads and mobile places: Disentangling place, space and mobility', *Identities: Global Studies in Culture and Power*, 19(2): 210–228.

Kiesling, S. (2011), 'The interactional construction of desire as gender', in B. McElhinny and A. Weatherall (eds.), *Gender and Language*, 211–238, Sheffield: Equinox.

Kiesling, S. (2018), 'Masculine stances and the linguistics of affect: on masculine ease', NORMA, DOI: 10.1080/18902138.2018.1431756.

Knowles, C. and Alexander, C. (2005), *Making race matter: bodies, space and identity*, Houndsmill, Basingstoke: Palgrave Macmillan.

Knowles, M. and Moon, R. (2004), *Introducing Metaphor*, London/New York: Routledge.

Kockelman, P. (2017), 'Semiotic agency' in N. Enfield and P. Kockelman (eds.), *Distributed Agency*, 25–38, Oxford: Oxford University Press.

Korpela, K. (1989), 'Place-identity as a product of environmental self-regulation', *Journal of Environmental Psychology*, 9: 241–256.

Koven, M. (2019), 'Narrating desire for place: Chronotopes of desire for the Portuguese homeland before and after "return"', in R. Piazza (ed), *Discourses of Identity in Liminal Places and Spaces*, 42–63, London/New York: Routledge.

Kramer, A. (2014), 'The observers and the observed: The "dual vision" of the mass observation project', *Sociological Research Online*, 19(3): 7, http://www.socresonline.org.uk/19/3/7.html.

Kristeva, J. (1980), *Desire in Language: A Semiotic Approach to Literature and Art*, London: Backwell.

Kulick D. (2000), 'Gay and lesbian language', *Annu. Rev. Anthropol.* 29: 243–85.

Kulick D. (2014), 'Language and desire', in S. Ehrlich, M. Meyerhoff and J. Holmes (eds.), *The Handbook of Language, Gender and Sexuality*, 68–84, Malden, MA: Wiley-Blackwell.

Labov, W. (1963), 'The social motivation of a sound change', *word*, 19:3, 273–309.

Labov, W. and Waletzky, J. (1997), 'Narrative analysis: oral versions of personal experience', *Journal of Narrative & Life History*, 7(1–4): 3–38.

Lacan, J. (1977), *The mirror stage as formative of the I. E crits: A selection*, (A. Sheridan, Trans.), New York, NY: W. W. Norton.

Lahlou, S. (2017), 'How agency is distributed through installations', in N. Enfield and P. Kockelman (eds.), *Distributed Agency*, 221–229, Oxford: Oxford University Press.

Lawless, E. (1993) *Holy Women, Wholly Women: Sharing Ministries through Life Stories and Reciprocal Ethnography*. Boston, University of Pennsylvania Press.

Lefebvre, H. (1974/1984), *The Production of Space*, translated by Donald Nicholson-Smith, Oxford: Blackwell.

Lefebvre, H. (1991), *The Production of Space*, Oxford: Blackwell.

Lemke, J. (2008), 'Identity, development and desire: Critical questions', in C. R. Caldas-Coulthard and R. Ledema (eds.), *Identity Trouble*, 17–42, Houndmills, Basingstoke: Palgrave.

Liebscher, G. and Dailey-O'Cain, J. (2013), *Language, Space and Identity in Migration*, London: Palgrave.

Llamas, C. and Watt, D. (2012), 'Introduction', in C. Llamas and D. Watt (eds.), *Language and Identities*, 1–8, Edinburgh: Edinburgh University Press.

Llamas, C. and Watt, D. eds. (2012), *Language and Identities*, Edinburgh: Edinburgh University Press.

Low, S. (2001), 'The edge and the center: Gated communities and the discourse of urban fear', *American Anthropologist*, 103(1): 45–58.

Low, S. (2008), 'The gated community as heterotopia', in M. Dehaene and L. De Cauter (eds.), *Heterotopia and the city: Public space in a postcivil society*, 153–163, Milton Park, England: Routledge.

Low, S. (2014), 'Spatializing culture', in J. J Gieseking et al. (eds.), *The People, Place and Space Reader*, 34–38, New York/London: Routledge.

Lyotard, F. (1984), *The Postmodern Condition: A Report on Knowledge*, Translated by G. Bennington and B. Massumi. Minneapolis: University of Minnesota Press.

Mair A, (1986), 'The homeless and the post-industrial city', *Political Geography Quarterly*, 5:351–368.

Malkki, L. H. (1992), 'National Geographic: The rooting of peoples and the territorialisation of national identity among scholars and refugees', *Cultural Anthropology*, 7(1): 24–44.

Manning, K. (2000), *Rituals, Ceremonies, and Cultural Meaning In Higher Education*, Westport, CT/London: Bergin & Garvey.

Martin Rojo, L. (2014) 'Taking over the square', *Journal of Language and Politics*, 13(4): 623–652.

Martin Rojo, L. (2016), *Occupy: The Spatial Dynamics of Discourse in Global Protest Movements*, Amsterdam/Philadelphia: John Benjamins.

Martin, J. R., Matthiessen, C. and Painter, C. (1997), *Working with Functional Grammar*, London: Arnold.

Martin, J. and White, P. (2005), *The Language of Evaluation*, London: Palgrave.

Maruna, S. (2011), 'Re-entry as a rite of passage', *Punishment & Society*, 13(1): 3–28.

Maslow, A. H. (1954, 2nd Ed, 1970), *Motivation and Personality*, New York: Harper and Row.

Massey, D. (1985), 'New directions in space. Social relations and spatial structures', in D. Gregory and J. Urry (eds.), *Social Relations and Spatial Structures*, 9–19, London: Palgrave.

Massey, D. (1992), 'Politics and Space/Time', *New Left Review*: 65–84.

Massey, D. (2005), *For Space,* London: Sage Publications.

Massey, D. (2013), *Space, Place and Gender*, Hoboken, NJ: John Wiley & Sons.

Matthews, Z. and Velleman, R. (1997), '"New Age" Travellers, urban slum dwellers, Aborigines and drug users: experiences of collecting sensitive data from marginalised communities', *Bull Méthodologie Sociologique*, 57: 65–85.

McGarry, A. (2017), *Romaphobia. The Last Acceptable Form of Racism,* Chicago: University of Chicago Press.

McNamara, T. (2019), *Language and Subjectivity*, Cambridge: Cambridge University Press.

Mendoza-Denton, N. (2002), 'Language and Identity', in J. K. Chambers et al. (eds.), *The Handbook of Language Variation and Change*, 475–499, Malden, MA/Oxford: Blackwell.

Milani, T. (2015), 'Sexual citizenship: Discourses, spaces and bodies at Joburg Pride 2012', *Journal of Language and Politics*, 14(3): 431–454.

Mills, J. (2003), 'Whitehead's Unconscious Ontology', *Theory & Psychology,* 13(2): 209–238.

Mitchell, K. (1997), 'Different diasporas and the hype of hybridity', *Environment and Planning D: Society and Space,* 15: 533–553.

Mitzen, J. (2006), 'Ontological Security in World Politics: State Identity and the Security Dilemma', *European Journal of International Relations,* 12 (3): 341–370.

Moita-Lopes, L. P. (2006), 'On being white, heterosexual and male in a Brazilian school: Multiple positionings in oral narratives' in A. De Fina A et al. (eds.), *Discourse and Identity*, 288–313, Cambridge: Cambridge University Press.

Molina, M. E. (2006), 'Transformaciones Histórico Culturales del Concepto de Maternidad y sus Repercusiones en la Identidad de la Mujer [Historical and cultural transformations of the concept of maternity and their repercusions in woman's identity]', *Psykhe,* 15(2): 93–103.

Morris, R. (2000), 'Gypsies, Travellers and the Media: Press Regulation and Racism in the UK', *Communications Law*, 5(6): 213–219.

Moss, P. and Dyck, I. (2003), *Women, Body, Illness: Space and Identity in the Everyday Lives of Women with Chronic Illness*', Lanhan: Rowman & Littlefield Publishers.

Mostowska, M. (2013), 'Migration and homelessness: the social networks of homeless Poles in Oslo', *Journal of Ethnic and Migration Studies*, 39(7): 1125–1140.

Motha, S. and Lin, A. (2014), '"Non-coercive rearrangements": Theorizing desire', *TESOL Quarterly*, 48(2): 331–359.

Mulcahy, A. (2011), '"Alright in their own place": Policing and the spatial regulation of Irish Travellers', *Criminology & Criminal Justice*, 12(3): 307–327.

Murdoch, A. and C. Johnson (2004), 'Introduction' in C. Johnson and M. Willers (eds.), *Gypsy and Traveller Law*, 1–20, London: Legal Action Group.

Murray, N. et al. eds. (2007), *Desire Lines: Space, Memory and Identity in the Post-Apartheid City*, London/New York: Routledge.
Naegels, T. and Blomme, M. (2010), *Volk*, Antwerpen: Uitgeverij Epo.
Nochlin, L. (1971), *Realism*, London: Penguin.
Norris, C. (2010), 'Frankfurt on Second-Order Desires and the Concept of a Person', *Prolegomena*, 9 (2): 199–242.
Norton B ed (1997), 'Language and identity' [special issue], *TESOL Quarterly* 31(3).
Nunes, M. (1999), 'Virtual topographies: Smooth and striated cyberspace' at http://www.cyberhead2010.net/nunes.html accessed -0/01/2020 (originally printed in M. L. Ryan (ed), *Cyberspace Textuality*, Bloomington: Indiana UP).
Ochs, E. (1992), 'Indexing Gender', in A. Duranti and C. Goodwin (eds.) *Rethinking Context: Language as an Interactive Phenomenon*, 335–58, Cambridge: Cambridge University Press.
Ochs, E. (1993), 'Constructing Social Identity: A Language Socialization Perspective', *Research on Language and Social Interaction* 26(3): 287–306.
Ochs, E. and Capps, L. (1996), 'Narrating the self', *Annual Review of Anthropology*, 25: 19–43.
Ochs, E. and Capps, L. (2009), *Living Narrative: Creating Lives in Everyday Storytelling*, Cambridge, Mass/London: Harvard University Press.
Ochs, E. et al. (1996), 'Socializing taste', *Ethnos. Journal of Anthropology*, 61(1/2): 5–42.
Okely, J. (2014), 'Recycled (mis) representations: Gypsies, Travellers or Roma treated as objects, rarely subjects', *People, Place & Policy*, 8/1: 65–85.
Oliveira, M. (1999), 'The function of self-aggrandizement in storytelling', *Narrative Inquiry*, 9 (1): 25–47.
Osborne, R (2002), '"I May be Homeless, But I'm Not Helpless": The Costs and Benefits of Identifying with Homelessness', *Self and Identity*, 1(1): 43–52.
Östman, J.-O. (1981), *You know: A discourse functional approach*, Amsterdam/Philadelphia: John Benjamins.
Palladino, M. (2016), '"It's a freedom thing": Heterotopias and gypsy travellers' spatiality', in M. Palladino and J. Miller (eds.), *The Gobalization of Space: Foucault and Heterotopia*, 65–80, London: Routledge.
Park, L. and Crocker, J. (2005), 'Interpersonal Consequences of Seeking Self-Esteem', *Personality and Social Psychology Bulletin*, 31(11): 1587–1598.
Parliamentary inquiry on equality of GRT https://www.parliament.uk/business/committees/committees-a-z/commons-select/women-and-equalities-committee/inquiries/parliament-2017/inequalities-faced-by-gypsy-roma-and-traveller-communities-17-19
Parliamentary-travellers-media-seminar-briefing%20(2).pdf) 2012, 'A Briefing: Gypsies, Roma and Irish Travellers in the media', https://www.nuj.org.uk/documents/briefing-gypsies-roma-and-irish-travellers-in-the-media/
Parsell, C. (2010), '"Homeless is what I am, not who I am" Insights from an inner-city Brisbane study', *Urban Policy and Research*, 28(2): 181–194.

Parsell, C. (2018), *The Homeless Person in Contemporary Society*, London: Routledge.

Perrino, S. (2011), 'Chronotopes of story and storytelling event in interviews', *Language in Society*, 40: 91–103.

Perrino, S. (2015), 'Chronotopes', in A. De Fina and A, Georgakopoulou (eds.), *The Handbook of Narrative Analysis*, 140–159, Malden, MA: Wiley.

Pew Research Center (2014), *A Fragile Rebound for EU Image on Eve of European Parliament Elections*, Washington, DC: Pew Research Center.

Phillips R. (2000), 'Performativity in practice: some recent work in cultural geography, *Progress in Human Geography*, 24: 653–664.

Piazza, R. (2015a), 'The representation of travellers in television documentaries: dispelling stigma while dealing with infotainment demands', in Piazza, R. et al. (eds.), *Values and Choices in Television. A View from Both Sides of the Screen*, 132–157, London: Palgrave.

Piazza, R. (2015b), '"Since Big Fat Wedding [...] now [people]... understand more 'cos of that programme": Irish Travellers' identity between stigmatisation and self-image', in R. Piazza and A. Fasulo (eds.), *Marked Identities*, 16–42, London: Palgrave.

Piazza, R. (2017), 'Ideology in the multimodal discourse of television documentaries on Irish travellers' and gypsies' communities in the UK', *Critical Approaches to Discourse Analysis across Disciplines*, 9 (1): 63–90.

Piazza, R. (2019), 'With and without Zanzibar: liminal diaspora voices and the memory of the Revolution', *Narrative Inquiry*, 29(1): 99–136.

Piazza, R. and Fasulo, A. eds. (2015), *Marked Identities*, London: Palgrave.

Piazza, R. and Morgan, P. eds. (2018), *Irish Travellers. The Unknown Residents of Horsdean*, Brighton: Sixth Floor Publishing.

Piazza, R. and Rubino, A. (2015) '"Racial laws turned our lives positively": Agentivity and chirality in the identity of a group of Italian Jewish witnesses', in R. Piazza and A. Fasulo (eds.), *Marked Identities*, 98–122, London: Palgrave.

Pidd, H. (2009), '"We're not squatters," says art group occupying Mayfair mansion', *The Guardian*, December 29.

Piotrowski, G. and Polanska, D. (2016), 'Radical urban movements in Poland –the case of squatting', *Miscellanea Anthropologica et Sociologica* 2016, 17 (1): 53–69.

Pomerantz, A. (2000), 'Interviews and identity: A critical discourse perspective', *working Papers in Educational Linguistics*, 16(1): 25–37.

Potter, J. and Mulkay, M. (1985), 'Scientists' interview talk: Interviews as a technique for revealing participants' interpretative practices', in M. Brenner, J. Brown and D. Canter (eds.), *The Research Interview: Uses and Approaches*, 247–69, London: Academic Press.

Prior, M. (2016), *Emotion and Discourse in L2 Narrative Research*, Bristol: Multilingual Matters.

Proshansky, H. et al. (1983), 'Place-identity: Physical world socialization of the self', *Journal of Environmental Psychology* 3(1): 57–83.

Queensborough Community College Definition for Diversity (http://www.qcc.cuny.edu/diversity/definition.html).

Rampton, B. (2007), 'Linguistic ethnography, interactional sociolinguistics and the study of identities', *Working Papers in Urban Language and Literacies,* 43: 1–14.

Rampton, B. et al. (2004), 'UK linguistic ethnography: A discussion paper', Retrieved from http://www.ling-ethnog.org.uk/documents/discussion_paper_jan_05.pdf

Reisigl, M. and Wodak, R. (2009), 'The discourse-historical approach', in R. Wodak and M. Meyer (eds.), *Methods of Critical Discourse Analysis,* 87–121, London, UK: Sage.

Reynolds, J. and Taylor, S. (2005), 'Narrating singleness: Life stories and deficit identities', *Narrative Inquiry* 15(2): 197–215.

Richardson, J. E. (2007), *Analysing Newspapers: An Approach from Critical Discourse Analysis,* Basingstoke and New York: Palgrave Macmillan.

Ricoeur, P. (1981), 'Narrative time', in W. Mitchell (ed), *On Narrative,* 165–186, Chicago, IL: University of Chicago Press.

Riggins, S. (1997), 'The Rhetoric of Othering', in S. Riggins (ed), *The Language and Politics of Exclusion: Others in Discourse,* 1–31, Thousand Oaks, CA: Sage.

Riggins, S. ed (1997), *The Language and Politics of Exclusion. Others in discourse,* Thousand Oaks: Sage.

Rollin, K. (2006), 'The Bias Paradox in Feminist Standpoint Epistemology', *Episteme: A Journal of Social Epistemology,* 3(1–2): 125–136.

Ross, F. (2005), 'Model Communities and Respectable Residents? Home and Housing in a Low-income Residential Estate in the Western Cape, South Africa', *Journal of Southern African Studies,* 31(3): 631–648.

Rowles, G. (1983), 'Place and personal identity in old age: Observations from Appalachia', *Journal of Environmental Psychology,* 3(4): 299–313.

Ruddick, S. (1990), 'Heterotopias of the homeless: strategies and tactics of placemaking in Los Angeles', *Strategies,* 3: 184–201.

Rushton, S. (2003), 'Two preservice teachers' growth in self-efficacy while teaching in an inner-city school', *The Urban Review,* 35(3): 167–18.

Sack, R. (1997), *Homo Geographicus: A Framework for Action, Awareness, and Moral Concern,* Baltimore/London: Johns Hopkins.

Sacks, H. (1972), 'An initial investigation of the usability of conversational data for doing sociology', in D. Sudnow (ed), *Studies in Social Interaction,* 31–74, New York: Free Press.

Sacks, H. (1992), *Lectures on conversation* (2 vol. ed), Edited by G. Jefferson, introduction by E. Schegloff, Oxford: Blackwell, [Combined vols. ed, 1995].

Sacks, H. et al. (1974), 'A simplest systematics for the organization of turn-talking in conversation', *Language,* 50(4): 696–735.

Sarbin, T. (1983), 'Place identity as a component of self: An addendum', *Journal of Environmental Psychology,* 3: 337–342.

Sartre, J. P (2018), *Being and Nothingness: An Essay in Phenomenological Ontology',* translated by Sarah Richmond, Abingdon: Routledge.

Schegloff, E.A. (2007), 'Categories in action: Person-reference and membership categorization', *Discourse Studies,* 9(4): 433–461.

Schiffrin, D. (1996), 'Narrative as self-portrait: Sociolinguistic constructions of identity', *Language in Society*, 25(2): 167–203.

Schwartz, R. and Halegoua, G. (2015), 'The spatial self: Location-based identity performance on social media', *New Media and Society*, DOI: 10.1177/1461444814531364.

Scully, M. (2019), 'Challenging peripherality: Cornwall in pan-Celtic narrative of place', in R. Piazza (ed), *Discourses of Identity in Liminal Places and Spaces*, 147–165, London/New York: Routledge.

Seul, J. (1999), '"Ours is the Way of God": Religion, Identity, and Intergroup Conflict', *Journal of Peace Research,* 36(5): 553–569.

Shane, G. (2008), Heterotopias of illusion in M. Dehaene and L. De Cauter (eds.), *Heterotopia and the City*, 259–271, London/New York: Routledge.

Sheehan, R. (2010), '"I'm protective of this yard": long-term homeless persons' construction of home place and workplace in a historical public space', *Social and Cultural Geography*, 11(6): 539–558.

Shelter factsheet at Shelterhttps://england.shelter.org.uk/__data/assets/pdf_file/0011/48458/Factsheet_Street_Homelessness_Aug_2006.pdf accessed 31/12/2019).

Shields, R. (2005), *Lefebvre, Love and Struggle: Spatial Dialectics*, London: Routledge.

Sibley, D. (1995), *Geographies of Exclusion,* London/New York: Routledge.

Sibley, D. (2006), 'Inclusions/exclusions in rural space', in P. Cloke et al. (eds.), *Handbook of Rural Studies*, 401–410, London: Sage.

Silverstein, M. (2003), 'Indexical order and the dialectics of sociolinguistic life', *Language & Communication*, 23: 193–229.

Simon, B. (2004), *Identity in Modern Society: A Social Psychological Perspective*, London: Blackwell.

Slater, T. (2002), 'Fear of the city 1882–1967: Edward Hopper and the discourse of anti-urbanism', *Social & Cultural Geography*, 3(2): 135–154.

Smith, N. (1993), 'Homeless/global: scaling places', in J. Bird et al. (eds.), *Mapping the Futures: Local Cultures, Global Change*, 87–119, London: Routledge, London.

Snow, D. and Anderson, L. (1987), 'Identity work among the homeless: the verbal construction and avowal of personal identities', *American Journal of Sociology*, 92(6): 1336–1371.

Snow, D. and Anderson, L. (1993), *Down on Their Luck: A Study of Homeless Street People*, Berkley: University of California Press.

Spivak, G. C. (1984–85), 'Criticism, feminism and the institution', *Thesis Eleven*, 10–11: 175–187.

Spivak, G.C. (1990), *The Post-Colonial Critic: Interviews, Strategies, Dialogues*, New York: Routledge.

Stein, J. (1996), 'Image, Identity, and Conflict Resolution', in C. A. Crocker and F. O. Hampson, (eds.), *Managing Global Chaos*, 93–101, Washington DC: US Institute of Peace Press.

Stephen, D. (2010), 'Young women construct themselves: Social identity, self-concept and psychosocial well-being in homeless facilities', *Journal of Youth Studies*, 3(4): 445–460.

Stokoe, E. (2003), 'Mothers, Single Women and Sluts: Gender, Morality and Membership Categorization in Neighbour Disputes', *Feminism & Psychology,* 13(3): 317–344.

Stoler, A. L. (1995), *Race and the Education of Desire: Foucault's History of Sexuality and the Colonial Order of Things*, Durham, NC: Duke University Press.

Stubbe, M. and Holmes, J. (1995), 'You know, eh and other "exasperating expressions": an analysis of social and stylistic variation in the use of pragmatic devices in a sample of New Zealand English', *Language and Communication,* 15(1): 63–88.

Tajfel, H. (1974), 'Social identity and intergroup behaviour International', *Social Science Council,* 13(2): 65–93.

Tajfel, H. and Turner, J. (1979), 'An Integrative Theory of Intergroup Conflict', in W. Austin, and S. Worchel (eds.), *The Social Psychology of Intergroup Relations,* Monterey, CA: Brooks/Cole.

Tajfel, H. and Turner, J.C. (1986), 'The social identity theory of intergroup behavior', in S. Worchel and W. Austin (eds.), *The Psychology of Intergroup Relations*, 7–24, Chicago, IL: Nelson-Hall.

Takahashi, L. et al. (2002), 'The sociospatial stigmatization of homeless women with children', *Urban Geography*, 23(4): 301–322.

Talmy, S. (2011), 'The interview as collaborative achievement: Interaction, identity, and ideology in a speech event', *Applied Linguistics,* 32(1): 25–42.

Tannen, D. (1993), 'What's in a frame? Surface evidence for underlying expectations', in Tannen, D. (ed), *Framing in Discourse*, 14–57, Oxford: Oxford University Press.

Tell, D. (2009), 'Jimmy Swaggart's Secular Confession', *Rhetoric Society Quarterly*, 39(2): 124–146.

Tempest, S. and Starkey, K. (2004), 'The effects of liminality on individual and organizational learning', *Organization Studies*, 25(4): 507–527.

Thomas, J. (1995), *Meaning in Interaction*, Harlow: Longman.

Toolan, M. (1997), 'What is critical discourse analysis and why are people saying such terrible things about it?', *Language & Literature,* 6(2), 83–103.

Tremlett, A. (2014), 'Making a difference without creating a difference: super-diversity as a new direction for research on Roma minorities', *Ethnicities,* 14(6): 830–848.

Trimingham, P. (2015), '"They paint everyone with the same brush but it just simply isn't the case": Reconstructing and redefining homeless identities', in R. Piazza and A. Fasulo (eds.), *Marked Identities*, 58–78, Houndsmill: Basingstoke.

Turner, J. C. (1987), A self-categorization theory, in J.C. Turner et al. (eds.), *Rediscovering the Social Group: A Self-Categorization Theory,* 42–67, Oxford: Basil Blackwell.

Turner, J. C. and Reynolds, K. (2011), 'Self-categorization theory', in P. Van Lange et al., *Handbook of Theories in Social Psychology,* (vol 2): 399–417.

Turner, V. ([1969] 1997), *The Ritual Process: Structure and Anti-Structure*, Abingdon, Oxon: Routledge.

Turner, V. (1967), 'Betwixt and between: The liminal period in rites de passage', in *The forest of symbols: Aspects of Ndembu Ritual*, Ithaca/NY: Cornell, 1967.

Turner, V. (1974), *Dramas, Fields and Metaphors*, Ithaca/London: Cornell University Press.

Tusting, K. and Maybin, J. (2007), 'Linguistic ethnography and interdisciplinarity: Opening the discussion', *Journal of Sociolinguistics*, 11(5): 575–583.

Urry, J. (2007), *Mobilities*, Cambridge: Polity.

Van de Mieroop, D. (2011), 'Identity negotiations in narrative accounts about poverty', *Discourse & Society*, 22(5): 565–591.

Van de Mieroop, D. et al. (2017), 'Mobilizing master narratives through categorical narratives and categorical statements when default identities are at stake', *Discourse and Communication*, 11(2): 179–198.

Van Dijk, T. (1993), 'Principles of Critical Discourse Analysis', *Discourse & Society*, 4(2): 249–283.

Van Leeuwen, T. (2008), *Discourse and Practice: New Tools for Critical Discourse Analysis*, New York: Oxford University Press.

Vasudevan, A. (2017), *The Autonomous City: A History of Urban Squatting*, New York: Verso.

Vertovec, S. (2007), 'Super-diversity and its implications', *Ethnic and Racial Studies*, 30:6, 1024–1054.

Villar, G. et al (2013), 'Linguistic indicators of a false confession', *Psychiatry, Psychology and Law*, 20(4): 504–518.

Wardhaugh, J. (1999), 'The Unaccommodated Woman: Home, Homelessness and Identity', *The Sociological Review*, 47, 1: 91–109.

Waters, J. (2014), 'Snowball sampling: a cautionary tale involving a study of older drug users', *International Journal of Social Research Methodology*, 18(4): 367–380.

Watt, D. et al. (2014), 'Language and identity on the Scottish/English border', in D. Watt and C. Llamas (eds.), *Language, Borders and Identity*, 8–26, Edinburgh: Edinburgh University Press.

Whitehead, A.N. (1960), *Religion in the Making*. New York: Meridian. (Original work published 1927.)

Whitehead, L. (2002), *Democratization: Theory and Experience*, Oxford: Oxford University Press.

Widdicombe, S. (1998), '"But you don't class yourself": The interactional management of category membership and non-membership', in C. Antaki and S. Widdicombe (eds.), *Identities in Talk*, 52–70, London: Sage.

Wierbizca, A. (2010), 'Cultural scripts and intercultural communication', in A. Trosborg (ed), *Pragmatics across Languages and Cultures*, 43–78, Berlin/New York: Walter de Gruyter.

Wolch, J. and Rowe, S. (1992), 'On the streets: mobility paths of the urban homeless', *City and Society*, 6: 115–140.

Wortham, S. (2000), 'Interactional Positioning and Narrative Self-Construction', *Narrative Inquiry*, 10: 157–184.
Wortham, S. (2001), *Narrative in Action*, New York: Teachers College Press.
Young, R. (1995), *Colonial Desire: Hybridity in Theory, Culture, and Race*, London: Routledge.
Zimmerman, D. H. (1998), 'Identity, context and interaction', in C. Antaki and S. Widdicombe (eds.), *Identities in Talk*, 87–106, London: Sage.

Index

agency 35, 40, 56, 59, 71, 115, 120, 122, 123, 126–129, 130, 132, 134, 144, 146–147, 151, 159, 163, 168, 170
Ahearn 163
Appadurai 17
Auer 7

Bakhtin 147
Bamberg and Georgakopoulou 67, 70
Baxter 39, 100, 105
Benwell and Stokoe 3, 4, 40
Berger and Luckmann 6, 7
Blommaert 5, 13, 23, 33–34, 37, 71, 81
Branigan 154
Brown and Levinson 161
Bucholtz and Hall 8, 9, 20, 56, 57, 58
Butler, 18, 28, 70

Cameron and Kulick 8, 28–29, 98
Casey et al. 140
Cenzatti 26–27, 54, 93, 95
chronotope 13, 71, 147
confession 122, 148, 159–162
contestation 4, 17–18, 25, 27, 30–31, 51, 53, 56, 64, 77, 82, 93–94, 166
counter-space 26–27, 60
Creese 6, 34, 42–43

De Fina 4, 10–12, 19, 21, 33, 39
De Fina and Georgakopoulou 12, 33
De Fina and Perrino 36
Dee and Debelle 49–51, 68
Dehaene and De Cauter 27, 53, 134
Deleuze and Guattari 24–25, 28, 95–96, 118
deontic 127–128
desire 3–5, 8, 10, 11, 17, 27, 28, 29, 51, 54, 56, 57, 63, 74, 77, 80, 97, 98, 107, 109, 116, 128, 168
Devereux 141, 142
diversity 1, 2, 5, 11, 17, 39, 54, 86, 124, 163, 165

Dixon and Durrheim 20–22, 47–48, 53

Eckert and McConnell-Ginet 9, 167
education 98, 101, 103, 104, 124, 129, 131
emplaced action 127
enclavization 128
ethnicity 2, 50, 85, 142

Friends, Family and Travellers (FFT) 94
Foucault 23, 26–28, 79, 91, 94, 133
frame 56, 60, 74–75, 77, 79

Georgakopoulou 12, 74
Giddens 18, 19, 98
Goffman 13, 22, 33, 67, 86, 104
Gumperz 97, 165

hate crime 90
hegemonic 3, 6, 10, 17, 23–25, 28, 30, 36, 41, 53, 62, 65, 83, 113, 133, 145, 165–166, 171
heteropia 3, 4, 17, 24, 26–31, 47, 51, 53–56, 58–62, 69, 74–75, 79, 81, 94, 96–97, 108–109, 128, 134, 151, 154–156, 169–170
heterotopic 27, 46, 58, 65–66, 74, 79–80, 94, 101, 104, 107, 112, 116, 124, 148, 155, 158, 168–169
Hirst and Humphreys 96–97
Human Rights Commission 89

Iveson and Cornish 141

James 43, 83, 87, 90
Johnstone 1, 7, 21, 38

Kiesling 97, 99, 101
Korpela 21, 47

Labov and Waletzky 11, 162
Lahlou 129
Lefebvre 22–23, 93, 112

liminality 3, 14, 17, 25–26, 30–31, 35, 56, 68-69, 74–75, 79–81, 109, 120, 163, 168, 170
Llamas and Watt 17, 167
Low 23, 61, 116, 118
Lyotard 12, 166

Martin and White 47, 71, 75, 160
Massey 47, 90, 166
Milani 94, 97, 98
modal(s) 59, 124, 127, 129, 155, 167

narrative 10–13, 21, 39, 37, 40, 50, 52, 66, 67, 70, 73, 86, 112, 125, 136, 154, 157, 162, 166, 170
normal 100, 101, 124, 134, 168, 170, 171

Ochs 9, 11, 20, 29, 74
Oliveira 63, 65, 109
othering 41, 65, 78, 146, 162

Palladino 22, 24, 26, 79
Parsell 138, 146
Piazza 9, 88
Piazza and Fasulo 13, 24, 43
Piazza and Morgan 44
Piazza and Rubino 13
place-identity 1, 6, 14, 17, 20–21, 23, 27–28, 30, 33, 37, 47–48, 80, 82, 86, 97, 115, 135
polyglossic 160
positioning 3, 9, 11, 12, 21, 67, 68, 70, 144, 157, 168

prime and marginal spaces 139
Prior 29, 34–35

Rampton 166
resistance, 3–4, 15, 35, 43, 51, 53, 55, 60, 74, 77, 83, 87, 90, 94, 140, 154
Ricoeur 71
Riggins 41, 78, 107
Ross 99, 109, 170

Sartre 83
self-aggandizement 63, 65
Shelter 135
small narrative(s) 72, 144, 152, 159, 161
smooth 25, 95–96, 118, 171–172
Snow and Anderson 139
social constructionist/ism 35, 52, 99, 163, 163
space of representation 95
striated 24, 95–96, 111–112, 118, 124, 134, 171–172
surveillance 87, 133

Tajfel and Turner 65, 151
Turner 14, 19, 25, 26 35, 65, 66 70, 75, 151, 170
Tusting and Maybin 166, 172

van De Mieroop 36, 62, 108
van Leeuwen 33–34, 59, 63
Vertovec 1, 2, 5, 54

Wardhaugh 137, 139, 140
Whitehead 97, 98

www.ingramcontent.com/pod-product-compliance
Lightning Source LLC
Chambersburg PA
CBHW072237290426
44111CB00012B/2127